THE ROUGH GUIDE to

Windows 7

1st Edition

by
Simon May

E

ROUGH
GUIDES

www.roughguides.com

Credits

The Rough Guide to Windows 7

Text editing, design and layout:
Andrew Clare
Proofreading: Susanne Hillen
Production: Rebecca Short

Acknowledgements

Thanks to Donna for unequivocal support, and Janet and J... ...Thanks to... Percy
and Andrew for the opportunity and guidance, and to everyone else who... ...Thank you.

Publishing Information

This first edition published October 2009 by
Rough Guides Ltd, 80 Strand, London WC2R 0RL
Email: mail@roughguides.com

Distributed by the Penguin Group:
Penguin Books Ltd, 80 Strand, London, WC2R 0RL
Penguin Group (USA), 375 Hudson Street, NY 10014, USA
Penguin Group (Australia), 250 Camberwell Road, Camberwell, Victoria 3124, Australia
Penguin Group (Canada), 90 Eglinton Avenue East, Suite 700, Toronto, Ontario, Canada M4P 2Y3
Penguin Group (New Zealand), Cnr Rosedale and Airborne Roads, Albany, Auckland, New Zealand

Printed and bound in Singapore by SNP Security Printing Pte Ltd
Typeset in Minion and Myriad
Cover image courtesy of HP. Other images courtesy of HP, Microsoft, Zyxel, Belkin and Cisco.
Illustrations on p.40 and pp.54–55 by Andrew Clare

300 pages; includes index
A catalogue record for this book is available from the British Library.
ISBN 13: 978-1-84836-277-2

1   3   5   7   9   8   6   4   2

Contents

Contents

SECURITY AND SAFETY

TROUBLESHOOTING

About this book

The chances are that if you've picked up this book you have an interest in using Windows 7. And why not; it's exciting! Windows 7 let's you do more work and have more fun with the latest PC technology, and in a far more intelligent way than ever before. Microsoft's latest operating system has changed fairly significantly compared to previous versions, so it's good to have a tour guide. Whether you're new to Windows, are considering buying a Windows 7 PC or are a Windows user about to upgrade, then this is the book for you.

These pages are peppered with Windows tips that I've picked up over the years; every one is as vitally relevant to Windows 7 as it was to previous versions. This book doesn't take the standard "this is what you get out of the box" or "here is this feature, here's that one…" approach; it's been designed to help you do the stuff that's important to you: sending e-mail, surfing the Internet, playing with pictures and enjoying your music, movies and games. Hopefully you'll reach an understanding of Windows 7 and be able to set it up just right for your needs, fix any problems you encounter and maybe even help your friends if they struggle.

I've tried to avoid complicated step-by-step tutorials and keep things easy to follow and explanatory. That way you know what you're doing and why you are doing it.

If you've not yet experienced Windows 7, now's the time to dive in, using this book as your guide.

Getting started

Frequently asked questions

What is Windows?

The operating system, or OS, is the piece of software on your computer that holds everything together. It lets you type on your keyboard and have things appear on screen; it lets you plug in your digital camera and copy pictures from it. Everything on your computer relies on your operating system; it controls the experience you have using your PC. Windows 7 is designed to be less daunting to use than any other OS Microsoft has ever released. It also allows you to connect some of the coolest new hardware, like multi-touch screens, play the very latest games and watch and record TV.

Windows has been around for a long time and is installed on millions of PCs. Almost everyone has used Windows at some point and they all use it in a variety of ways. You can use Windows for watching movies and TV, viewing photos and listening to music all over the home. You can pause the TV in the kitchen and continue to watch in the bedroom right where you left off. Businesses run on Windows, using it to run their e-mail servers, share data and keep in touch with customers. It's even used to run nuclear submarines and war ships!

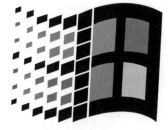

Now in its mid-twenties
Windows 1.0 was released in November 1985; that's a difference of 24 years between Windows 1.0 and Windows 7.

Frequently asked questions

Why Windows 7?

You might be thinking, "Where did Windows 7 come from? What about XP (version 5)? and Vista (version 6)?" Well, things have moved on a bit since those releases and Microsoft now describes them as legacy. What that means is that they'll be around for a little while longer, but support from Microsoft will gradually tail off. Further updates won't be made available so the latest technology won't work if you stick with them. XP was first released in October 2001, making it eight years old, while Vista was released in January 2007.

For Windows 7 Microsoft took a different branding approach, opting for something easier to understand, so names like XP – which meant eXPerience – and Vista have been dropped in favour of a much simpler "7".

The fantastic news is that with this simplicity comes compatibility. Almost all hardware that worked with Vista will be fine with Windows 7. If your printer, camera, TV card, scanner or other devices worked on Vista, they will probably work with Windows 7. Most stuff that worked with XP will work with Windows 7 too.

Windows 7 will also work on most PCs that ran Windows XP! For the first time ever the minimum requirements for running a newer version of the OS have actually dropped. That said, higher spec computers will run Windows 7 even faster.

With all these different versions of Windows being released you may be wondering if you should hold out for Windows 8, 9 or 10! Like buses, there's always going to be a "next" one and a *next next*" one on the distant horizion, but Windows 7 offers significant enough functionality and compatibility improvements for you to hop on right now.

The new Windows 7 Desktop allows you to be more productive, with gadgets to deliver information at a glance, quick access to programs and functions from the taskbar and the ability to see behind transparent windows to the Desktop.

Which Windows 7 should I choose?

There are two versions of Windows 7 available in stores. Windows 7 Home Premium is the version intended for use in the home. It contains the most media-friendly features that let you listen to music and watch TV and videos on your PC as well as having a pretty interface. It doesn't do some of the more business-like stuff, such as allowing central administration of PCs on a network using something called Active Directory. Some encryption features aren't available either. Those extra features come with Windows 7 Professional, which is intended for business use. Windows 7 Professional still includes all the good stuff for home use because it's built on top of Home Premium. Either of these versions is a good choice for the home and they will be found on most PCs that come with Windows 7 preinstalled. Upgrades to these versions from Windows Vista are available in stores or from **microsoftstore.com**.

Will Windows 7 run on my PC?

To run Windows 7 on a PC requires the following minimum hardware requirements:

▸ 1GHz processor.

▸ 1GB RAM (32-bit) or 2GB RAM (64-bit).

▸ 16GB of available disk space (32-bit) or 20GB of available disk space (64-bit).

▸ DirectX 9 graphics device with WDDM 1.0 or higher driver.

Frequently asked questions

There are a couple of other versions that it's worth knowing about. Enterprise and Ultimate are the most complete versions, and they include far more bells and whistles than most people will need. Unless you're provided with a Windows 7 PC by the company you work for it's unlikely that you'll see Enterprise. If it is installed on a PC you've just bought it's a warning sign to check it's legal. Ultimate is probably overkill for most but is designed for the home. It includes advanced features for encryption and stuff that enthusiasts like to have; see **microsoft.com/windows** for the specifics.

The last version available has fewer features than Home Premium. Windows 7 Starter is intended for low-power computers, and may come installed on a netbook. To make sure that the low-powered hardware runs ok, a maximum of just 3 applications can run at the same time. That's quite a limitation.

What is Windows Genuine Advantage?

It's important that your version of Windows is not a pirate copy. There are a few reasons, but the most important ones revolve around safety. It's not uncommon for illegal copies of Windows to come bundled with other illegal software, increasing the possibility of spyware on your system that could put your important information in the hands of people out to steal your identity.

Windows 7 becomes the centre of your digital world. It's where you store all your family photos, keep your collection of rare music, and manage your finances with Internet banking. Naturally it's a place you want to keep safe. Windows Genuine Advantage is Microsoft's software to help you do that. So if you find you've been duped into buying a high-quality forgery, Microsoft has a program to give you a complimentary copy of Windows.

After installing Windows it must be activated. Contrary to what you may have been told this doesn't allow Microsoft to "track your every movement" or anything like that. In fact it doesn't send them any personal information at all. And as a bonus, an activated copy of Windows allows you get your hands on some great free software from Microsoft.

Links:

Microsoft downloads:
microsoft.com/downloads

Microsoft Genuine Advantage:
microsoft.com/genuine

32 bit or 64 bit – what does that mean?

There are two editions of Windows designed to work with slightly different types of hardware, 32 bit and the more modern 64 bit. The difference between 32 and 64 bit is too complicated and mathematical to get into, but essentially the advantage to a 64-bit PC is that the maximum amount of memory (RAM) that can be installed is much higher. The disadvantage is that because it's newer not all hardware makers have driver software available for the 64-bit version, so some things, like that 7-year-old scanner, might not play ball. Another point to note is that the 64-bit version will only run with a 64-bit processor (CPU), which more or less includes most new processors, but not those found in netbooks. Generally, 64 bit will be found on brand-new, high-end PCs built for gaming, entertainment or specialist purposes like graphics work, while 32 bit is installed on most desktops, laptops and netbooks with 4gb or less memory (RAM). Both versions are installed and used in the same way.

Tip: A good website to keep up with the latest developments is tomshardware.com. It has in-depth hardware reviews that are always clear and easy to understand. Another good way to learn about hardware is to buy a PC or Windows magazine; these offer a valuable resource of reviews, tips and solutions to real-life computing problems.

How to decide which to get

Deciding which version to go with is actually quite simple, and the decision will have been taken for you already if you buy a new PC with Windows 7 preinstalled. Assuming you have a 64-bit processor there is one further factor in favour of either 32 bit or 64 bit that will push you over the edge in making a decision.

Get 32 bit if...

You are reliant on older hardware that doesn't have 64-bit drivers (you can find out if this is the case from the manufacturer's website). If so, you'll want to stick with 32 bit. If you do fit into this category then you probably don't need the extra memory capacity that 64 bit delivers anyway. The maximum 4gb of memory that you probably have is more than enough for everyday tasks.

Get 64 bit if...

You're going to use memory-hungry applications, like HD video editing, games or computer aided design (CAD). With 64 bit you can use much, much more memory than 32 bit, meaning that the PC will run more smoothly when working with massive files or running lots of applications simultaneously.

But generally...

Most people will go for the perfectly adequate 32 bit edition and 4gb or less RAM.

Any advice on buying a new PC?

The choice of available PCs is massive; it can be a daunting experience deciding what to buy. PCs come in a dizzying variety of forms and each have their good and bad points.

Laptops Currently the most popular type of PC sold around the world. They offer flexibility, being totally portable and coming from bijou 12" models to gargantuan 20" monsters that are considered "desktop replacements". The physical size of a laptop is determined by the screen. Laptops are often less powerful than their desktop equivalents because their processors have to consume less electricity in order to extend the time it can run from a battery. Special considerations for laptops include size, battery life and weight.

Netbooks A rapidly growing new segment of the laptop market. Designed to be very small, lightweight and portable, they're generally less powerful than laptops, but start up in a matter of seconds. They're relatively cheap and great for Internet stuff.

Desktops There's almost no end to the computing power of a desktop PC. There are no real limits to how physically big or small they can be, depending on what's crammed into them. Typically a modern desktop will have at least a dual core processor – effectively two processors in one – while top-end desktops can stretch to eight cores! Desktops can hold any amount of RAM from 1GB (any less is pretty useless these days) to 64GB (way, way over the top

Frequently asked questions

Can I run Windows on a Mac?

Apple Computers use an operating system called Mac OSX. Apple or Mac computers are known for looking nice and shiny, for their attention to detail, and often for their higher price tag when compared to a PC. The Mac hardware can also run Windows 7.

Macs with the Leopard release of OSX include an application called Boot-Camp which lets you install Windows on a separate part of the hard drive, giving the option to boot up to either Windows 7 or OSX.

Virtual Machine software, like Parallels or Virtual Box, run a second virtual computer within Leopard. This approach delivers the best of both worlds, allowing OSX and Windows to be accessible simultaneously.

for most needs). They need an external monitor, but some swanky models have the computer built into the monitor, something you may want to avoid if you're the kind of person who'd like to tinker and expand their hardware later on down the line.

Installing Windows 7

Installation options

Have you just bought a new PC or do you want to install Windows on a computer that already has a previous version? Chances are a new PC will come with Windows 7 pre-installed, in which case there's not much to do. It will probably need to be customized a bit, which you can find out how to do later in this chapter.

If you've just bought a new PC with Windows 7 pre-installed, skip ahead to page 23. If, however, there is another operating system on the PC, take a few moments to think about just how to install Windows 7. You have two options:

▸ Install Windows 7 from scratch. This is the only way to move to Windows 7 from Windows XP or earlier versions. It totally wipes the old operating system, removing any settings and, more importantly, all files (photos, videos, documents, everything). The advantage of this is that any unreliability of your old system should also be lost. It'll be like starting over with a new computer, so any applications such as Office or e-mail software will have to be reinstalled.

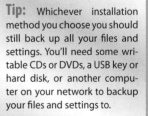

Tip: Whichever installation method you choose you should still back up all your files and settings. You'll need some writable CDs or DVDs, a USB key or hard disk, or another computer on your network to backup your files and settings to.

See later in this chapter for advice on how to back up.

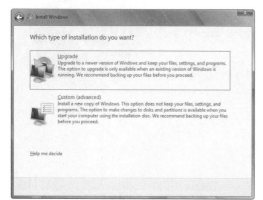

▶ Upgrade from Vista. This involves keeping all your settings, files and programs already installed, but possibly inheriting any problems the PC had gained over time. Of course, you could choose to perform an installation from scratch with Vista too, if you'd prefer.

For the first time ever Microsoft has made Windows 7 available as a download from their website. The downloaded files need to be burnt onto a DVD before installation.

Can't boot from DVD?

If your PC doesn't prompt you to boot from the DVD, then there's probably a problem with the PC's BIOS (a special piece of software that lives on the computer's motherboard). Configuring the BIOS is different on every computer, so consult the instructions that came with the PC. As a general rule, pressing F2 when booting up should reveal the BIOS. Then look for "boot order" and ensuring that CD/DVD is listed as the first device to boot from. Be careful not to change any other settings unless you know what you're doing. Finally, save and exit.

Custom installation, or installing from scratch

When installing from scratch everything on the PC will be wiped clean. Make sure you have a backup first of all the files on the PC that are worth keeping!

Starting the installation

To start installing from scratch, put your Windows 7 DVD into your PC's drive, turn on the PC and follow the prompts to boot from the DVD.

When done successfully a screen will appear saying "Windows is loading files". This isn't actually installing Windows; it's just getting ready to run the installation. After this the real setup starts.

Setup requires a bit of information like what language to display and what time zone you're in. The "End User License Agreement" must also be agreed to. Then you'll be presented with some installation options. Choose to perform a **Custom** installation, otherwise known as a clean installation.

Setup can organize the hard disk for you in a number of ways. It'll prompt with **Where do you want to install Windows?** Generally just accept the defaults. It is possible to do far more complicated things at this stage; to find out what and how, take a look at the Microsoft website. Once the chosen drive has been automatically formatted, Windows will start installing. It'll take a while so grab yourself a cup of coffee.

Giving the PC a name

After a couple of reboots Windows will be installed and ready for you to start configuring it. You'll be asked for a Windows username; this might end up being one of a few on your PC if more than one person will use it. It's probably best to use some variation on your own name to make it easy to identify.

A name for the computer is also needed. Windows automatically creates one from your username, but that might not be something you want to call the PC itself. If setting up Windows 7 on a laptop that'll be used in a public WiFi location, like in a coffee shop, think twice about calling it "John-PC" for privacy and security reasons. The names of animals, colours or countries make for fun alternatives.

You'll also be asked to invent a password. Make sure it's easy for you to remember but complicated enough that no one else can work it out.

Activation

Next, the Product Key for Windows 7 will be required. You'll find it on the inside of the DVD case, or if you downloaded the install files it will have been made available at that stage. If the key isn't immediately to hand Windows can be used for up to thirty days without it. Open **Start > Activate Windows** once the installation is finished to activate Windows 7 permanently.

When installing Windows a name is needed for the PC and to identify you. Don't make the name of the PC too obviously linked to your identity if WiFi cafés are a regular haunt. Select a name that won't stand out, such as a colour.

Tip: For the strongest password use a combination of letters, numbers, characters (such as #,./!"£$%^&) and upper and lower case. A great way to do this can be to take a household product and turn some of the letters into numbers. For example detergent might become D3t3rg3nt#, making it really hard for anyone to guess, even if they knew you were a cleaning freak! You'll have to enter the password twice, and select a hint that reminds you of the password; something like "cleans dishes" could work.

Why activate?

To prevent software piracy Microsoft requires that Windows is activated (registered) with them. The information that they keep isn't personal, it just describes the PC to them, mainly its serial numbers.

Unless Windows is activated it will disable itself after thirty days and will not allow any access other than to activate Windows.

Keeping Windows up to date

Microsoft has a massive catalogue of solutions to help out with any problems you might encounter. They need to collect some information from the PC about what went wrong in order to make use of that information. It's important to keep Windows up to date to reduce the chances that any malware (malicious software like viruses and spyware) infects your PC. With this in mind select one of the following options during setup:

▶ Use Recommended Settings – sends Microsoft details of problems and makes sure Windows is always up to date.
▶ Install important updates only – to make sure Windows 7 gets just security and major updates.
▶ Ask Me Later – does as it says: continually nags about turning updates on. It's not at all recommended to leave your PC vulnerable in this way for long.

Network settings

Windows 7 has three profiles that help manage security settings depending upon the type of network your PC's connected to.

▶ Home Network is the least tightly controlled of the three, giving you more freedom, so it's perfect for use at home. It enables **HomeGroup** so you can connect to other computers around the home, sharing things like movies, pictures, videos and music.
▶ Work Network allows connection to other computers on a network, but it won't allow you to join or set up a HomeGroup.
▶ Public Network is the most tightly controlled, and also prevents sharing your media with a HomeGroup or any other computers. It's the profile to use when you're in a public place, like a WiFi enabled coffee shop.

All done!

The installation of Windows 7 will now finalize and reboot, ready to use.

Upgrading from Windows Vista

You'll need to have some time set aside for doing an upgrade. It can take anything up to four hours depending on how many applications are installed on the PC and how much data there is. Make sure you close every application running on your PC before you start the installation, otherwise the upgrade will fail.

Starting installation

Either insert the installation DVD or burn the downloaded ISO image (a soft copy) of the DVD using your DVD-burning software. The installation should start automatically, but if it doesn't or if Auto Run is turned off, browse to your DVD drive and run **setup.exe**.

Once setup starts the first thing you'll see will be a big button that says simply, **Install Now**. Give it a click! A message that says "Setup is copying temporary files" appears, followed by "Setup is starting".

The setup process gathers some basic information to get Windows 7 up and running. First it'll prompt to get installation updates from the Internet. In the main you'll want to do this as you'll get a more up-to-date and secure installation (and automatic update won't have as much to do later). If you have an Internet connection, select **Go online to get the latest updates for installation (recommended)**. Setup will then spend some time searching for updates from the Internet. If, however, the PC isn't connected to the Internet, then select **Do not get the latest updates for installation**.

The first screen of the Windows install can be used to set your language and location. Selecting a foreign language doesn't make for a good way to learn one, just a very hard way to use a PC.

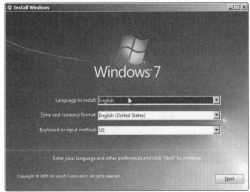

The next thing to do is accept the license agreement, having read it. Then select the **Upgrade** option when asked what type of installation you want. Setup will then begin copying installation files to the PC, installing Windows 7 and transferring your documents and settings into the new Windows 7 Libraries structure. The PC will reboot and restart with a Windows 7 logo a few times as it continues the installation.

Activation

Next, the Product Key for Windows 7 will be required. You'll find it on the inside of the DVD case or, if you downloaded the install files, it will have been made available at that stage. If the key isn't immediately to hand Windows can be used for up to thirty days without it. Open **Start > Activate Windows** once the installation is finished to activate permanently.

Windows can keep itself up to date, and will use information about how you use your PC to help improve itself. If sending information to Microsoft bothers you then opt out by selecting Install important updates only.

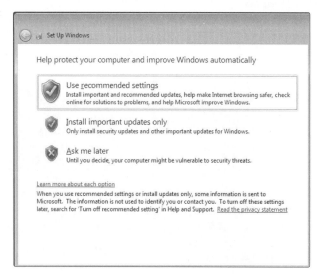

Keeping Windows up to date

Microsoft has a massive catalogue of solutions to help out with any problems you might encounter. They need to collect some information from the PC about what went wrong in order to make use of that information. It's important to keep Windows up to date to reduce the chances that any malware (malicious software like viruses and spyware) infects your PC. With this in mind select one of the following options:

▸ Use Recommended Settings – sends Microsoft details of problems and makes sure Windows is always up to date.

▸ Install important updates only – to make sure Windows 7 gets just security and major updates.

▸ Ask Me Later – does as it says: continually nags about turning updates on. It's not at all recommended to leave your PC vulnerable in this way for long.

Network settings

Windows 7 has three profiles that help manage security settings depending upon the type of network your PC's connected to.

▸ Home Network is the least tightly controlled of the three, giving you more freedom, so it's perfect for use at home. It enables **HomeGroup** so you can connect to other computers around the home, sharing things like movies, pictures, videos and music.

▸ Work Network allows connection to other computers on a network, but it won't allow you to join or set up a HomeGroup.

▸ Public Network is the most tightly controlled, and also prevents sharing your media with a HomeGroup or any other computers. It's the profile to use when you're in a public place, like a WiFi enabled coffee shop.

All done!

Soon the log on screen will appear; your old username and password from Windows Vista is all that's needed. A few minutes after you've logged on, your PC will be ready to play with.

Buying a PC with Windows 7 preinstalled

If Windows 7 is preinstalled there's very little you will need to do to get up and running. But this will vary by manufacturer. If the PC was bought from one of the larger ones there will be a few more essential steps to complete your setup. Most likely they will have left most of the setup choices up to you. If this is the case then the first

Tip: Lots of new PCs come bundled with extra software from the manufacturer. A lot of this software doesn't do much of any use and has come to be known as "crapware".

A great application to get rid of crapware is PC Decrapifier. It searches a new PC, gathers all the unwanted software and asks if it should remove it. Available from pcdecrapifier.com.

thing you'll see is a screen asking you to name your PC. If you do then refer to the previous section in this chapter on custom installations. You will be asked everything from "Giving the PC a name" onward, but the process will be much faster.

If the PC hasn't been set up in this way then it's likely that someone has already customized it, in which case you'll need to do a few things manually. First, you will need to know the name of an account with Administrator access; hopefully you have this, but if not go back to the person who sold you the PC. Next consider doing the following:

▸ Changing the PC name – **Go to Start > Control Panel > All Control Panel Items > System** then select **Advanced system settings** from the left panel. In the window that appears select the **Computer Name** tab and then click the **Change** button.

▸ Change the time and time zone – Click the clock in the bottom right-hand corner of the screen, and select **Change date and time settings.**

▸ Set up extra User Accounts and change passwords – go to **Start > Control Panel > All Control Panel Items > User Accounts**. It's a good idea to change any passwords that were given to you when you received the PC.

▸ Activate Windows – In the search box on the Start menu type "activate" and hit enter, then follow the wizard.

It's also useful to play with the **Getting Started** program to help customize the PC to your tastes; this should be at the top of the Start menu.

Getting up and running

Getting your PC working just right is a great way to familiarize yourself with Windows. Restoring settings and files from a previous PC, making sure all the hardware works and getting the screen set up properly are all essential.

Deciding what features you need

Windows 7 automatically installs the most commonly required features so your PC is set up to do most things immediately. There are, however, a few things that can be tweaked – for example, a Web server can be installed.

Go to **Start > Control Panel > Programs and Features > Turn Windows Features On or Off**. Here, toggle features on or off using the tick boxes. Quite a few features are designed for corporate use and typically can be ignored.

Setting up hardware

Having installed Windows, and especially if you've done a custom installation, you may find that there are a couple of bits of hardware that aren't working. This is because Windows doesn't yet know how to deal with them. Every bit of hardware in the PC has something called a "driver" that acts like a manual. This driver tells Windows

Device Manager is a useful tool for checking the hardware inside your PC and seeing if there are any problems with missing drivers.

how to use the hardware. Windows already has drivers for tens of thousands of devices, but any new kit might need something extra.

New hardware usually ships with a CD containing relevant drivers. Equally, Windows can often find missing drivers on the Internet automatically. If it can't find a driver either locally or online then Action Center will pop up to say that the driver needs to be downloaded from the vendor's website, and normally it'll point you in the right direction. If not, then consult the manual that came with the device to see if it says where to get drivers. Failing that, Google the name of the manufacturer and look for the "support" or "drivers" pages on their website.

What's missing

The easiest way to find out what's missing is to consult Device Manager. Select **Start**, type "device manager" into the search box and hit enter. Any device not working will have a yellow exclamation mark next to it. Right click and select **Update Driver Software**, then either have Windows search for the driver, or if you've downloaded it, point to the location where it's been saved.

Another way to check on your devices is via **Start > Devices and Printers**. This only shows what's installed, not what's missing.

Connecting to the Internet

One of the first things you'll need to finish setting up your PC is access to the Internet. How you connect depends upon how your home network is configured or if you're connecting directly via a modem. To learn more about setting up home networks look to Chapter 22.

It should then be a simple process to get online. Depending on your situation, refer to one of the following as a guide:

> **Tip:** A good way to find missing drivers is to use driver-hunting software. These applications analyse your system hardware and then search the Internet for matching drivers. Although this sounds like the same thing that Windows already does, it uses looser search criteria and might find something Windows can't. drivermax.com has a solid application for doing this.

Wired network

This is the simplest way to connect to the Internet with Windows 7. If you already have a wired network then all that's needed is to plug the Ethernet cable into the PC.

Wireless network

Look to the bottom right of the screen, next to the clock. There you will see a bar graph that shows the wireless signal. (If it's not there then there's probably a problem with your PC's wireless network card; see Chapter 31 for help.) Click the graph and a pop-up will appear showing available wireless networks. Highlight the one to connect to, click the **Connect** button and enter the network password.

Directly connected to broadband via a modem

Broadband modems connect to the PC either via USB or Ethernet. If the USB variety, some drivers will be required for it; a CD from your Internet service provider should complete the setup for you.

If the Ethernet variety, then all you need to do is connect the modem to your PC via the Ethernet port and you should be able to get online. The modem might first need turning off and on again.

Dial-up

This is the oldest form of Internet connection and should only be considered if you can't get broadband. Your PC may have a modem port built in (it's not the same as a broadband modem). You'll need to know the phone number of the Internet service provider (ISP) and your username and password. Next plug the modem cable into the phone line and into the PC. Go to **Control Panel > All Control Panel Items > Network and Sharing Center > Set up a new connection or network > Connect to the Internet > Set up a new connection now > Dial-up**. Finally enter the username, password and phone number and click Connect.

Mobile broadband
To connect via mobile broadband follow the instructions provided by the wireless carrier. The settings and software that they use to make the connection varies dramatically, but you will need to install software and drivers before it will work.

Tip: If you have a laptop, first check that wireless is actually turned on, as many notebook PCs have a physical switch for security.

Tip: If you have problems setting up your network or getting online take a look at Chapter 31.

Getting the screen resolution just right

Among other improvements in Windows 7 it's now much easier to change display settings and customize the Desktop. To change screen resolution (the size of things on the screen) **right click** anywhere on the Desktop and select **Screen Resolution**.

There are a few things you can do with the resolution options. Firstly the **Detect** button helps find any new monitors (displays) that have been connected to the PC. The **Identify** button slaps a great big 1, 2 or 3 up on each screen depending on how many are attached. This helps to show which of the little monitors in the configuration window is which monitor in real life.

The **Resolution** and **Orientation** drop-down menus allow you to manually adjust the appropriate settings for each monitor. Why is it useful to change them? Well, Windows may not have defaulted to the best settings for you. It's a matter of personal preference; some people just like everything bigger.

Resolution is all about what can fit on the screen. Numbers like 1024x768 or 1600x800 are often quoted and refer to the maximum pixel-width and pixel-height that the display supports. The higher the numbers, the higher the resolution. The higher the resolution, the more you can fit on screen but the smaller each thing on screen becomes. Refer to the display manufacturer's specs to see what it can support because running at their recommended settings will give you the sharpest picture.

The help files are particularly good at explaining how to get the best resolution. Select **What display settings should I choose?**

Setting the screen resolution correctly makes Windows much more usable; the higher the numbers the more there is on screen. Check what your monitor can support, though.

Getting the latest updates

Windows is constantly being updated, normally on what is referred to as "patch Tuesday", which is the second Tuesday of every month. If the patch is urgent Microsoft will release it sooner. These updates are important for keeping Windows 7 secure. Not installing these updates vastly increases your risk of getting hit by a virus or attack. Antivirus software is great, and that's a must too, but update patches ensure things are completely secure. As well as dealing with emerging security threats Microsoft Update can also add tiny bits of functionality and fix residual problems, or "bugs", within the operating system.

By default, Windows 7 should have Automatic Updates turned on, and if not you will see near-constant nagging messages. Compared to older versions of Windows, nag messages are something you see a lot less of in Windows 7, but these ones remain – they're that important!

There is an easy way to find out if Windows Update is turned on and to enable it if not. Go to **Control Panel > System and Security > Action Center**. If Windows Update is switched off the security drop-down menu will automatically be expanded, and a big red section will appear telling you as much. Either choose to **Have Windows install updates automatically** or **Let me choose**. The second option allows selection of exactly which updates are installed, but the first option is highly recommended.

Wherever this icon is shown it has something to do with Windows Update, the process of keeping Windows constantly protected. Occasionally it will appear in the notification area next to the clock if there are updates ready to be installed.

Moving settings over from an old PC

There's a great way to transfer settings from an old PC to a new one. Easy Transfer backs up documents, music, and e-mail – in fact, virtually everything from the old PC. It will even recommend which additional programs to install on the Windows 7 machine to access all your files, and tell you how much disk space you're about to use up.

Tip: Easy Transfer can be used to copy all the files and settings from any previous version of Windows across to Windows 7. Another option if you want to use both computers at the same time is synchronization software like Live Mesh (mesh. com) or Windows Live Synch (synch.live.com). Both of these applications will keep "mirror" copies of the same file on two PCs so that when one copy is updated, both are!

The ways to move stuff are:

▸ Via an Easy Transfer cable, a special cable that connects two PCs via their USB ports on each.
▸ Over your network, either wired or wireless.
▸ Using a USB key or USB hard drive.

To start the Easy Transfer process select **Start > All Programs > Accessories > System Tools > Windows Easy Transfer**.

If using an Easy Transfer cable, connect both PCs together, install the software on the accompanying CD on the old PC and select the **An Easy Transfer Cable** option.

When using the **A Network** or **An external hard disk or USB flash** options to transfer settings, the wizard will ask where to copy

the backup tool installation files. Put them somewhere you'll be able to find them on the network or
on your USB key and then install it onto the old PC
from there.

The wizard walks you through transferring everything from the old PC and says how much it's about
to copy. After it's analyzed all your files you'll be given
the option to **Customize**. This allows you to select
or de-select what's copied. For more precise control
over exactly what gets copied, select the **Advanced**
option.

After the Easy Transfer Wizard is done copying, it'll
tell you what to do next on the new PC. Once everything is transferred over it's not a bad idea to double-check that
you've copied everything you thought you had.

Working with User Accounts

If more than one person is going to be using your PC,
think about each person having their own User Account,
especially if kids are going to be using the same machine.
This way everyone can have individual personal settings,
different wallpapers and different colour schemes. It also
allows their documents and music collections to stay
separate, so you don't have to listen to your kids' music or
put up with their terrible Desktop wallpaper!

Adding User Accounts

To add extra User Accounts open **Control Panel > Add or Remove User Accounts**. All the User Accounts that are already
set up on the PC will show up.

Tip: If it's important for you to be able to
protect your kids when using the PC then
Parental Controls are just the job. These
are found in Control Panel > User Accounts
and Parental Controls. They allow control
of which games and applications kids can
access. You can also set how long they're
allowed to use the PC for and with the addition of an extra application, Windows Live
Family Safety, you can control what they're
able to access on the Web. It's also important to only give them standard User Accounts, not administrator, so that they can't
break the PC or mess with settings.

Getting up and running

Setting up extra User Accounts in Windows is a great idea when more than one person uses the PC. It keeps their documents and settings separate so they can have their own wallpaper or secret files!

To set up a new user, click **Create a new account** and give it a name; it can be anything that means something to both you and the other person who will be using the PC. The type of access that the new User Account has to the PC is important to consider. There are two basic account types within Windows 7 (there are other more advanced and complex types, but these two you'll find easily): **Administrators**, who can do anything on the PC, and **Standard Users**, who can do a lot less. It's a good idea to limit who has administrator access; kids might not need to be administrators as they could damage the PC or even lock out their parents! Administrators can add or remove User Accounts but standard users can't. It's far easier for an administrator to accidentally damage the PC, although something called User Account Control will normally pop up to prevent accidents. You can also set a password for the account if you like, but it's not mandatory.

Tip: The Guest account in Windows 7 is disabled by default, and if you can it's better to leave it that way for security. Normally it's only used when running something like a website from your PC. Enable it by opening Control Panel > User Accounts and Family Safety > Manage another account then select the Guest account. The first time you try to change the account it will be turned on. To turn it off select the account in the same way and select Turn off the Guest account.

The basics

Getting around in Windows 7

Windows 7 Basics

Windows 7 has been blessed with major visual enhancements which make it the easiest version of Windows to navigate. If you've ever used Windows before then it'll still feel familiar, although some things, like the notifications and the taskbar, have been tweaked considerably.

The Start menu

The Start menu in Windows 7 has undergone a complete overhaul. It's far more intelligent than previous versions, adapting itself constantly to what you're doing. From here you can access all the programs you have installed, power down your PC or put it on Standby, access folders and perform searches.

Using Windows 7

Windows 7 has the potential to significantly change the way we interact with computers. One of the main advances comes from the ability to prod and poke at your screen with your fingers to interact with your PC. In fact it's much more than just prodding and poking; with a compatible display you can move elements around on the screen and use gestures to make it even easier to navigate. In some cases you might not need to use the mouse at all!

Windows 7 can also be controlled with your voice. Like something out of *Star Trek*, you can literally talk to your PC (using specific commands) and tell it to do something. You can, for example, say "Start Paint" and have the paint application launch.

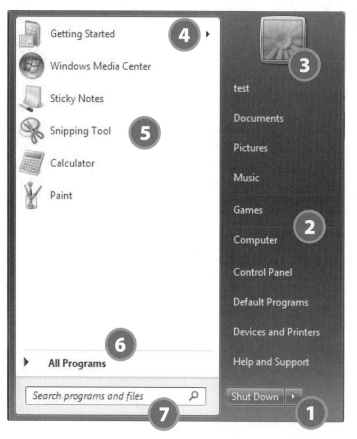

The Start menu:

1 **Power button** – Shut Down, Standby, Restart, Log Off and Switch user functions.

2 **Shortcuts** – access to common areas of Windows 7.

3 **Your account image** – a picture to represent you.

4 **Start menu item with Jump List** – the small arrow to the right can open files directly from the Start menu.

5 **Recently used Start menu items** – any recent programs appear here.

6 **All Programs** – Shortcuts to every program installed on your PC.

7 **Search** – quickly find and launch programs and files.

Useful icons to recognize

There are a plethora of beautiful new icons in Windows 7. It's not immediately obvious what they all do, so here's a quick guide.

 Libraries are where you store your documents, music, videos, pictures and other files in Windows 7.

  The Recycle bin works in exactly the same way as in previous versions of Windows. When you delete a file or folder it's moved to the recycle bin, not actually deleted. So you can restore any items that you've accidentally deleted. Of course the icon looks much better now and you can easily tell when it's full. To empty it quickly, **right click** on the icon and select Empty Recycle Bin.

 Internet Explorer 8 is the default Web browser that comes installed on Windows 7. It's much improved on previous versions and very well integrated. If you don't like it though (and many people don't), you can choose a different Web browser to be your default.

 There are two applications built into Windows 7 that will play your music and videos, and do other things too. **Windows Media Player 12**, an icon that looks like a play button, is the default. It's great for organising your media collections and can do a whole lot more. **Windows Media Center** will turn your PC into a TV. You can use

it with a remote control up to ten feet away from your computer. It's represented by a green orb.

 The back and forward buttons are used on many of the windows in Windows 7 to enable you to step back to the previous page when completing a task. The forward button is enabled when you have already gone back from a page. Normally there is a small drop-down menu next to the forward button to allow you to select a specifc place to go to. They appear in all file explorer windows and the back button now makes an appearance in Wizards.

Window controls

All windows (unless they have been heavily customised by the software makers) use the same three control buttons in Windows 7.

▸ **Minimize**, a small line – removes windows from view, sending them to an icon on the taskbar.

▸ **Maximize**, a small square – makes the window take up the full screen.

▸ **Close**, an X on a red background – closes the window completely.

The minimize, maximize and close buttons (left to right) are found to the top left of any window.

Getting around in Windows 7

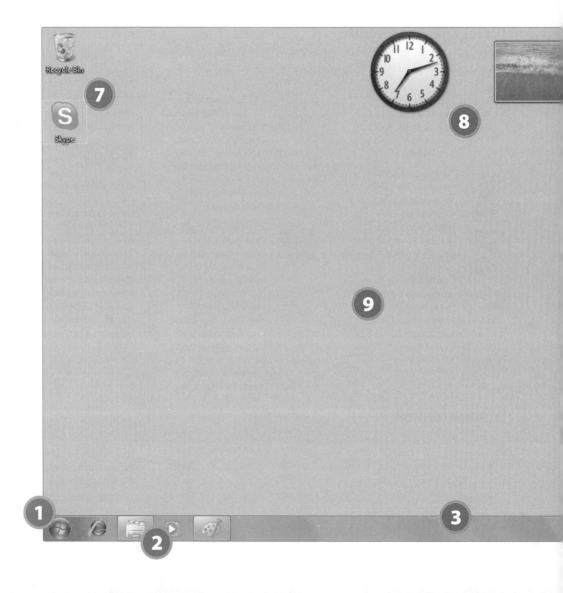

The Desktop:

A quick guide to the visual elements that make up the Windows 7 Desktop.

1 **Start menu** – shortcuts to programs and commonly accessed parts of Windows 7.

2 **Programs pinned to the taskbar** – applications that always sit on the taskbar for fast access.

3 **Taskbar** – a place to pin your most-used programs for fast access and for running programs.

4 **Notification Area** – shows status for applications running in the background.

5 **Date and time** – a bit of a no brainer!

6 **Show Desktop** – hides all the running programs so you can see your Desktop.

7 **Desktop Shortcuts** – shortcuts to programs used frequently.

8 **Desktop Gadgets** – information snippets running on your Desktop.

9 **Desktop** – where applications run and items like documents and gadgets can be placed.

The mouse and keyboard

The mouse and keyboard have been around since the Dark Ages, or at least it seems like they have! They've been around so long it's easy to take what they do for granted, but it's worth looking at a couple of simple techniques to get the most out of the mouse with Windows.

Left-click

To do most things in Windows a mouse is needed (unless Touch is being used). The left mouse button does lots of the work, and there are two techniques available. First, the single-click normally selects something, or if it's a button or a link you're clicking it will start the activity associated with that button or link. For example, clicking a button that says "Open" will open something; clicking an Internet link will go to where that link points.

If there isn't an immediate action associated with whatever is being clicked then a double-click is needed. Where single-clicking an icon on the Desktop will select it, double clicking will open it.

Right-click

The right mouse button is one of the fastest ways to access lots of features within Windows. Right-clicking on anything usually brings up a pop-up list of shortcut options for doing things associated with that item. For example, right-click on the Desktop to reveal options to change the view settings or move to the next wallpaper in a slide show. Right clicking on the taskbar or the Start menu or virtually anywhere within Windows will give you similar context-specific options. If an option is shown in bold it's the default, which normally means it's the action that will happen when using drag and drop.

Drag and drop

One of the most effective and intuitive ways to move things about in Windows is to drag and drop. Simply click on a movable object like a shortcut, a document or file, even text and pictures, then drag your mouse to where you want to put it and let go.

Shortcut keys

Lots of things can be achieved quickly in Windows with shortcut key combinations. For example, to copy and paste some text highlight the text and press **ctrl + c**, then to paste it somewhere put the mouse pointer there and press **ctrl + v**. There's a whole menagerie of useful keyboard shortcuts in Windows 7; try the Windows key ▓ and **tab** for a very cool way to switch tasks. There are more keyboard shortcuts inside the cover of this book.

Understanding the taskbar and Start menu

The taskbar is another feature to have been overhauled in Windows 7 and although it is still referred to as the taskbar it's also now known by the rather awesome title of "Superbar". It's far more intelligent and contextually responds to the task in hand. The Start menu and taskbar combine to provide a launch pad for all your applications, most recently accessed files and search requests.

The taskbar

The taskbar is where you can find all the applications and folders you currently have running or open; each one is represented by an icon and its name. In Windows 7 it's been further enhanced, allowing

> **Tip:** For fast access to the programs on your taskbar you can use the keyboard. Just press the Windows key and then a number. The numbers correspond only to applications that are pinned to your taskbar. By default the first icon is Internet Explorer so to start this you can hold down the Windows key while hitting 1.

Tip: You can close a window without having to first open it from the taskbar. Simply hover over its icon and in the top right of the thumbnail of the window's contents you'll see a red X. Click it to close that window.

If there is more than one window open for a particular application you'll get a visual clue on the taskbar in that the icons appear to be stacked for that application, as in this example for Windows Messenger.

Tip: You can change the order of any of the icons on the taskbar by simply dragging and dropping. This works for both pinned programs and programs that are running.

applications to be "pinned" to the taskbar, making them stay visible there all the time, running or not. This is a surprisingly big change to get used to, but persevere and it pays off. You can pin your most frequently used programs to the taskbar, so that they're always at hand. There are a couple of ways to pin an application.

▸ When it's running (and so already on the taskbar) simply right click and select **Pin this program to the taskbar**.

▸ Drag any shortcut to the taskbar, and then, whilst hovering over the taskbar, the **Pin this program to the taskbar** message will appear next to the cursor; simply drop the shortcut there.

▸ Select any shortcut on the Start menu, right click and select **Pin this program to the taskbar**.

Once programs are pinned to the taskbar you'll only get one icon per program appearing by default, even if you have multiple instances of the same program running.

The visual difference between pinned items and regular running items is a subtle box around the icon. One of the nicest things about Windows 7 is the attention to detail, and this wasn't spared on the taskbar. When hovering the pointer over an icon before clicking it, the background of the icon will shift in hue to one of the prevailing colours in that icon, which makes for a subtly beautiful effect.

When more than one window is open for a particular program, for example if you have two documents open in Microsoft Word, all the instances of Word will be grouped together under one icon. To access these individually, simply hover over the icon and select them from the pop-up thumbnail images of available windows. Another elegant feature is that when the mouse is moved over the icons on the taskbar, the previews transition into each other smoothly. If your PC isn't powerful enough to display the thumbnails then the names of the windows will pop up and can be selected just the same.

Show the Desktop (aka Aero Peek)

With all those cool gadgets and beautiful Desktop wallpapers it would be nice to be able to see them once in a while. Windows 7 has a cool feature called Aero Peek for doing just that (anything with "Aero" in the title just means it looks cool!). To the far right of the taskbar is a small panel; this is the **show Desktop button**. Hovering over the button "peeks" at the Desktop; all windows stay open but become transparent. But to be able to actually get to something on the Desktop, like a gadget, you have to click the **show the Desktop** button and everything will minimize out of the way.

> **Tip:** If you don't like the new "icons only" view of the taskbar and you'd prefer to display the names of the programs as well, right click an empty area of the taskbar (or the Start menu icon). Select Properties and change the taskbar buttons option to either Combine when taskbar is full or Never combine.

Notifications

Applications running on the PC don't necessarily take up space on the taskbar. The notification area, to the left of the clock on the taskbar, is where all the applications running in the background are hiding. It's much improved and less distracting than in previous versions of Windows. It won't hassle you with as many pop-up balloon messages either.

By default there's an Action Center icon. If you're connected to a Wifi network there'll also be an icon for that and you'll see a power status icon if you're using a laptop. Often this is where antivirus software will hide too. Clicking the little up arrow shows a pop-up that reveals other hidden applications that are running. At the bottom of this popup is a **Customize** link which controls how chatty the notifications are, and which ones are hidden.

Customize the notification area icons by opening Control Panel > All Control Panel Items > Notification Area Icons or by hitting Start and typing notification.

The Show Hidden Icons button will expand the notification area so you can see what programs you have running in the background.

The options for hiding icons are:

▶ **Show icon and notifications**, in which case the icon will appear in the notification area on the taskbar.

▶ Only show notifications, which will only show the icon when it has something to say.

▶ Hide icon and notifications, which basically tells the annoying little icon to go away! You can always find the hidden ones by clicking the up arrow next to the clock.

You can customize the Start menu if you don't like the new look. It's easy to set it back to a more familiar style.

The ultimate step backwards is achievable by selecting **Always show all icons and notifications on the taskbar**, which does just what it says. But beware, because in Windows 7 taskbar space is something of a commodity and although the taskbar can take up multiple lines it can become quite hard to use.

Start menu

The Start menu is the control centre where all your installed applications and Windows settings can be accessed. It's also an easy way to start searches. There are shortcuts to Documents, Music, Games and other devices on the network too. Microsoft got the Start menu almost right a long time ago, so improvements over time have been minor and mostly cosmetic. Windows 7 does have a couple of functional enhancements in this area though, notably the Search and Jump lists.

If the new Start menu doesn't suit your needs then issues with it are easily solved. Right click on the Start button or a blank area of the Start menu and select **Properties**. Click on **Customize** and you'll see a plethora of customization options, including the ability to bring back the **Run** command.

The most recently used applications will occupy the left-hand side of the Start menu, making finding them again much easier. A neat feature of Windows 7 is that this list only includes what's been launched from the actual Start menu or from a search. So it doesn't get cluttered with applications that are regularly launched from the taskbar and are already easily accessible.

You can also access the Help files from here. Just click **Start > Help and Support**.

The power of Search in Windows 7

Search in Windows 7 is fast and powerful. It very intelligently replaces the Run command from XP and earlier versions and does far more than a first glance may suggest. There is a Search box in almost every window; even when opening a file from an application there's a search box. It's a massive timesaver.

The contents of the Start menu are automatically searchable as are all the documents within the Libraries (even individual words within those documents are searchable!). On the Start menu Search provides a rapid and intelligent launcher function. So in Windows 7 when you need something, just search; it can be faster than going to get it manually.

To see the real power of Search on the Start menu just start typing. To quickly launch Paint, type "paint", then hit enter; there's no need to wait for it to find results. Paint will start up. If you aren't sure of the exact name just start to type part of it that you know. For example, to configure voice recognition, start typing "voice" and wait to select from the results. You don't even have to have the Search box selected; Windows will automatically focus to the search field when you start to press any keys if the Start menu is open! For a list of really useful searches see the inside cover.

> **Tip:** To quickly manage the current user's account just click the picture at the top of the Start menu; from there it's easy to change passwords or the profile picture. In fact almost all aspects of the User Account can be managed from there.

> **Handy Start menu searches**
>
> Type mail to find any e-mail applications on your PC. Your default should be the first one to appear (you can just press enter to launch it).
>
> Type internet to launch Internet Explorer.
>
> Type notes to launch the Sticky Notes application.
>
> Type media to launch Windows Media Center.
>
> Type player to launch Windows Media Player.

All Jump Lists on the taskbar let you close all the windows for the selected program or to pin or unpin items.

```
Tasks
        Go to MSN home page
        E-mail inbox
        View Windows Live Profile
        Send an instant message...
  ●     Available
        Busy
        Away
        Appear offline
        Sign out from here (SI-PC)

  ●     Windows Live Messenger
  ●     Unpin this program from taskbar
  ●     Close all windows
```

Jump Lists

One of the most productive new features of Windows 7 is Jump Lists; these appear on both the Start menu and the taskbar. Jump Lists are associated with programs and present a variety of options, like the ability to quickly open files that have recently been used by that application. This allows quick access to files in a way that's structured around *what* the documents are rather than *where* they are. It's yet another way Windows 7 lets you stop worrying about your filing, just like Search.

Jump Lists do other things that normally require the application to be opened first. Windows Live Messenger, for example, has a number of tasks that can be accessed via Jump Lists, including the ability to go online while setting your availability status as you go, or to open Hotmail. Live Messenger isn't part of Windows 7 by default but you can find out how to get it in Chapter 11.

There are two ways to access Jump Lists for items on the taskbar:
▸ Right click the mouse on the icon.
▸ Left click the mouse and drag upwards; the Jump List will drag with the mouse (even cooler with a touch screen where it moves up at the flick of a finger!).

On the Start menu Jump Lists appear as a small right-pointing arrow to the right-hand side of a program's name. For most programs they give access to the most frequently or recently used files. Windows Media Player, for example, would show music and videos that are frequently played, such as a favourite album. Jump Lists on the Start menu also perform functions within the program. The Windows Media Player Jump List can shuffle all the music in your collection. Great to listen to music quickly!

The Desktop

The Desktop is the area above the taskbar adorned with a background (wallpaper) of choice, some gadgets that display information and some shortcuts for easy access of applications and files, or the files themselves.

Creating shortcuts

Shortcuts are quick ways to launch applications or files. They don't just appear on the Desktop, they can also live in folders, on the taskbar and in the Start menu. They are essentially a way to put a link to anything on the PC somewhere that's convenient.

There are a few ways to make them but they must be created on the Desktop or in a folder:

▶ Right-click, select **New > Shortcut** and a wizard walks you through setting one up.

▶ Drag and drop the original file using the right mouse button, and a small pop-up menu with a **Create shortcut here** option will appear. The fact that it's in bold makes it the default, so just let go of the button and the shortcut will appear.

To open the gadget gallery quickly just hit the Start button and type gadget. Windows will automatically find and run the gadget gallery for you.

Add the weather gadget to the Desktop and save time looking out the window to see if it's raining. To find this and others, right click and select Gadgets.

Gadgets

Gadgets in Windows 7 are small, visually appealing programs running on the Desktop for specific tasks; normally they provide some sort of at-a-glance information such as up-to-date weather information, the time, CPU usage and so on. A number of gadgets come with Windows 7 by default and give a taste of what you can get.

To add gadgets to the Desktop **right click** an empty area of the Desktop and select **Gadgets** to view the gadget gallery. In the bottom right you'll find a link to **Get more gadgets online** which launches the Windows Live Gallery website, where hundreds of other gadgets are available to download. They've been created by all sorts of media companies, like Sky News and ESPN, as well as private software writers.

Gadgets themselves can be placed anywhere on your Desktop. The entire Desktop could be covered with little information snippets from around the globe, but that would obscure the lovely wallpaper.

There are four basic controls for gadgets:
- ▶ Drag gadget – you can grab by this to move it anywhere on your Desktop.
- ▶ Settings – some gadgets have options for customizing the information they display.
- ▶ Larger / Smaller Size – most gadgets have two displays: large (which typically shows more information) and small.
- ▶ Close – this gets rid of the gadget from the Desktop.

Snap! (or how to quickly resize windows)

A neat feature of Windows 7 and one which is even cooler when using a multi-touch display is Aero Snap. Snap makes it easy to resize windows. Say there are two documents open and a side-by-side comparison is needed; minutes could be spent resizing both windows so that they sit evenly. But now you can slam one window to the left side of the Desktop and the other to the right; it takes only a second. Anything moved and dropped on the far left of the screen automatically takes up the left half of the Desktop, and the same with anything dropped on the right.

Snapping doesn't end there; maximize any window (making it take up the whole screen) by simply dragging it to the top of the Desktop and dropping it there.

Aero Snap can make a window take up half the screen. Simply drag it to the left or right edge and drop. Useful for side-by-side comparison of documents.

Tip: If you've got your wallpaper set to a slide show and you don't like the current one, right click the Desktop and select Next Desktop Background Picture.

Tip: When you're browsing the Internet, most browsers will allow you to select any picture you come across and make it your Desktop wallpaper. This can be a great way to discover interesting pictures; you could try your friends on Facebook, or photo-sharing websites such as flickr.com.

Tip: After creating a theme share it with other people by sending them the .theme file. Just search for your theme's name with .theme suffix at the end.

Shake!

Another neat feature for manipulating windows is Aero Shake. Simply click the top of a window where the title is and shake it. If there are multiple windows open the first time you shake a window all the other windows minimize and vanish. Shake again to restore the other windows. Whoa there shaky!

Making the Desktop more personal

Your PC is all about you: it's got all your important documents, your treasured photos and movies on, so why shouldn't it reflect your personality too? Right click on the Desktop and select **Personalize** and it can! There are all sorts of things to change, from the colour of the frosting on the Aero glass effects or window colours to mouse pointers, screensavers, sounds and account pictures – you can really make Windows your own.

One of the coolest new features is the ability to have a picture slide show as your Desktop wallpaper. Select **Desktop Background** and then select more than one picture and they will rotate through at set intervals. That way every day can be a new picture, or every minute!

Themes allow you to build up a style for the Desktop that includes colours, sounds, wallpaper and screensavers. Build themes by changing everything through **Personalize** and then selecting **Save theme**. There are some really great themes built in, and loads more available online for free by selecting **Get more themes online**.

Working with multiple monitors

Having more than one monitor attached to a computer can make it even more productive. Windows can be open on different monitors at the same time using each for a specific task, each with their own sizes and resolutions. The PC needs to have two video connections to be able to do this but it's a good way to make use of older monitors, and Windows will have no trouble dealing with the different display settings of each. To configure multiple monitors right click on the Desktop and select **Screen Resolution**.

Files, folders and Libraries

A folder is just like its name suggests: a group of things (documents) that you want kept together. In previous versions of Windows this meant a folder for documents, music, videos etc. Folders can contain more than one type of file, so videos and music can be in the same folder, for example.

Libraries are a new feature of Windows 7 and they make it really easy to manage all the files and folders on the PC. There is a Libraries icon on the taskbar; it looks like a group of folders. Libraries bring files and folders from all over the PC (and in fact other PCs on the network) into a single view. From there it's just like managing files in a folder. By default Windows 7 comes with four Libraries to organize files:

▶ Documents – to hold CVs, letters, spreadsheets etc.
▶ Music – oddly enough to hold music.
▶ Video – for films, home movies, that sort of thing.
▶ Pictures – to hold that massive archive of holiday photos.

There is also a Library created automatically if the PC is used as a TV to store recorded TV programs. By default Libraries include all of your own folders and folders that everyone on the PC can access, called "public folders", combining them all into a single view. If the PC is part of a HomeGroup then folders from other PCs in the HomeGroup are included automatically (learn more about Home-Groups in Chapter 22).

Create Libraries by clicking the **New Library** button in the Libraries window. Then select the folders to appear in the Library;

> **Tip:** If you have one very large monitor and one much smaller monitor or you often work on long documents it can be useful to have one display set to portrait and another in landscape mode. This is simple to set up through Control Panel > Appearance and Personalization > Display > Screen Resolution.

The Desktop

If you right click on a Library you can also change which folders belong to that Library and how that Library is arranged; for example, for pictures, music, video or documents.

Tip: It's really easy to share your Libraries with anyone on your computer or your network. Just select the Library you want to share and click the Share with button. Then you can choose who has access to your Libraries and how much access they have.

they can be any folder on the PC or even on another PC on your network. To add network folders (if the PCs aren't in a HomeGroup) enter the name as a network and share path like this:

\\the-name-of-the-computer\the-share-on-the-computer

A share is a folder on another PC that has been made available to other computers on the network. To add more folders to or remove folders from the existing Libraries, go into that Library and click the **Includes: x Library locations link**.

Enhanced user interface

6

Windows Touch

One of the coolest new features of Windows 7 is support for touch screens. Most of what can be done with the mouse, and more, can be done with just a light touch on the screen, which feels much more natural than it sounds. PCs with a touch screen often come with a pen too, making it possible to actually write on the screen – don't worry, the pen doesn't have any ink in it so it won't leave marks!

To set up touch screen and pen support go to **Control Panel > All Control Panel Items** and select **Pen and Touch**. From here it's possible to customize exactly what happens when the screen is touched either by fingers or the pen. The **Flicks** tab is where most of the clever settings are; flicks are gestures of the fingers that can make navigation and other tasks much quicker, explored on the next page.

Using the pen it's possible to write freehand on a special area of the screen. Tap the screen once and the tablet input tool appears at the left-hand edge of the screen; tap or drag the tool into a usable position and start writing on it. Anything written in this area will be converted into text; Windows learns your handwriting and gets more accurate over time.

Enhanced user interface

The flicks

One finger placed on screen then moved swiftly to the right is **back.**

One finger placed on screen and moved up slowly **scrolls down.**

One finger placed on screen then moved swiftly left is **forward.**

One finger placed on screen and moved down slowly **scrolls up.**

With a bit of training you can get Windows to recognize your handwriting and convert it into text.

Generally when using Touch it's best to imagine that your finger is the mouse pointer. So to select something on screen simply touch it once; a touch is like a click. To do a mouse double click touch the screen rapidly twice. There are some simple "flicks" and gestures that are well worth understanding to get the most out of Touch; they're obvious when you think about them, but they aren't available on the mouse. It's great fun exploring Windows

Zooming in on a webpage or picture is achieved by pinching two fingers together and expanding them.

Zooming out is the opposite of zooming in.

Rotating pictures is achieved by touching the picture with one finger and drawing an arc around it with another.

Rightclicking is done by placing one finger on screen and tapping the screen with another finger or by keeping the first finger pressed on the screen (a circle draws around your finger in a clockwise direction; when you've touched the screen long enough and the circle is fully drawn a right click occurs).

with Touch. Media Center works brilliantly and the taskbar is very logical; just drag an icon up to get to its Jump List.

Voice recognition

One fun way to make Windows 7 even more productive is to use the built-in voice recognition technology. With a little practice and a microphone you can actually interact with your computer just by talking to it. It may seem like a fun gimmick for impressing friends, but actually it's possible to dictate all those e-mails or that really long letter.

Setting up voice recognition is just a case of opening **Control Panel > Ease of Access > Speech recognition options**. There are

Enhanced user interface

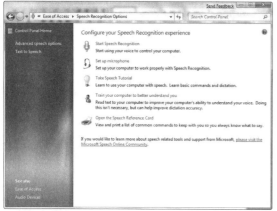

a couple of things you need to do. First, set up a microphone to check that Windows can hear clearly. It's best to use a headset microphone as they don't tend to pick up background noise as much as other types (use a Bluetooth one for that authentic "Uhuru" from *Star Trek* look). The odd background noise isn't too important, but if someone else is in the vicinity who thinks it's clever to keep shouting "Start! Shut down!" then it's probably better to invest in a headset mic. The wizard will calibrate the sound for different types of microphone to try to get the best from them.

Spend fifteen minutes working through the tutorial to learn and familiarize yourself with the commands for speech recognition; it's far better than a trial-and-error approach. If you and your computer just don't seem to be talking the same language, though, there's a way to reach a deeper understanding. Within **Control Panel > Speech recognition options** select **Train your computer to better understand you**; this provides another tutorial to run through which will train your computer and also give tips on ways to use voice recognition more effectively. If you ever get stuck and can't remember what the speech recognition commands are, you can open up **Control Panel >Speech recognition options** and select **Open the speech reference card**.

Configure speech recognition to be able to use the PC just by talking to it. Say "Start, open Internet Explorer" to start browsing the Web.

This toolbar appears whenever speech recognition is enabled. The centre display provides help when things aren't totally clear.

Advanced settings

Control Panel

The Control Panel in Windows is your one-stop shop for changing any of the settings on your PC. There are plenty of other ways to get into the Control Panel, but the main one is to go through Start > Control Panel. Control Panel in Windows 7 has two basic views:

▸ The Home view groups similar components together, making navigation much more intuitive but slightly slower.
▸ The All Control Panel Items view shows you every individual component that makes up the Control Panel.

Click **All Control Panel Items** at the bottom of the initial Control Panel window to change to that view, and to switch back click the **Control Panel Home** icon on the left of the Control Panel.

Ease of Access

Windows 7 aims to be the most accessible version of Windows for people with a variety of physical impairments. The Ease of Access Center allows you to optimize Windows for people with blindness or vision difficulties, hearing difficulties and difficulties using the keyboard and mouse. To access these settings open **Control Panel > Ease of Access**

Control Panel

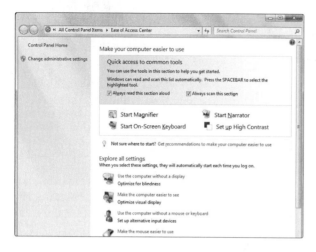

> **Ease of Access Center**. This is also where you can configure voice control of your PC. One of the important things to do for people who need this optimization is to make it easy for them to log on. This requires clicking on the **Change administrative settings** link on the left sidebar. Without it the accessibility optimizations will only take effect after the person has logged on, something they may not be able to do successfully.

Setting program defaults

Default programs are programs used to open specific types of files for specific tasks. For example, Internet Explorer is used when a Web page is opened. Windows allows the default programs to be changed easily to accommodate a preference for a different application. Firefox could be used as an alternative to Internet Explorer, for example. To see what the defaults are or to change them go to **Control Panel > All Control Panel Items > Default Programs**.

One word of warning: when you open the Ease of Access Center your PC will automatically start talking to you. It can be a little disconcerting the first time, so turn your speakers down.

To select things like a default browser and e-mail program, go to **Set program access and computer defaults**. It's also possible to select which application will open a specific file type, like a ".doc" file, but it's normally best to just let the applications manage that themselves.

Putting a CD or DVD into a drive makes things happen automatically via AutoPlay. Exactly what happens when can be set according to preference. For example, when inserting a CD you might always want it to be ripped (copied) to your music collection rather than having it play. Different activities can happen when different things are inserted. A DVD movie might always play, but a DVD with enhanced content (extras just for the PC) will open a window to view the disk's contents. **Change AutoPlay settings** allows all this to be customized.

Action Center

Action Center is the place to go to find out about the health and status of Windows. It keeps information about the security and maintenance of your PC. It's available from **Control Panel > All Control Panel Items > Action Center** or **Control Panel > System and Security>Action Center** or the flag icon in the notification area.

The **Security** drop-down in **Action Center** shows the status of antivirus, anti-spyware, firewall, Windows updates and other security measures. The **Maintenance** drop-down shows the status of backups and any problems with previous backups.

Action Center is also a springboard to other areas of Control Panel like User Account control, Troubleshooting and Recovery.

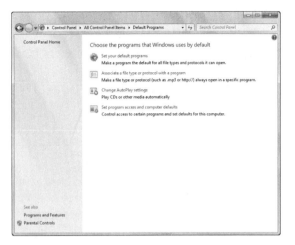

Don't like your default Web browser? Program Defaults is the place to change it.

User Account Control

User Account Control (UAC) is a security measure that helps prevent accidental or malicious damage to Windows. UAC stops software on websites or within Windows from running on your PC without you first accepting that it's okay. If a dodgy website has code embedded in it to make changes to the PC, UAC will pop up asking if it's okay to proceed. Without UAC it's possible that a website could have made a change to your computer without your knowledge. Most websites wouldn't do that, but it's a risk that the PC is protected against with Windows 7.

UAC is also visible on menus and buttons that make changes to the PC's configuration. It's a visual warning of a small blue and yellow shield icon indicating it's possible to do accidental damage. This is an improvement over Windows Vista where UAC became one of

Tip: Some applications can't yet cope with UAC and you'll need to disable it in order to use them without any problems. It's easy to do just by going into User Account Control Settings and setting the slider to Never notify.

Control Panel

User Account Controls help protect the PC from malicious applications or accidental damage. Control how much it nags with a simple slider.

the most unpopular, derided and ultimately **turned off** features of Windows. Microsoft made great efforts to make UAC far less annoying in Windows 7 and most people will now be able to leave it turned on.

To change or view UAC settings open **Control Panel > All Control Panel Items > Action Center > User Account Control settings**. UAC is easy to control now thanks to a slider that makes it more or less chatty (or annoying). Slide to the top for a more annoying PC (and more secure) and to the bottom to effectively disable UAC. It's best to leave it at the default in most circumstances.

Troubleshooting

Also available through the Action Center, troubleshooting helps fix PC problems using a variety of wizards. Each walks you through a series of small changes in order to diagnose a problem. It can be used to fix issues with:

▶ Programs.
▶ Hardware.
▶ Network and Internet connections.
▶ The way your PC looks.
▶ The security of your PC. (If, for example. you've lost access to a folder.)

The wizards are simple to follow and everything they do can be easily undone. For more information on fixing Windows problems see the Troubleshooting section at the end of this book.

Tip: If you click the Windows Experience Index link it will give you a detailed breakdown and tell you how you can improve your score.

Recovery

Recovery gives access to a feature called System Restore, basically a Windows time machine for use when something's gone wrong. Use it to step back in time to when the PC was last working. System Restore creates a restore point before you install any applications, so if something screws up the PC generally it's possible to undo it.

The part of System Restore that Recovery gives access to is not the whole story. You can do more, like configure when restore points are made or manually make your own restore point. To get to this part of System Restore go to **Control Panel > System and Security > System > Advanced system settings**.

System

System shows all sorts of things about the PC, an indication of what it's capable of, details about the processor, how much memory there is and whether a bona fide copy of Windows is installed. It's accessed from **Control Panel > System and Security > System**.

Once you get there you'll see the Windows Experience Index, showing how capable your PC is in terms of its hardware. The higher the Windows Experience Index score the better equipped the PC is for multitasking, running games smoothly and so on. The highest score possible in Windows 7 is 7.9; to get that requires a really fast processor with massive amounts of memory, a huge video card and lightning fast components connecting it all together. It can be a lot of fun upgrading your PC to get to that 7.9 score, but it can also be very, very expensive!

This is also the place you can change the name of your PC (remember you set this when you were installing Windows), to manage your hardware or to get really nitty gritty with your peripheral devices (all the other stuff you have attached to your computer). You'll need Administrator access to manage your system settings properly.

> **Tip:** You can also get into System by right clicking on Computer on the Start menu and selecting Properties.

Control Panel

Side Show

Side Show connects devices like small screens or even some mobile phones to the PC to display specific information, like what's currently playing in Media Player or what e-mails are in your inbox. A Side Show device will come with instructions on how to set up Side Show as it varies device by device. What can be shown in a Side Show depends on the Side Show gadgets installed on the PC. Only a couple come as standard but there are loads more available online by selecting **Get more gadgets online** from the left of the Control Panel window. Some laptops come with a small Side Show screen on the outside of the laptop, so it's possible to see if any new mails have come in without opening it. A Windows Phone running Windows Mobile 6.5 can be added as a Side Show remote control for Windows Media Center too.

Getting speakers set up just right is really important, especially for games. Use the Sound Control Panel to tweak the speaker setup of your PC.

Sounds

Configuring sound can take a little time if you want to get it just right. Get to the settings through **Control Panel > All Control Panel Items > Sound**, to show the audio devices set up on the PC. On the Playback tab is the main sound device; double-click or highlight it and select **Configure**. A wizard will then help you configure the speakers, making sure the speakers are located correctly and the correct sound is coming from each, especially useful with a complicated 7.1 surround setup. Clicking **Properties** shows which connection jack is which on the PC and configures volume levels and special enhancements, like creating the effect of being in an opera house. The **Advanced** tab will let you configure sound quality. This is something not many people will need to play with, and it's normally best to leave it set to the highest quality possible.

Managing User Accounts

User Accounts have lots of different settings, from the password right through to the profile picture. Managing them is easy. Open Control Panel > User Accounts > Manage another User Account. From here you can change the name of the account, change or even remove the password (or set one on a new account), change the profile picture, configure Parental Controls or change the access that the account has.

To manage your own account open **Control Panel > User Accounts and Family Safety** and follow the quick links to **Change your account picture** or **Change your Windows password**.

Linking your Windows User Account to online IDs
Linking the User Account on your PC to an online user ID makes it easier to manage and for people to share things with you. Once the local User Account is linked to an online ID, like a Windows Live ID, then the online ID is the only ID you need give to people. Even if people on your local network want to share files with you, they can use the online ID and Windows will sort out the rest. So if someone wants to share something with you they don't need to know your username, which frankly could be anything, just your e-mail

Tip: Every account on Windows has an account picture that helps identify the user when signing in to the PC; by default when you set up an account it will be assigned a picture. You can assign any picture in your collection to be your account picture. Just click the account picture at the top of the Start menu to change it.

Tip: For the strongest password use a combination of letters, numbers, characters (like ##,./!"£$%^&) and upper and lower case.

Managing User Accounts

address. Also if you use two PCs in the house the User Accounts may have different names – one could be Bob1 and another could be Bob2. It's possible to link the accounts for these separate machines to the same online ID. So logged onto one PC as Bob1, you can access your files on the other PC under the Bob2 account just by connecting over the network with the Bob2 details.

To set this up, you will first need an online ID; go to **get.live.com** to sign up. Then go to **Control Panel > All Control Panel Items > User Accounts > Link Online IDs**. Then select the **Add an online ID provider** link at the bottom of the window. This launches a webpage listing the available ID providers, follow the instructions to install a small package that will link to that provider. Finally go back to **Control Panel > All Control Panel Items > User Accounts > Link Online IDs** where a new option will have appeared for Online ID Providers. Click the **Add Linked ID** link, enter log on details for the ID provider and you're all set.

Why not change the default profile picture for your account? Go to Control Panel > All Control Panel Items > User Accounts **then** select Change your picture **and** browse your photo collection for something more personal.

Tip: Manage each set of credentials just by clicking on the little down arrow to the right of the credential. If you want to add new credentials select the Add a link under each section.

Managing stored credentials

When logging in to a website through Internet Explorer, Windows can remember your username and password combination to save having to log in to the site again. **Control Panel > All Control Panel Items > User Accounts > Manage your credentials** allows control of those accounts and allows you to back up your credentials. There are three types of credentials:

▸ Windows credentials are accounts that you use to access other Windows resources, like another PC that has a different user name and password combination.

▸ Certificate-Based credentials is where you can store certificates for sites that require high levels of security and issue you with a certificate to verify your identity – these are quite few and far between.

▸ Generic Credentials are probably the most used type; they allow you to store credentials for websites you visit frequently and the like.

It's a good idea to back up your credentials if you have a lot of them, as they can easily be forgotten. This is as easy as going to **Control Panel > User Accounts and Family Safety > Credential Manager** and selecting **Backup Vault**.

Enter a location for the vault to be saved to; it's best to make this a removal disk of some type, like a USB key (but be sure to take care of it). Next it will prompt to press the **ctrl** and **alt** and **del** keys on the keyboard at the same time.

The screen will go blank and only a password entry screen will appear. Enter a really strong password with upper case and lower case letters, numbers and symbols – don't forget this one file has all your passwords in it! The backup will then be saved.

To restore your vault go to **Control Panel > User Accounts and Family Safety > Credential Manager** and select **Restore Vault**. Browse to the location of the backup vault and click **next**. Press **CTRL + ALT + DEL** when prompted, then enter the password for the vault; once done the restore should complete in an instant.

Online IDs

Online ID providers are organisations that give you access to Internet-based tools and services. The best example is Windows Live. With a Windows Live ID you can access all of Microsoft's online services from a single account. Normally an online ID takes the form of an e-mail address which is linked to stuff like Messenger, online storage, calendars, a blog, photo sharing, Zune, Xbox etc. It can represent every facet of your online existence.

Backing up passwords

It's a good idea to back up your passwords, just in case you ever get locked out of your PC. It's simple to do. Open Control Panel > User Accounts and Family Safety then select User Accounts and finally from the quick list on the left select Create a password reset disk. A USB key or a floppy disk is needed. Read the first screen of the wizard, click next and enter the location that you want to back up to. Click next again and enter the password for the account you are currently signed on with and click next again. Once it completes you'll have a backup of your account password that can be used to recover all your other passwords.

User switching: how can more than one person use my PC?

If more than one person will be using the computer it's a good idea to create a separate account for each person. This will keep individuals' documents and settings separate. To access their own stuff each person will need to log on to the PC. Switching accounts between users is very straightforward. There are two ways:

▶ Log off – essentially this shuts down everything being worked on and gives the other person total access to the PC. To do this select **Start** then click the arrow to the right of the power button on the Start menu and select **Log off**.

▶ Switch user – this keeps all applications open and lets someone else log on and use the PC. It has the downside of slightly lower performance since everything is still running. To do this select **Start** then click the arrow to the right of the power button on the Start menu and select **Switch user**.

Switch user is really handy if the other person only needs to use the PC for a short period of time. If someone has switched users and tries to shut the PC down, they'll be told that someone is still logged on and might have unsaved files. If they are an Administrator they can shut down anyway – another reason to restrict who are Administrators!

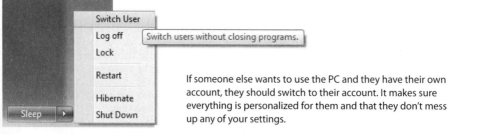

If someone else wants to use the PC and they have their own account, they should switch to their account. It makes sure everything is personalized for them and that they don't mess up any of your settings.

The Internet

Internet Explorer and the Web

9

The Internet is a massive group of interconnected computers all over the world. Originally invented for the military, it has evolved far beyond its original purpose. What does remain, however, is its basic stability. It's always there. What we normally think of as the Internet is actually the World Wide Web, sort of the front end to the Internet. There's more to it than that but that's basically what most of us use every day. To understand the Internet it's a good idea to have a grasp of some basic terms:

- ▸ Webpage – a page of information that exists on the Internet. It can be made up of pictures, words, video, sounds and countless other things.
- ▸ Website – a collection of webpages.
- ▸ Address – this is the location on the Internet of a website or a webpage. It's also known as a URL (which means Uniform Resource Locator, but you'll probably never hear that mentioned).
- ▸ Domain name – forms part of the address of a website. It's the "roughguides.com" in an address. Domain names allow a website address to easily become memorable and to associate it with a brand. Every domain name must be unique.

▶ **Hyperlink** – often just called a link. These sit on webpages and are pointers to other websites or other pages within a website. Links are usually highlighted within the text or pictures on a site and will often change appearance when you hover over them with the mouse pointer. Behind any hyperlink is an address.

▶ **Internet browser** – software that lives on the computer (such as Internet Explorer) that allows viewing or "browsing" of webpages.

▶ **Download** – the process of taking something from the Internet and storing it somewhere on the PC.

▶ **Upload** – the process of taking something from the PC and storing it on the Internet.

▶ **Search engine** – there is so much information on the Internet that it's hard to find things. Search engines constantly watch webpages for changes and can be searched for specific terms or words. Google is currently the most popular and famous.

Web 2.0 and social networking

Fact: If Facebook were a country it would be the sixth biggest in the world with a population of over 175 million active users. Some say there is more information on Facebook now than on the rest of the Internet!

A term you hear a lot these days is "Web 2.0". It refers to websites made up of "user-generated content", meaning the information people go there for isn't created by one person or one group but by the people who use the website. Some great examples are YouTube, Twitter and Wikipedia.

Social networking is a form of Web 2.0 that also gets a lot of press. There are all kinds of social networking sites, Bebo, Facebook and MySpace being some of the largest. Facebook is actually the most popular website in many countries around the world. Social networking sites allow users to "share" things with their friends. Friends can be either people they know in the real world or people they have met online. At one time this "networking" was thought to be the retreat for sad, lonely people with nothing better to do. These days, though, everyone is doing it, even the US president!

Internet Explorer 8

The most installed and used Internet browser on the planet is Microsoft Internet Explorer. This is largely because it ships as the default browser on most new PCs. Internet Explorer 8 (IE8) comes with Windows 7 and has some massive improvements in both how it is used and the more open standards it supports. This poses a challenge to many websites which were heavily customized to support previous versions of Internet Explorer. The more standards-based IE8 doesn't actually display them very well. There are ways around that, though.

You can launch IE8 from its icons on either the taskbar or Start menu. Once open it's immediately quite different in appearance from IE6, which is still in massive use and accounts for about forty percent of all Internet traffic. The look is similar to IE7 but there are many improvements.

Tabs

Tabs are one of IE8's most useful features. Tabbed browsing will be familiar to anyone who's used Firefox or Internet Explorer 7. Within one window it's possible to have lots of webpages open, each in its own tab. It might not be immediately obvious why that's a good idea, but it reduces clutter on the taskbar dramatically. It integrates nicely with the taskbar and shows each open tab as a separate preview thumbnail when hovering over the IE8 icon. Tabs have exactly the same functionality as webpages opened in separate windows.

By default in IE8 one tab opens automatically to display your home page and the name of the website is shown on the tab, along with a little icon or "favicon". Extra tabs can be opened by clicking the smaller tab to the right of the open tabs.

Internet Explorer and the Web

Internet Explorer toolbar:

1 Forward and back buttons – these are the main way to navigate; the back button is probably the more useful of the two and allows you to retrace your steps. The back-space key on your keyboard does the same thing.

2 Address bar – where you type the address, like roughguides.com, of a website you want to visit. Type in a non-Web address like just "rough guides" and a search for rough guides will start. ALT + D is a quick way to focus on the address bar.

3 (left to right) **Compatibility mode** opens pages as if using an older browser. Refresh the current page reloads everything on the webpage you're looking at. Stop prevents a webpage from loading fully – useful if you've gone to the wrong place.

4 Search bar – lets you quickly search for things on the Web. The drop-down to the right allows different searches like Wikipedia or Google to be used if they're installed.

5 Access to favorite websites – a collection of links to the places you like to go.

6 Tabs – webpages can be opened in their own tabs, making browsing neater and much more efficient.

> ### Tip:
> You can add all sorts of toolbars to IE. There are plenty available from Microsoft, Google and Yahoo! But anyone who wants to make one can. Sometimes they bring something useful to the party but often they don't unless you're hooked on the services of the company providing it. The Windows live toolbar, downloads.live.com, allows your Favorites to sync with Live.com as well as fast access to Live.com features. The Google toolbar, (google.com/toolbar) does the same thing, and there are ways to extend this further with widgets. The Yahoo! toolbar (toolbar.yahoo.com) has some extra features to make browsing safer.

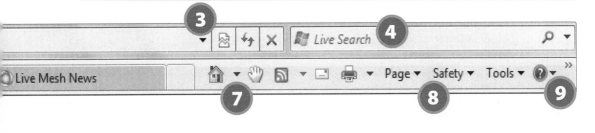

7 (left to right) **Go to the home page, open a feed** (highlights orange when there's a feed on the page), **send the webpage in an e-mail, print the webpage.**

8 **Menu options** – these three menus for more advanced options are good to get to know, especially the **Safety** menu. There are many hidden gems here.

9 **Help button** in case you get stuck.

The status bar:

1 **Current status** – describes what's happening. If it's loading a page, it will say "waiting", "downloading" and "Done" when it's all over. Handily it'll inform you how many items on the page are remaining to download, and will count down as each loads.

2 **Notifications** – icons appear in this area when there's something you need to know, such as when SmartScreen has found a problem or when a popup has been blocked.

3 **The current Zone** – security in Internet Explorer is based on Zones; the Internet Zone has the highest level of security.

4 **Zoom** – Clicking this area lets you zoom in and out, making the text and pictures larger or smaller – handy if you encounter something in a tiny font. It's also possible to do this with **CTRL +** and **CTRL –** or with a pinch/unpinch motion if you have a touch screen. Have a look at Chapter 6 for some more detailed info on doing that.

Internet | Protected Mode: On   🔍 100% ▾

Sometimes it's useful to open a second copy of a webpage, to follow a specific link from the site, for example. To do that right click on the tab and select Duplicate Tab.

> **Tip:** Tabs can be moved around and reordered on the tab bar. Select a tab and hold down the left mouse button while dragging it horizontally to shuffle it around.

When a link on a webpage is clicked, that page will open in the current tab, replacing what's already there. To open the page in a new tab, **right-click** the link and select **Open in New Tab**. You can also do this a bit quicker by holding down the **CTRL** key while left-clicking on the link.

When more than one tab is open a tab can be closed by clicking the **X** on the tab or by pressing **CTRL + W** on the keyboard. It can be annoying accidentally closing a tab, but that's not a problem with IE8. Just open a new tab and a **What do you want to do next?** page appears with three sections, one of which is **Reopen closed tabs**. This section shows all the tabs that have been closed during the browsing session. Just click on the page that was accidentally closed to reopen it. It's a total lifesaver.

Moving around and searching

Navigation in IE8 is just the same as in any other browser. To open a page click the link on a webpage, and the new page will load in place of the one you are currently viewing. IE8 keeps a history for each tab, so if at any point you want to go back to a previous page, just click the **Back** arrow button. Unsurprisingly, you use the **Forward** arrow button to go forward again.

> **Tip:** Press CTRL + Q to view all the open tabs in a grid with previews of what's on each page. If you have lots of open tabs it makes navigation a cinch.

To go to a specific Web address (also known as a URL), type the address into the address bar and hit **enter**. Addresses have historically been preceded by **www** but for most sites you can omit this when typing into the address bar. For example, **www.bbc.co.uk** or **www.google.com** can also be reached simply with **bbc.co.uk** or **google.com**.

The most common way to find things on the Internet is to use a search engine. Google is king of the hill at the moment, finding the most relevant results in fractions of a second. Interestingly, Google only actually indexes about one percent of the whole Internet, but that's more than enough for most. Microsoft also has a search engine, called Live Search. In some ways it's better than Google (you can get paid to use it for shopping, for example!) and it can often root out some different results to Google. Internet Explorer is set up to use Live Search, and there's a search area in the top right of the browser to make searches easier. Just type in what you're looking for and hit **enter**.

Favorites

Many of us go to the same webpages over and over again. A good way to make it easier to get there rather than having to type the address in every time is to add it as a favorite. The Favorites button on the toolbar brings up a list of your currently stored faves. It also reveals the **Add to Favorites** button that'll add the currently open webpage to your Favorites list. You can also add Favorites from the keyboard by pressing **CTRL + D**.

After adding a favorite a more friendly name can be added for the webpage (the page title is used by default). Favorites can be organized into folders and moved around by dragging and dropping them within the folders pane.

The **Favorites Bar** is a special folder within Favorites. Anything in this folder will appear on a toolbar called, funnily enough, the Fa-

> **Tip:** It's easy to add other search engines to IE8. Click the drop-down to the right of the search box and select Find More Providers Select one from the list and a popup asking Do you want to add this search provider? appears, click Add to add it and make it the default if you wish. That way Google, Yahoo!, Ask, Live or even Wikipedia can be used directly from the search box.

Sometimes it can be a bit tricky to view the text on a website. If things are too small then zoom in! Select Tools > Zoom > Zoom In to make things bigger or Tools > Zoom > Zoom Out to make them smaller. Another quick way is CTRL + and CTRL -. If your computer has a touch screen you can zoom in by placing two pinched fingers on screen and moving them apart (pinch them back again to zoom out)!

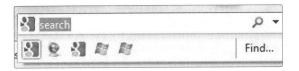

vorites Bar. It's a handy way to access websites that are used daily in just one click. To turn it on, right click anywhere on the toolbar area and select **Favorites Bar**.

Suggested sites

IE8 has an inbuilt feature to help you discover new websites you might find of interest. It uses your browsing history to suggest sites that are similar to places you have already been. To enable it, go into **Favorites** and click **Turn on Suggested Sites** at the bottom of the pane. It takes a little while before it knows you well enough to start feeding you useful sites. Once it is enabled you can get suggestions by going back into **Favorites** and clicking **See Suggested Sites** at the bottom of the pane.

Compatibility View

IE8 supports more open Web standards, which is a good move by Microsoft since it makes webpages easier to build. Unfortunately Internet Explorer has been the standard for so long that many websites customized themselves to work with previous versions. Consequently some pages look a little messed up in IE8, but you can get around this by using Compatibility View.

Compatibility View displays websites as if using IE7. It's a bit of a backwards step, but most sites will catch up as they eventually get updated with new designs. To activate it, click the broken page icon in the address bar. Once one webpage for a domain (like roughguides.co.uk) has been opened in Compatibility View all other pages there will open in Compatibility View. IE8 remembers this between sessions too so you won't have to do it more than once for any problem sites.

Favorites in IE8 are great if you just want to keep track of Favorites on your own, but there can be far more to Favorites than that. Del.icio.us is a fantastic website for sharing Favorites (also known as Bookmarks) with friends, through something called social bookmarking. The idea is that friends are interested in the same stuff as you and by sharing you all get to see more of the Web. Find out more at delicious.com; it's free.

Tip: A fast way to check if there is anything new on a page is to hit F5 on the keyboard to refresh the open webpage.

Printing

There might be times when it's handy to print out a webpage, for example after getting some directions from **maps.live.com.** In IE8 you can conveniently print the current webpage by clicking the printer icon in the toolbar. Additional options are in the drop-down just to the right of this. **Print Preview** opens a view of the page as it will print. It's always good to do this because what prints out might not be exactly what's expected. **Page Setup** allows options like a header with the address of the webpage to be printed too.

Popups

A popup is a simple idea that went badly wrong. When surfing the net it's easy to come across a site that will throw up a window with an advert or something else unwanted in it. As a result, pop-up windows are blocked in IE8; generally that's a good thing. When it happens a bar will appear at the bottom of the toolbar letting you know a popup was blocked, but it's subtle and easily missed. There will naturally be sites you go to all the time that you trust not to pop up something unwanted. To that end, you can configure pop-up blocking by going to **Tools > Pop-up Blocker**. It can be turned off (not recommended) or configured with **Pop-up Blocker Settings**. The Pop-up Blocker is rules-based, much like everything in IE8. Adding a site means that popups will always be allowed to appear there. It's possible to add whole domains, like this ***.roughguides. co.uk**, but only do that if the site can be trusted.

Is that website real?

For some uses, like Internet banking, security is paramount. All sites of this nature have something called a "certificate" that proves they are who they say they are. This stops people putting up a fake website claiming to be someone else. Not all sites need a certificate, but

Some websites won't display properly in Internet Explorer 8 because they've been built for older versions. The compatibility view button, to the right of the address bar, forces IE8 to display the page correctly.

Tip: Printing webpages can be wasteful; there's often lots of stuff on them that we don't need. Hewlett Packard (HP) have an excellent application called "HP Smart Web Printing" that comes with their printers and is available for free from their website hp.com (just search for HP Smart Web Printing). It makes it possible to compose a printed page from lots of different webpages very simply, saving paper and ink. You don't even need to have an HP printer.

Tip: Many antivirus packages, including free ones like AVG (free.avg.com), include an application that will "rate" the security of websites. This often appears as a green tick or a red X next to search results from Google or Live Search.

Tip: IE8 integrates cleverly with the taskbar so that when downloading a file the background of the IE8 icon there will fill with green from left to right to indicate download progress – handy if you have another window open over the top of Internet Explorer.

never use a service like Internet banking or a site where you have to disclose personal information without one.

▶ If a site has a valid certificate, the address bar goes green and a locked padlock appears.
▶ If a site has a certificate, but something is wrong with it, the bar will go red, an indication that the site might be a fake, so unless you have good reason to believe that the red bar is a mistake don't log on!

How Internet Explorer prevents phishing

Phishing is when a website pretends to be something it's not in order to steal critical information about you. For example, there are often scams where a website will pretend to be your bank in order to get your banking details. As well as the security certificates described above, IE8 has an additional feature called "SmartScreen Filter". When this is turned on through **Safety > SmartScreen Filter > Turn On SmartScreen Filter** it checks the pages you're viewing to see if there's anything fishy (or phishy) about them. It looks for particular bits of code on the page that aren't quite as they should be or that match up to a specific set of criteria. SmartScreen Filter also checks against Microsoft's hourly updated list of dodgy sites to see if your browser is being redirected to somewhere bad.

If a website is malicious a pop-up message will let you know; it has lots of red on it so it'll be hard to miss. You'll be given the option to continue anyway or to just get out of Dodge. If you happen across a site whilst surfing that you know is doing something wrong you can report it. It's through these reports that Microsoft can enhance their list of dodgy sites. To file a report go to **Safety > SmartScreen Filter > Report Unsafe Website**. The list of unsafe sites is vetted so you should only get a warning when you've been somewhere that really is a nasty.

At any time you can confirm your suspicions about a website by forcing a check; to do that go to **Safety > SmartScreen Filter > Check this website**.

InPrivate browsing

There are many reasons why one might not like others to know what they've been looking at on the Internet. Perhaps it's buying a present for a spouse or the kids and is a secret till a special day. IE8 includes a feature called InPrivate browsing that helps with this.

Every page that's visited in Internet Explorer is held in the history; that's why it's possible to go back and forward through pages. Many pages also store "cookies" on the computer to save settings used on their websites or track the time between visits. This makes it possible for people to snoop.

InPrivate Browsing stops IE8 from creating a history or saving cookies. To switch it on select **Safety > InPrivate Browsing**. A separate IE8 window will open that is private and an InPrivate symbol will be displayed to the left of the address bar.

> **Tip:** InPrivate browsing is great, but occasionally it can be a bit annoying. Because it doesn't store cookies, (small packets of information about what you have done on a website), sites can behave differently to how you'd usually expect. For example, If an ad pops up and you click a button to "ignore", it will just keep popping back up at you as the browser can't store a cookie telling it to ignore that popup.

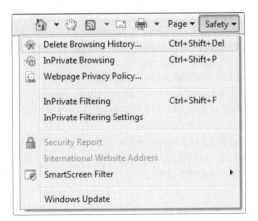

A fast way to start InPrivate browsing is CTRL + SHIFT + P.

Covering your tracks

When browsing normally it's possible to remove some of the footprints that are left behind. Go to **Safety > Delete Browsing History** and select exactly which things you want to remove and keep private.

Accelerators

IE8 has a handy new feature that makes doing things with the information on a webpage even easier. Called accelerators, they either allow something to be done with the whole page or with some selected text. Accelerators are activated by **right-clicking** and selecting one from the pop-up menu. Some accelerators are already built-in for tasks like translating words on a page, searching or looking up more details on a subject in Microsoft Encarta (Microsoft's encyclopedia).

Webpage accelerators, which affect the whole page, are located by right clicking anywhere on the page. **Translate with Windows Live**, for example, will translate the whole page to another language.

The other way to use an accelerator is to select some text, then **right-click** and select an accelerator like **Define with Encarta**. As well as right-clicking you can also find accelerators in the small blue box that appears to the top right of any text you select on a webpage.

Not all accelerators are immediately visible, but anywhere the accelerators appear there will be an **All Accelerators** option that will show more.

Choose carefully which parts of your browsing history to wipe out. Deleting passwords may not be a great idea. Do you really know all your website passwords?

Delete Browsing History — Send Feedback

☑ **Preserve Favorites website data**
Keep cookies and temporary Internet files that enable your favorite websites to retain preferences and display faster.

☑ **Temporary Internet files**
Copies of webpages, images, and media that are saved for faster viewing.

☑ **Cookies**
Files stored on your computer by websites to save preferences such as login information.

☑ **History**
List of websites you have visited.

☐ **Form data**
Saved information that you have typed into forms.

☐ **Passwords**
Saved passwords that are automatically filled in when you sign in to a website you've previously visited.

☐ **InPrivate Blocking data**
Saved data used by InPrivate Blocking to detect where websites may be automatically sharing details about your visit.

About deleting browsing history — Delete — Cancel

Web Slices

Often there'll be a website that you visit regularly for updated information. It might be a graph of your stocks and shares, or it might be a weather site. IE8 includes a feature called Web Slices, which are sections of a website that it'll automatically get updates for and let you know when they've changed. When a Web Slice is added it appears in the Favorites Bar along with your Favorites and suggested sites. More and more websites are adding Web Slices to their homepages, but there are loads available at **ieaddons.com**.

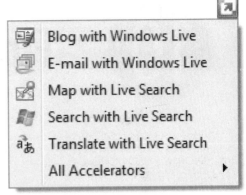

Removing Internet Explorer

Windows 7 is the first version of Windows ever to allow Internet Explorer to be removed. This is actually a huge step for the operating system. It's been possible to opt out of using Internet Explorer for some time, but now you can actually tell it to "be gone!". Kissing goodbye to Internet Explorer, though, does take a little thinking about.

Accelerators can be added to by going to ieaddons.com. There are some great ones out there, particularly the Wikipedia search and the Twitter and Facebook sharing accelerators.

First there is the question of how you'll live without it. Removing it without slotting something else in its place will lead to a total lack of access to the Web. Bearing in mind that downloading another browser is the most obvious way to get one, make sure it's been downloaded before you remove Internet Explorer.

The next question you need to answer is "Do any of the sites that I rely on require Internet Explorer?". If the answer to that is yes, then it's best to leave it installed; it still doesn't preclude using another browser. It's likely that you won't know the answer to the above question if you've never tried other browsers. If you do fancy the idea of not using Internet Explorer then try running two browsers side by side before removing it. There are still some sites out there that only work well with Internet Explorer.

10 Firefox

Internet Explorer isn't the only option when it comes to Internet browsers on Windows 7. The second most popular browser available today is Mozilla Firefox. The latest release of Firefox (version 3) can be downloaded for free from mozilla.org and installation is simple.

Firefox is considered by many to be more secure than Internet Explorer because there have historically been fewer problems or vulnerabilities associated with it. That said, for the first time ever in 2008 Firefox fared worse than Internet Explorer for vulnerability, but these issues were fixed faster than the equivalent Internet Explorer flaw.

Firefox 3 holds the Guinness World Record for the most downloads on a single day. On 18 June 2008 more than eight million downloads were recorded in 24 hours, showing just how popular an alternative it is!

What's different to IE8

Firefox functions in almost the same way as IE8; it uses tabs and windows just the same. It looks quite different, and some of the features have different names, but it only takes a short while to get used to.

One of the most obvious differences is that Favorites are called bookmarks in Firefox, which is actually a far more standard term across the Internet.

Speed is a less obvious difference. Usually Firefox will load pages a few seconds faster than Internet Explorer, which doesn't seem like much, but makes a big difference while you're browsing.

Other than those slight differences an Internet browser is an Internet browser, and Firefox does basically the same things as Internet Explorer.

Installing Firefox

Installing Firefox is just like any other installation on your PC, so there's nothing scary about it. First off go to the website of the organization that makes it, mozilla.com, where you'll see a big button that says Download Firefox – Free. If there isn't then click Products > Firefox at the top of the webpage.

Internet Explorer will ask what to do with the file. Click **Run** and as soon as the installation files have downloaded it will start. It's always useful to do this with installations from the Web, since it prevents having to remember to clean up!

When the installation begins, it's the usual "Standard or Custom" question. At the bottom of the wizard though is an important tick box: **Use Firefox as my default Web browser**. If it's checked, Firefox will replace Internet Explorer as the default, meaning that webpages will automatically be opened in Firefox. So, for example, when you get an e-mail and click a link in it, the webpage will open with Firefox. This can be changed later, by going to **Control Panel > All Control Panel Items > Default Programs > Set Default Programs**.

Firefox

The first time Firefox is launched it takes you to the Fashion Your Firefox page, which lets you download pre-configured packs to customize Firefox based on the type of Web surfing you like.

From here on if the Standard option was selected it's just a case of clicking the **Next**, **Install** and **Finish** buttons. If Custom was selected then it's just the same, but before that it'll ask where Firefox should install to and where the icons should go.

Starting Firefox for the first time

The first time it starts, Firefox will ask if you want to import all your settings from Internet Explorer. If you've been using Internet Explorer then it's a good idea as it gets you up and running faster. There's an option to use Firefox's slightly dull but quick-loading homepage, but if you have one you prefer then stick with that. Otherwise dull but quick is as good a starting place as any. There's a useful page that opens the first time Firefox runs, with some handy links to learn a bit more about Mozilla.

Removing Internet Explorer

It is possible for both Internet Explorer and Firefox to live happily on the same PC, and can actually be pretty useful; some sites don't play very nicely with Firefox because they've been heavily customized for IE. Have a look in the add-ons section of this chapter to find out how to simulate Internet Explorer from within Firefox. And

Tip: A word of warning about removing Internet Explorer: get something else first! Although removing Internet Explorer isn't a one-way street (just reverse the process to get it back) it's rather annoying when you come to realize you have no way to get online. That in turn probably means there's no way to get another browser.

if you do have a passionate hatred for Internet Explorer it's easily removed in Windows 7.

Open **Control Panel > All Control Panel Items > Programs and Features** and select **Turn Windows features on or off** from the left-hand panel. In the dialogue that appears uncheck Internet Explorer 8 and it will be removed.

Keeping Firefox up to date

Much like Internet Explorer, Mozilla regularly releases updates to keep Firefox secure. It's important that these get installed to keep the PC safe. Firefox checks Mozilla for developments quickly each time it starts, and will automatically download and install any updates for itself or any third-party add-ons you have installed.

Using Firefox 3

Much of the way that Firefox works is just like Internet Explorer, although some of the commands have different names and locations. The first and most obvious thing is that Favorites are called bookmarks. Really they're just the same thing: a collection of links to the websites and pages you like to visit most.

Bookmarks are a central feature of Firefox and can be added quickly with either the **CTRL + D** keyboard shortcut or by clicking the star to the right of the address bar. They can be organized from the **Bookmarks > Organize Bookmarks** menu.

The Awesome bar!

The address bar in Firefox is called the Awesome bar. It actually is quite awesome, or quite clever at the very least. It'll take the usual straightforward address for a website, like **google.com**, but it can cope with other things too. If you don't know the specific address

Tip: There is another way to get Firefox without having to install it on your PC: portable-apps.com is home to a set of tools that can be used without actually installing them. Normally when something is installed on Windows it updates something called the "registry" and it hooks itself into different parts of the system. The programs at Portable Apps have been re-engineered to remove the requirements for all those hooks. What that means is that the applications install into a folder which can just be copied somewhere else, like a USB stick. If you try that with a normal application it will probably malfunction.

Firefox

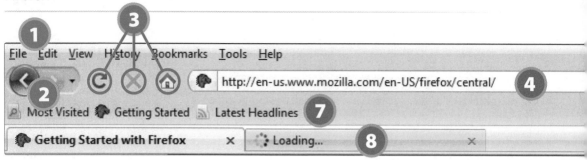

Tip: There are far more productive things that can be done with the homepage of your Internet browser. Imagine a custom homepage that gives you all the information you need every day, like the news headlines, your stocks and shares and the weather for the next couple of days. That's got to be a better way to start the day than a search box! netvibes. com, google.com/i and home. live.com are some of the best.

1 The menu bar – the menu bar offers access to all the most detailed features. Some options are replicated with buttons on the toolbar, but the menu bar offers the most consistent way to find things. This is especially important when a theme has been applied that changes the way the browser looks.

2 Back and forward – the back button is (cleverly) much bigger since it's the one that's used more often. There is a setting in Tools > Options to make both buttons the same size.

3 Refresh, stop and home – they do exactly the same as any other browser and exactly what their name suggests. Refresh reloads the page. Stop prevents a page from finishing loading. Home goes to your homepage.

4 The address bar – aka the Awesome bar. It will accept a Web address, or if you just type in some words it will do a Google search and take you to the first result.

5 The search bar – does what it says on the tin. By default it searches Google, but other search providers can be added by going to addons. mozilla.com.

Transferring data from en-us.www.mozilla.com...

6 **Page loading** – when a page is loading this symbol moves and each dot "lights" up. It lets you know that something's going on. Looking at the status bar at the bottom is the other way to find out.

7 **Bookmarks** – any bookmarks that you have can appear on the Bookmark bar. They have to be added through Bookmarks > Organize Bookmarks or by dragging the icon from the address bar above when you are on a page you want to keep on the bookmark bar.

8 **Tabs** – each tab can hold a different website or page and behaves like a separate browser window. If you close a tab by accident and want to get that page back, press CTRL +SHIFT + T to reopen it.

9 **Status information** – shows what's currently happening with loading the page; when the page has loaded it will say Done.

10 **Progress bar** – the progress of loading each element of the page is shown here.

Tip: There are many ways to customize Firefox, and the way that sidebars work can be changed too. **Sidebar on Right** is an extension that moves the sidebar from the left, where it always appears, to the right. It's a small change but it suits some people better. You can find it among hundreds of other extensions at addons.mozilla.org.

Tip: The last option on the dropdown is Google, which makes it easy to integrate with Google reader or a custom Google homepage. Go to google.com/reader or google.com/i to find out more.

of a site you're looking for, but it's likely to be something fairly obvious, just type it in. For example, "rough guides" typed into the address bar will go straight to **roughguides.com**. What's actually happening is a Google search behind the scenes; it's like typing "rough guides"into Google and hitting the search engine's **I'm feeling lucky** button.

Another "awesome" thing is that if a site is in your browsing history or bookmarks, typing any part of its name will bring up a dropdown list to select the bookmark or history item from. So if **roughguides.com** is in your history, typing "guide" in the address bar will bring up a selection of sites including **roughguides.com**.

Sidebars

Sidebars aren't turned on by default, but they can make browsing much easier. There are inbuilt sidebars for both Bookmarks and History; to turn them on go to **View > Sidebar**. Those two sidebars themselves aren't actually that cool. What is cool, though, is that any bookmark can be turned into a sidebar. So you can view your favourite news webpage constantly whilst surfing.

To create your own sidebar:
▶ Go to **Bookmarks > Organize Bookmarks**.
▶ On the left select **Bookmarks menu**.
▶ On the left-hand side of the window right click and select **New Bookmark**.
▶ Enter the details of the page to put in the sidebar and tick **Load this bookmark in the sidebar**.

Feeds

In Firefox bookmarks can also be created from RSS feeds. **Latest Headlines,** found on the Bookmarks toolbar, is just that. Each bookmark under Latest Headlines is just an entry in the feed, and selecting one opens the source of the feed item. This is called a **Live Bookmark**.

Live Bookmarks are the default way to view feeds. When you come across a site with a feed on it, just like in IE the orange feed icon will appear, except in Firefox it's to the right of the address bar. Click it and the feed will open, giving you some options for how to subscribe. Live Bookmarks is the default, but other methods are available from the drop-down list at the top of the feeds page. Just under this is a tick box which changes the default method of opening a feed. To change it back go to **Tools > Options > Applications**.

Wiping out footprints again

Just like Internet Explorer, Firefox provides the option to remove traces of which sites you've visted. It's done through **Tools > Clear Private Data** or **CTRL + SHIFT + DEL**. This removes much of the same things as Internet Explorer. Note that this information isn't shared between Internet Explorer and Firefox, so if both have been used, tracks from both will need to be cleared separately.

Security

There are a few other security features that are worth a mention besides just being able to clean up after you. Just like Internet Explorer, Firefox stores all the passwords for all the sites you go to. However, it can put an umbrella password around those saved passwords for extra security. Go to **Tools > Options > Security** and tick **Use Master Password** to set one up. Once Firefox has started, if someone goes to a site for which there is a stored password it will prompt for this master password. If the correct password is given then the passwords for all sites are unlocked, until Firefox is closed. If your PC is shared, all your passwords are stored securely as long as you remember to close Firefox.

Tip: Unlike with Internet Explorer, passwords for Firefox aren't stored within Windows. That means that they don't form part of the backups available from Control Panel. Instead use an add-on like "FEBE" to back them up. You can find it along with the other add-ons mentioned in this chapter at the Mozilla extensions site. addons.mozilla.org.

Tip: A great place to find add-ons for Firefox is lifehacker.com/tag/firefox-extensions. Life Hacker often reviews new add-ons and compiles frequent lists of the best ones for specific purposes.

Similar features for protecting the PC and your information from malicious sites are also part of Firefox. Going to a site with a valid security certificate (such as your Internet banking site) makes part of the address bar go green. Visiting sites that have an invalid security certificate make it go red. It's important to look out for this if you're entering sensitive information like credit card details.

Add-ons

The area where Firefox really excels is in just how customizable it is. For example, it's possible to completely change the way it looks by adding a theme. You can also add all kinds of functionality with add-on extensions. There are hundreds of different add-ons available from the website.

From within Firefox go to **Bookmarks > Mozilla Firefox > Customize Firefox** to go to the Mozilla website that holds all the extensions. Anything is possible.

To say that there are one or two add-ons available for Firefox would be an understatement. There are well over four thousand available! Anyone can develop an extension, and many people do. lifehacker.org is a great blog to find excellent extensions. Search the blog for "Firefox" and a wealth of recommendations will appear.

Among those available for download, there are add-ons that will:
▸ Improve download management.
▸ Turn Firefox into a blogging tool.
▸ Preview a link without opening the page.
▸ Synchronize bookmarks.
▸ Help you discover new websites.
▸ Remove banner ads from webpages.

Some of the best

The Mozilla website has some great suggestions for the best add-ons, but "Fashion Your Firefox" (**tinyurl.com/6kqnhf**) is a scheme that they run to highlight some of the better ones. In just a few clicks it's possible to make the browser do much more. This part of the site arranges the add-ons around your surfing habits, so it's a handy way to track down the stuff you'll find useful.

StumbleUpon

Sometimes you don't know what you're looking for until you find it. StumbleUpon points you at sites that other people have, ahem, stumbled upon. A simple toolbar allows you to rate sites you've visited and will then show you similar sites that other users have recommended.

Facebook toolbar

Facebook is a great place to share things with friends, to chat with or catch up with people you've not seen for a while. The Facebook toolbar makes it even easier to update your status and share Web content.

ColorfulTabs

If you feel like the Firefox interface is a little drab for your tastes then add-ons like ColorfulTabs are great for spicing it up. This add-on changes the background colour of tabs, making them easier to distinguish from each other, which makes browsing faster.

eBay sidebar for Firefox

The Firefox sidebar really comes into its own with this add-on, allowing to have your eBay watch list open while browsing around elsewhere – ideal for keeping an eye on closing auctions or comparing prices between eBay and online stores.

FEBE

FEBE is an add-on that backs up all your other add-ons, passwords and virtually any setting within Firefox. It's a great way to keep your Web setup safe, or to move it to another PC via a memory stick.

Download Status Bar

Firefox normally launches a small window to tell you about the progress of a download you've started. This add-on simplifies things by adding a download bar to the bottom of the Firefox window. It's a cleaner approach and makes it easy to browse the Web while something downloads in the background.

IETab

The beginning of this chapter alluded to being able to use Internet Explorer from within Firefox, and this add-on does just that, allowing you to view pages as Internet Explorer would see them without having to switch browsers. Internet Explorer still needs to be installed, though, so don't remove it if you want to use this.

Grease Monkey

A fantastic add-on which can actually customize the webpage being viewed. It's surprisingly liberating being able to change a website at will to meet your own needs. All you need is Greasemonkey and an easy-to-install script from **userscripts.org**. Don't like seeing ads? Get a script. Don't like that your homepage has a search box? Get a script. Want the word "fish" replaced with "chips"? Get a script. If a certain webpage bugs you, it will have bugged someone else too and there will probably be a script to fix it.

Windows Live Essentials

Windows 7 doesn't ship with any applications for e-mail, editing movies, uploading or managing photos and some other common tasks. Microsoft does, however, provide totally free applications to do all this and more as part of the Windows Live Essentials package. Distributing them separately allows Microsoft to update the programs without releasing a new version of Windows.

Although these applications don't come with Windows 7, the name, "essentials" suggests that they might be quite useful. They are in fact the applications that used to ship with earlier versions of Windows, and you'll probably miss some of their functionality if you don't download them. There are, of course, similar applications available from other vendors that will do the exact same things, and more, but nowhere else do they come in one simple-to-install package.

Go to download.live.com to get the very latest version of Windows Live Essentials.

Windows Live Essentials

Tip: It's not essential to use e-mail software on your PC. It might be easier to just use the Web-based access that an e-mail service provides. There are also some fantastic, free Web-based e-mail solutions. Three of the best are GMail gmail. com (also known as Google Mail), Hotmail hotmail.com, and Yahoo Mail yahoo.com/mail – great if you are using a netbook with limited hard disk space. Obviously if using this method you'll need to be connected to the Internet in order to access your messages.

Windows Live Essentials is made up of:

▶ Mail – check mail accounts with Hotmail or virtually any other e-mail provider, as well as accessing calendars, newsgroups, feeds and managing contacts.
▶ Messenger – chat and make voice and video calls with friends all over the world for free.
▶ Gallery – manage photo collections, add descriptive tags, make simple edits and share them online.
▶ Movies – create and edit simple but effective videos.
▶ Writer – create and maintain a blog, a simple website to talk about anything.
▶ Toolbar – increase the power of Internet Explorer with favorite backup, better search and fast access to Windows Live Essentials features.
▶ Family safety – better protection and monitoring for your family's Web browsing.

Installation is straightforward: just select which of the above is needed and follow the wizard. It's almost impossible to go wrong!

E-mail

The Internet offers a variety of ways to communicate and share things. E-mail is the most notable example; millions of e-mails are sent all over the world every day. It's now the primary communication method for many people.

Hotmail is one of the most established and popular e-mail services in the world. Microsoft has undertaken a major overhaul of Hotmail and it's now better than ever. You can access it at home in front of your PC or from anywhere else on the planet. It will also integrate with virtually any POP3 or IMAP4 e-mail service; in other words you can configure it to access your messages from almost any other e-mail accounts you have!

Using Windows Live Mail

This chapter concentrates mainly on getting you up and e-mailing using Windows Live Mail. It's much like using any other e-mail program, and the general techniques in this chapter are applicable to almost any e-mail program. See the sidebar for some alternatives.

Tip: There are lots of other e-mail programs out there besides Live Mail. Mozilla, who make the very popular Firefox Internet browser (an alternative to Internet Explorer), also produce an e-mail client called Thunderbird. It doesn't integrate as well with Hotmail but it's simple, secure and free. Get it at mozilla.com.

Tip: If the option to use SSL to access your e-mail is available, do it. SSL provides greater security to prevent people snooping and it won't slow anything down.

E-mail

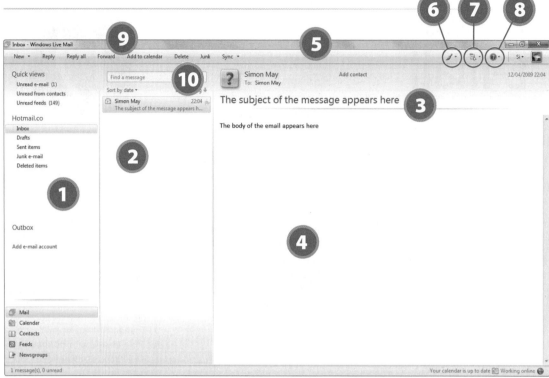

Select a folder to view from the folder pane; normally e-mail will come into the Inbox. Select the message to view in the message pane. The e-mail will appear in the reading pane.

The Windows Live Mail pane

1 **The folder pane** – this is where all mail folders, newsgroups and feeds are listed by name. Selecting a folder displays its contents in the message list (2). Messages can organized by dragging and dropping them into folders.

2 **The message list** – when a folder is selected in the folder pane (1) its contents appear here with each message listed separately. Right-click a message for more options.

3 **The message header** – displays information about the message, who it's from, who else it's being sent to, the subject etc.

4 **The reading pane** – this is where the body of a message is displayed.

5 **The tool bar** – buttons that perform common tasks such as checking for new mail or forwarding messages. Some buttons have a small downward pointing arrow next to them which reveals more options.

6 **Colorizer** – customize the colours used throughout Windows Live Mail to your taste.

7 **Menus button** – fast access to some of the options on the menu bar; select **Show menu bar** to reveal the rest of the options.

8 **Help** – when something doesn't seem to be possible or isn't working as expected, click the **help** button to learn more about it.

9 **Menu bar** – more in-depth access to program features such as account settings.

10 **Search Bar** – type anything here to search the sender, subjects, other recipients or body of any e-mail. Make sure the right folder is selected in the folder pane, though.

E-mail

Adding an e-mail account to Windows Live Mail often requires just three bits of information: your e-mail address, your password and a name that people will see when they recieve an e-mail from you. The name you use can be anything, but your own is probably best!

Tip: Don't become too reliant on your e-mail provider's storage; back it up once in a while by downloading it all. If you read the terms and conditions carefully they most likely won't look after saved e-mails if they have a crash.

Setting up

Once Windows Live Mail is installed as part of Windows Live Essentials, a wizard steps you through setting up access to your e-mail accounts. If you don't have an e-mail account already then get a Hotmail account by clicking the **Get a free E-Mail account** link.

It's not completely necessary to know the finer details of your account settings; Live Mail will be able to work out most of the complicated things for the average account. But there are a few bits of information you'll need:

▸ The e-mail **address** you want to access.
▸ The **password** to that e-mail account.
▸ Your **display name**: the name other people will see when they receive an e-mail from you. Normally this would just be your own name but you can set it to anything you like.

Windows Live Mail then does most of the setup automatically. If, however, the e-mail provider is more obscure, or has a custom domain name, then a little more information is needed. Your e-mail service provider will be able to supply all those details. Check their website for recommended e-mail settings.

Setting up more e-mail accounts
More than one e-mail account can be kept in sync and mail sent from any accounts that are set up. After adding the first account setting up another is as easy as clicking the **Add another account option** in the left pane of the window.

Reading e-mails

Getting around is very easy; there are three main components called panes. The panes work in the same way throughout the program, not just for mail but for feeds and newsgroups.

Every time a new e-mail is received an unread count appears next to the folder that the unread messages are in. It's a good visual indicator that you have e-mail.

New mail is shown in a number of ways; a small envelope icon appears next to the taskbar icon, a "ping" sounds each time a new message hits your inbox, or if you're using Windows Live Messenger under the same account a popup will appear for each new mail received, whether Live Mail is running or not!

Dealing with junk mail

Incoming e-mails might also appear in the **Junk E-Mail** folder. Hotmail has the added benefit of junk e-mail or "spam" filters that should weed out any unwanted messages. You can fine-tune which e-mails are automatically moved into the Junk folder based on simple rules.

When a junk e-mail is received right click on it and select **Junk e-mail**. You can then set rules for how to deal with e-mail like the one selected:

▸ Add to blocked senders list – If you don't know the person who sent the mail (or don't trust them!).

▸ Add sender's domain – If you don't know the organization that sent the e-mail or you don't trust everyone there. Any e-mail from that organization will then end up in your Junk E-Mail box. Don't add domains like hotmail.com or google-mail.com or other common e-mail domains to the blocked senders list or e-mail from friends might stop coming in.

The new mail icon in the taskbar.

Tip: If the pictures don't appear in an e-mail straight away don't worry, it's simply a measure to protect your PC. If a message has pictures missing there will be a yellow or red bar in the message header with a Show Images link. Simply click it and the pictures will appear.

Tip: If someone says that they've sent you an e-mail and it hasn't arrived, it probably found its way into the Junk e-mail folder. To stop that happening again right click the e-mail and select Junk E-Mail > Add to safe senders list.

Add sender to safe senders list	
Add sender's domain (@example.com) to safe senders list	
Add sender to blocked senders list	
Add sender's domain (@example.com) to blocked senders list	
Mark as junk	Ctrl+Alt+J
Mark as not junk	
Unblock	

Junk an e-mail by selecting it and using the CTRL + ALT + j keyboard combination. There is also a Junk button on the toolbar to do exactly the same thing.

Tip: By default the Junk e-mail folder isn't emptied automatically; things can live there forever. Be sure to empty it every so often or it'll start to consume a lot of disk space!

This also works the other way around. If you find legitimate e-mails turning up in the Junk folder you can add individual senders or the sender's domain to the **Safe senders list**. That way their messages will always reach the inbox safely.

The last two options for sending mail to Junk are just for individual messages. **Mark as Junk** simply moves the e-mail into the Junk folder. Within the Junk folder the option becomes **Mark as not Junk** and restores the message to its original location.

To get into the nuts and bolts of managing junk mail go to **Safety Options** from the **Menus** button. Here you can choose how much Windows Live Mail manages your junk mail for you, from not at all right through to the extreme of only allowing specific people (your Allowed list) to send you mail. You can also choose to permanently delete suspected junk e-mail instead of moving it to the Junk folder, but once it's gone, it's gone! For person-by-person level filtering, The **Blocked Senders** and **Safe Senders** tabs give you complete control over who does and doesn't make it into your inbox.

Sending an e-mail

To send a mail click the **New** button on the toolbar. The first thing to do is address the e-mail to one or more recipients. If you know the person's e-mail address (it will look like **name@example.com**)just type it into the **To:** area of the message; you can add more than one address by separating them with a semicolon (;). A cool feature is that it automatically searches your contacts when you start to type a name, even if it's not in e-mail address format. So type in "John" and a selection of Johns from your contacts will appear. Or to select someone directly from your contacts simply click the **To:** button.

Tip: Always consider the person who will be receiving the e-mail. Will that complaint really be taken seriously if sent with a puppy-dog paw print background? Is a tiny size 4 font going to be easy for them to read, or will a large size 24 overwhelm them?

Tip: Although almost every Internet-based (sometimes called "webmail") e-mail service uses POP3 or IMAP4, sometimes access must be turned on for those services from your e-mail account. If Windows Live Mail knows about your e-mail provider it will let you know what needs changing in order to give it access.

Tip: To send really large files consider using a service like getdropbox.com or skydrive.live.com. These services allow uploaded files to be shared with anyone just by including a link in an e-mail.

The subject line of the e-mail is a brief description of what it's about. "Hello" isn't particularly descriptive and something like "Family newsletter" is much clearer for the recipient.

In the message body enter the main part of your message. It's possible to get creative with text formatting here, using different sizes and typefaces, text colours and highlights. Lists can be created using bullets and numbers and you can include any number of smileys ☺, all available from the message toolbar.

Other formatting options, including background images and sounds, are available if the Menu Bar is turned on: click **Menu > Show menu bar**.

Stationery is a selection of predefined backgrounds and templates for jazzing up messages. **Dinosaurs**, for example, is especially fun for sending to kids! If sending to an adult it is best not to bother as it's rather overwhelming for the person reading the mail.

Links can be included in e-mails in a couple of ways. To have the address of a website appear in the e-mail message simply type it in. Anything typed that starts with **www.** or **http://** will automatically be linked to the text that follows, so **www.microsoft.com** automatically creates a link, as does **http://microsoft.com**. Another way to do this is to highlight a section of text and click the **link** button, then enter the address of the website. The advantage is

There are two other ways to add re-cipients to an e-mail. CC or Carbon Copy is used to send an e-mail to people who might also be inter-ested in the message. BCC or Blind Carbon Copy is used to do the same but will hide the fact that you're also sending the message to these people. To activate these boxes click the Show Cc & Bcc link to the right of the subject box.

that **http://www.roughguides.co.uk** could be hidden behind the words "Rough Guide" which looks much nicer in the message.

Creating custom stationery makes it easy to apply a similar look and feel to all e-mails. Create one e-mail with the background you want (changed with **Format > Background**) then go to **File > Save as stationery** and save it somewhere sensible such as your Documents Library.

Click the **Attach** button to attach a file to the e-mail: you can at-tach a document, video, music file – literally anything. The person receiving the e-mail will need to have the right software for the attachment to be able to use it on their PC.

Sending pictures in an e-mail

Cicking **Add Pictures** opens a window to browse for images to add to your message. It automatically opens to the Pictures Library. Find the one you want and click **Add** to pop it into the message. You can add as many pictures as you like. Once you're done, close the window and go back to the e-mail by clicking **Done**.

After adding a picture to the message you can have fun add-ing effects to it. You can add frames and change the frame colour from the toolbar. The **Autocorrect** button automatically adjusts the balance and contrast of a picture to make it more pleasing to the eye. Each picture in the message can be given a caption by selecting the picture and typing in the little grey box below.

One of the most important considerations when sending photos in an e-mail is the size of the picture – not the space that it consumes on the screen but the disk space it takes up. The bigger the picture the longer it can take to download the e-mail. There are three easy-to-understand options for setting this from the toolbar.

▶ Medium – the default, this is a good general setting for making pictures clear and quick to download.
▶ Low – makes the picture a smaller size and lower quality but much faster to download.
▶ High – preserves the original size of the file but makes downloading it slower.

Take care sending pictures in high; remember the person receiving the picture. A picture sent in high might take them a long time to download if they have a slower dial-up connection. The toolbar will give you a handy indication of roughly how long your pictures will take to download.

The Layout button gives the option of organizing the pictures in the message into many different styles. Images can be automatically resized to take up more or less space on screen and captions added or removed.

Message priority, read receipts and signatures

Sometimes e-mails in the inbox appear with an exclamation mark (!) to their left. This indicates an e-mail message is of high importance. You can set a new message as important by clicking the **High** button on the toolbar. Using it all the time it just like crying wolf! So only use it on messages that will actually be important to the recipient. It's also possible to mark e-mails as low priority with the **Low** button, but not many people bother with it.

If it's important to know that the recipient received your e-mail it's possible to make the e-mail "phone home" when it's been opened. This is activated on an individual e-mail from **Tools > Re-**

E-mail

quest read receipt. It's considered a little excessive to do this for every e-mail, and some people consider it rude so use it sparingly.

Signing off an e-mail with contact details and having to type them over and over again soon gets boring! Luckily **signatures** come to the rescue. A signature can include contact details such as a phone number or address, can be formatted with different fonts and colours and include links and pictures. To set signatures select **Tools > Options > Signatures** from the main window. Here you can create any number of signatures with different details: one for work, one for friends, one for family. A simple text-only signature can be typed in the text box on the **Signatures** tab, or a more complicated HTML signature (one formatted like a webpage) can be added.

A little bit of e-mail etiquette

Some simple tips for sending e-mail:

▶ **Keep the recipient in mind**; get to the point quickly and stick to it. And don't be terse.

▶ **Don't abuse High Priority e-mail stamps**; it should be high priority to the recipient and not just the sender.

▶ **Don't send e-mails to everyone**, just to the people who need to read them.

▶ **Don't bombard people with jokes**; everyone likes a joke, but forwarding tons of them and nothing else will eventually make people pay less attention to your messages.

▶ **Keep pictures small** unless you know the person at the other end wants the bigger versions.

▶ **Avoid unnecessary formatting**; colourful backgrounds and flashing pictures might be fun, but consider whether the person getting the mail will think so.

More than just e-mail

Don't forget the calendar

Calendar keeps track of appointments, birthdays and other events in your life. If linked to a Live account everything done locally is available online too. To get to calendars click the **Calendar** button at the bottom of the folders pane. To create an entry, select the day you want the event to take place and click **New**. To invite others to the event click **Send** in e-mail.

Subscribe to other calendars from calendars.live.com to keep up to date with what your friends or colleagues are doing. Just click the Subscribe link. An even easier way is to receive an ICS file from someone in an e-mail; opening that will subscribe you to their calendar. Any groups on Live.com can also have a calendar that you can subscribe to.

E-mail

Tip: Contacts are linked to people.live.com if you're using a Hotmail account. Any changes made to contacts on the PC are automatically synchronized to the Web, and vice versa. If you use Hotmail to update a contact it will automatically appear on the PC the next time you sync your mail. This means you only have to update your contacts once, and they're backed up for you automatically.

Microsoft has some active and well-managed newsgroups which are great for getting help with problems and talking to experts in the Microsoft community. Add a new newsgroup account and use msnews.microsoft.com as the news (NNTP) server.

Contacts

With lots of people to keep in contact with it can be tough to keep track of all their information. Luckily the Contacts feature is here to help. To create a new contact, click the **Contacts** button at the bottom of the folder pane, then click **New**. Now enter as much or as little information about the person as you like and click **Save** to add their details.

There might be a collection of people you think of as being part of the same group such as friends from work, family or customers. Using categories can help organize your contacts to make them easier to find. To create a category click the small drop-down arrow to the right of **New** and select **Category**, then add contacts by selecting them and clicking **Save**.

Contacts also manages friends within Windows Live Messenger (formerly MSN Messenger). Each contact has an IM box and will display the online status of any Live Messenger friends whose details you have saved.

Newsgroups

Newsgroups have been around for a long time and are much like public e-mails or forums, letting people share information and ask questions. They're declining in popularity but can still be a great resource. Sending messages is almost identical to sending e-mail messages.

To read newsgroups access to a news server is required; your Internet Service Provider (ISP) probably has one. Most ISPs will provide a news server address in the advanced set-up information on their website. To set one up select the **Add newsgroup account** link from the folder pane. The wizard will walk you through entering all the relevant details, the most critical of which is the News (NNTP) server name. News-groups don't tend to be well managed; it's often easy to accidentally find salacious content so it's worth monitoring kids' activity.

Feeds

Feeds are a way to publish information in a continually flowing stream for anyone to get regular updates on. They're usually used for services like distributing news and updates to blogs. Many news organizations like the BBC, CNN and hundreds of thousands of other websites distribute updates using this technology. Windows Live Mail can catch these feeds for you and tell you when they've been updated by "subscribing" to them. Click the **Feeds** button at the bottom of the folders pane.

It can be difficult to subscribe directly from Windows Live Mail since the address of the feed is needed, and it's not always the same as the address of the website. A far simpler way is to use Internet Explorer to subscribe to the feeds and then use Windows Live Mail to read them. In Internet Explorer 8 any site that has a feed associated with it will cause the feed button on the toolbar to highlight. Simply click this button and select the **Subscribe to this feed** link.

Manage Feeds on the toolbar will allow you to add or remove subscribed feeds and control how often it'll check for updates. Removing a subscription is a case of highlighting the feed and clicking **Delete**. Don't worry if the wrong one is deleted; it just moves to the Deleted items folder. For more information on feeds take a look at Chapter 15.

> **Tip:** There are other more intuitive ways of working with RSS feeds out there. google.com/reader is one of the best. Google Reader is great for managing hundreds of feeds and it updates constantly. It also suggests new feeds that might be of interest based on existing subscriptions.

There are two types of feed: ATOM and RSS. They are technically different but for all intents and purposes do the same thing.

Advanced techniques

There are a few things you can do to make your e-mail use more productive. It's likely that some of the mail you receive won't need to be read right away, but some will, so it would be handy to have a way to prioritize e-mails that need to be read immediately and ignore those that can wait. It's also a good idea to back up your e-mail because over time you will find the need to refer back to it. Services like Google Mail and Windows Live Hotmail hand out virtually unlimited storage for free and it can be useful to have a strategy for working with that.

Automatically dealing with incoming e-mail

Over time, giving your e-mail address to friends, signing up for newsletters, getting log ons for different websites and generally using e-mail, you will start to get lots of it. All of sudden twenty, thirty or forty e-mails per day arrive and it becomes a chore looking through it all. This is where rules come in.

Similar to the rules for junk mail, Windows Live Mail includes rules to sort your incoming e-mail. Most of the big Web-based mail providers have this kind of sorting built in too. Rules can look at virtually anything including the sender, the subject, the message itself, who else the e-mail went to, how big the e-mail is, and then do something with it. What it does with the e-mail is up to you. Every mail that comes from your mom could be highlighted pink, every mail that comes from your ex-boyfriend could be automatically deleted. Or you could cause trouble and automatically forward it to his new partner!

Setting up rules in Windows Live Mail is much the same process as if you were using most any other e-mail client or online e-mail service.

Select **Tools > Message rules > Mail**. The window that appears

Tip: Having your incoming e-mail sorted into folders is like having someone read everything for you. Set up rules to move generic things, such as newsletters or special offers from online stores, into a separate folder. That way when an e-mail comes from a friend, it's easier to see, and you can spend more time doing what you like doing best.

is split into three horizontal sections. The first box is to select the conditions that an e-mail needs to meet in order for the rule to apply. Conditions include things like the sender, the subject or the size of the e-mail. More than one condition can be selected. The second box is what happens to e-mails that meet the conditions of that rule. Selections include moving to a specific folder, deleting the mail or forwarding it to someone else. The last box is a plain English description of what will happen; anything that is highlighted blue and underlined can be changed. This is where the specifics, such as names of senders, can be added and where the folders that mails will be moved to are set. Finally, there's a box to enter a name for your new rule.

All rules are applied as e-mail is received. It's also possible to set rules for news items in much the same way: choose the condition and set the required action.

Archive

The massive amounts of e-mail that can be stored with online e-mail services mean that nothing ever needs to be deleted. It's fine just to move your read mails into the archive folder (you may need to create one first) and never have to think about filing since these services often include brilliant search engines. Google Mail is especially good in this regard. Many of these services actually find it harder to root out all the e-mails on a specific subject if you have a good filing system in place with things neatly tucked away in their own folders, so it may be better not to bother!

Generally, if you have unlimited storage space the best way to manage e-mail is to never delete mails, but instead move them to an archive. If you ever need to refer back to something, search the archive. To do this in Windows Live Mail just select the **archive** folder in the folders pane, and then at the top of the message pane type in what you need to find. Keep everything in one folder in the archive.

E-mail

Backing up and restoring e-mail

With all this unlimited e-mail space that online services provide, it's very easy to just expect everything to be there. For the most part it will be, but what happens if something goes wrong? What happens if there's a major problem and your e-mail provider loses your mail? Whose responsibility is it to get it back? The chances are that it's not actually theirs. When signing up to their service there was probably a set of terms and conditions that you should have read, but probably didn't. In those conditions it would have said that they don't have any responsibility to keep your e-mails.

It's probably best to consider your e-mail provider storing everything for you as a useful bonus rather than a guaranteed reliable system. Windows Live Mail includes the ability to export and import mail messages to an online service, and this can be used to create a backup of your online mails on your actual computer and vice versa.

After setting up your mail account, go to **File > Export > Messages**. A wizard will take you through the process of exporting all your mail messages. Select which folders to export and where to export them to, and a folder with all the messages selected will be created – a simple backup.

Restoring is just as easy. Go to **File > Import > Messages** and a wizard will walk you through it. When the import has finished everything will appear within **Storage folders > Imported Folder** in the folders pane.

Account settings can be backed up too by clicking on **File > Export > Accounts**. This can be useful to back up complicated things such as news servers. To restore them go to **Tools > Accounts** and click the **Import** button.

Scheduling to follow up an e-mail

There will be times when an e-mail comes in and something needs to be done with it by a specific date. A simple way to make sure that happens is to add it to the calendar. Select the message and click the **Add to Calendar** button on the toolbar. A window will appear setting up an event; the detail will be the body of the e-mail. It's just like adding any event to the calendar; all the same settings are there. It's a good idea to set a reminder, so that a dialogue box will pop up at a specified time to remind you what you need to be doing.

Working offline

One of the benefits of using e-mail software such as Windows Live Mail as opposed to just using a Web-based service is that an Internet connection isn't always required. **File > Work Offline** sets the program into a disconnected mode; it no longer needs an Internet connection. Everything works in just the same way; you can write e-mails and read any that have already been downloaded. Events can be added to the calendar, feeds that have downloaded can be read as can any newsgroup. Replying to newsgroups or e-mails is done in the same way … but how do people get those replies?

Well, the next time there's an Internet connection available go to **File > Work Online**. Everything that's been done whilst offline will then be sent: calendars on the Internet will get updated, newsgroup posts and e-mails will be sent. It's a useful feature if you have a laptop and have to get on a train or plane, if your Internet connection goes down or if you only have dial-up access.

Instant messaging and Skype

Instant messaging is a more immediate way of communicating online, allowing a series of short, more conversational messages to pass back and forth between people. It's less formal and more immediate than an e-mail, and normally the other person's responses are visible as they are typing them. The most popular instant messaging platform is Windows Live Messenger, the latest version of which includes a host of other cool features.

Windows Live Messenger does more than communicate through short typed messages; it also supports free voice and video chat. Text chat is enhanced too, with features like the ability to send pictures and smileys.

First run

To use Windows Live Messenger you'll need to have a Live account set up (also used for Hotmail or Xbox Live). The first time you start it you'll be asked for the account username and password. If you don't already have a Live account there's the opportunity to sign up for one. There's an option to save the

In Windows 7, Windows Live Messenger runs from the taskbar. Previous versions of Windows had it confined to the notification area. If you prefer it the old way you can force the program to run in "Vista Compatibility Mode". Create a shortcut to Windows Live Messenger, right click and select Troubleshoot compatibility, then tell the wizard to treat the program as if it's running on Vista.

password or to forget it. If the PC is being shared between people who don't have individual User Accounts it's a good idea not to save by unchecking Remember me and Remember my password.

Once installed, Windows Live Messenger will start automatically and appear in the taskbar every time the PC is turned on. If the idea of having the program start every time doesn't appeal, you can turn it off by opening Windows Live Messenger and selecting **Show Menu > Tools > Options**, then on the **Sign In** tab uncheck **Automatically run Windows Live Messenger when I log onto Windows**.

Adding people to chat to

If you've used Messenger before, or if you have contacts with IM information in their details, then your contact list will be prepopulated with those people. There are a couple of ways to add a new contact depending whether or not you know the e-mail address that person uses to identify themselves when instant messaging.

Instant messaging and Skype

The easiest way is to click the **Add a contact or group** button and select **Add a contact**. For this approach you need to know the person's e-mail address. After entering the e-mail address an invitation is sent allowing them to acknowledge that they know you. If the other person isn't set up on Messenger yet there is the option of sending them an e-mail inviting them to join. If they accept the invitation their status will be visible in your contact list; until then they will appear as offline.

When someone adds you on their Messenger you will be on the receiving end of the invite. If you accept their request they can be added to your contacts and dropped into a group.

To start chatting with someone, double click their name in the contact list.

If you're using a shared computer it's possible to make Windows Live Messenger forget your details. There is a Forget me link on the log on screen. Click the drop-down arrow at the bottom of the sign-in area to expose it.

Organizing people with groups

Just like in Windows Live Mail people can be managed by putting them into groups. It's handy in Windows Live Messenger as you don't have to keep scrolling down to find people. Groups can be collapsed so that only the name of the group is visible. They also allow you to chat with the whole group instead of just one person at a time. To create a group click **Add a contact or group > Create a group**, give it a name and add people to it from your existing contacts. They'll receive an invitation and will have to accept it to join the group.

Chatting

Tip: Just like having a chat with one person the same can be done with lots of people with a group. Double click the group to start a group chat with everyone in the group who is online. Be careful not to do it by accident!

To start a chat double click on a person or group and the chat window will appear. There is space for a picture of everyone who's chatting next to their name. At the bottom of the window is where your message is entered and any smileys are converted from plain text to a fun icon ☺. It's also easy to send someone a file or photo on Messenger; just click Photos or Files and browse for the one to send.

Messenger will also do voice and video calling from the chat window. To make video calls a webcam needs to be connected to the PC. A microphone isn't completely necessary as you can still type messages, but having one at both ends will make for a much better experience.

A microphone and speakers will definitely be required for a voice call, though; there's not a lot of point in one without!

If a microphone, speakers or webcam are connected to the PC they should work without any fussing, but settings can be tweaked in **Show Menu > Tools > Audio and video setup**.

Putting a face to the name

To set up a personal picture that will represent you to the people you're chatting with, double click the picture area at the top of the window. The standard profile pictures can be used, or if you have a webcam attached to the PC you can use it to capture one. A fun feature is the ability to have a dynamic picture, which makes a different picture appear for different moods. So a ☺ smiley inserted into your message can change your

Just like you can have a personal ring tone on a phone for each caller, your contacts can have their own sound.

Sounds for Donna dialog

When chatting with a friend you can see their picture. Of course, they might be using one of the stock pictures like the puppy, which is a bit boring.

Tip: A webcam might well be built into your PC, especially if you have a laptop. But if not Microsoft make a range especially built to work well with Windows Live Messenger. Virtually any manufacturer's webcam will work. Just make sure it has a Windows 7 logo on the box.

Tip: Extra pictures and characters can be found online from services like weemee.com. You'll find links to more images on the Web in the Display Picture window just below the pictures already available on your PC.

profile picture to one of you with a beaming smile. The **Dynamic Picture** button starts a wizard to get all the required shots; even video clips can be used so the angry face can really come to life!

Getting help from friends, playing games and other fun stuff

A handy feature is the ability to request remote assistance from friends. Many of us have a friend who's more technically minded than we are. With remote assistance they can be invited to connect to your PC and help fix a problem. Select **Activities > Request Remote Assistance** and an invite is sent in the chat window. Once accepted a message will appear on your screen with a connection password. For security purposes tell them the password over the phone rather than via the chat window, just to make sure you've got the right person. Once the password is entered at their end

Dynamic profile pictures are a really fun way to add personality to a chat. Connect a webcam and double click your profile picture in the Windows Messenger friends list. Select **Dynamic Picture**, then take a picture for each emotion or record a short video clip.

they'll be able to see your screen and help you out. It's even possible for them to control your screen if you allow them to.

You can play games too! There's checkers, tic tac toe and even a jigsaw that you can play on-line with friends in your contact list. Subscription-based games can can also be added. The **Games** button in a chat window opens a panel where all the available games can be selected. Chat stays open so the conversation can continue around the game.

You can also watch movie trailers with friends where everyone can comment on what's happening. To reveal other interactive pursuits click the **Activities** button.

Get a friend to help if you encounter a problem using your PC. When in a chat select Activities > Request Remote Assistance, then just follow the instructions – it's secure because they need to enter a code like this.

Making phone calls with Skype

The most popular way to make phone calls over the Internet is to use Skype. It's a free service (for the most part) that lets you talk to people anywhere in the world. It's just like using Live Messenger to make a call except that it's very much geared towards making calls rather than text chatting.

Because it's so popular there are lots of people you probably already know who might be on Skype.

Although for Skype-to-Skype calls the service is free, there's the option to pay for a service that doesn't actually require that both people have Skype. "Skype out" is a feature that makes it possible to use Skype to call a regular phone number, not just a Skype user. "Skype in" is almost the same; it lets you have a real phone number that goes to your Skype phone. While you do actually have to pay for these kinds of calls, it can still make international calling cheaper and easier. You can choose to pay as you go or pay a monthly subscription to these services if you want to take advantage of them. To learn more visit **skype.com**.

The one call that Skype can't make is an emergency call, so it's also a good idea to keep your land line for this reason.

What you need

To use Skype you'll need a microphone and some headphones or speakers. Most laptops come with microphone and speakers built in, but you'll get a better experience if you can use a headset. Using a microphone that is closer to the mouth makes it much easier for the person at the other end of the call to hear what you're saying.

It's also possible to get Skype handsets that work just like a regular phone handset, but connect to your PC via a USB cable or wireless. The best place to look for compatible kit is in the Skype shop; go to **skype.com/shop**.

It's not just voice chat that works over Skype; video works too. There are lots of suggestions in the Skype shop for video hardware.

Setting up

The first thing to do to set up Skype is to visit **skype.com** to get the software. Download the latest version and run the installation file.

When the install has finished you can set about configuring the software. The first thing that appears is a dialogue to sign up for a new account. There's also a link to **Sign in** at the top of this dialogue if you already have a Skype account. When you're signing up, Skype will create an account for you then load the welcome screen.

The welcome screen makes it easy to set up sound (and video, if you have a webcam attached) and find some friends to talk to. This can all be changed later, but it's a convenient way to get started.

Skype can search your Outlook, Outlook Express or Yahoo! Accounts for contacts. If you use Windows Live Mail, Hotmail, Gmail or anything other than Yahoo! on Windows 7 for e-mail, then you'll have to search for individuals by typing their name in.

Making calls

To make a call select a contact and a panel will open up to show their details. Just click the green **Call** button to make the call.

The first call you should make is to "Echo", the call-testing service, which helps to make sure everything is working properly. The call will be answered by an automated service and you'll be asked to leave a message. The

Tip: Occasionally there might be someone who becomes annoying and you want to stop getting calls from them. Just like in Windows Live Messenger they can be blocked. Select the person in the contacts list, right click them and select Block this Person. They will no longer be able to call you or see your online status.

When you create a Skype account use details that are recognizable to people who know you. Using a name such as "fluffybunny5098" might seem like a good idea, but not if you never get a phone call!

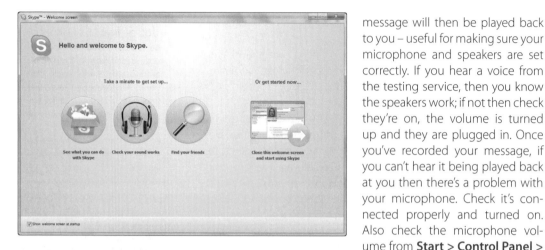

Once installed, Skype will help to get your microphone and webcam set up.

message will then be played back to you – useful for making sure your microphone and speakers are set correctly. If you hear a voice from the testing service, then you know the speakers work; if not then check they're on, the volume is turned up and they are plugged in. Once you've recorded your message, if you can't hear it being played back at you then there's a problem with your microphone. Check it's connected properly and turned on. Also check the microphone volume from **Start > Control Panel > All Control Panel Items > Sound**. If you have a headset microphone it should be about two inches from your mouth. If using a desk or lapel mic, make sure your mouth is close enough to it for it to pick up your voice. A little trial and error should help you settle on a good distance.

You can dial a regular phone number too. Select **Call phones** from the left-hand menu and a dial pad will appear. Enter the number and click **Call**; if your account has credit then the call will go through.

Calling from a website

One of the great things about Skype is that it integrates a little with your Internet Browser. Whenever a telephone number is displayed on a website Skype will jump in and allow you to call that number just by clicking on it. Again, you'll need some Skype credit as it still counts as a call to a regular phone number.

Tip: Just like in Windows Live Messenger there are games available to play with friends whilst chatting. These are hiding in the Tools > Extras. There are loads of other extras that can be installed, making it possible to do things like record phone calls.

Doing more

Skype logs all the calls you make, so it's easy to go back and get the number of that pizza company you called last week. Just select **Conversations** from the left-hand menu and the log will appear. To go even further back in time select **Show History** and every call, the length and who it was to will pop up.

Just like in Windows Live Messenger you can set your current availability status. By default you'll be set to **available** so if you don't want to be disturbed with calls you can change this status by going to **Skype > Online Status** and select **Away**. This menu also allows you to configure call forwarding.

Call forwarding works just the same as on a regular phone, sending the call somewhere else. Again it requires you to buy credits, but you may find that if you're away from your PC it's useful to have Skype calls directed to your mobile. Another option is to set up voicemail so that people can leave you messages. If you want to send voicemail to someone else, in the contacts list right click the person to send the message to and select **Send Voicemail**. You can only send voicemail to people who've paid for Skype credits and who have actually set up voicemail.

From the **Skype > Profile** menu it's possible to change various aspects of your profile, including adding a photo. This can make it easier for friends to find you on Skype, but always be careful about how much information you reveal about yourself online.

> **Tip:** If the sound quality of a phone call isn't up to much then go to **Call > Learn about Call Quality** to pick up some great tips about making calls better.

A quick way to change your status is to right click the Skype icon in the notification area (it might be hidden so use the up arrow). Changing status here is just the same as doing it from within the application; all the same options are available, but it's faster than opening the application first.

Photos, videos and blogging

Gone are the days of posting a photo or album to friends overseas or delivering a boring slide show of that last holiday to Spain. We can now send them a link to the photographs online, or even let them watch the video as we're recording it!

Managing and sharing photos

Windows Live Photo Gallery enables you to edit, share and display photos. It has powerful features often seen in gallery applications that accompany high-end graphics suites, but makes them very easy to use.

The first time it's launched it'll provide the option to sign in to Windows Live!, which gives access to online features like photo sharing. If it's not already, the program will ask if it can be the default for opening a variety of different picture types. Unless you plan to have another program do this say **Yes**. It can always be changed later through **Start > Default programs**.

Like Internet Explorer there is only one window to the application so it includes forward and back buttons for navigation. To get back to the main view click the **back** button a couple of times.

Organizing

Every photo in the gallery has a thumbnail view and properties associated with it that define how it can be organized. Lots of this information, like the date and location (if your camera has GPS) will be filled in automatically. Some information, like who's in the photo or what's been photographed, needs to

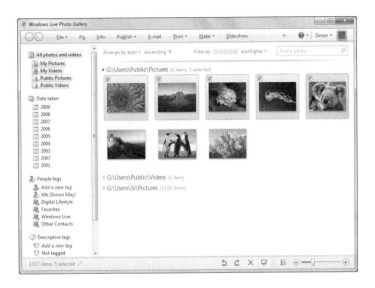

be added by you. These details can be used to quickly find photos in your collection.

Pictures can be clicked and dragged between folders, which are shown in the left-hand folder pane. To move more than one picture at a time select the tick boxes to the top left of the photos.

Organizing with tags is best achieved on an individual photo-by-photo basis since the contents of each will generally vary. When you open a photo you'll see an info panel over to the right. If it's not there click the **Info** button on the toolbar. From here tags can be added to the image by selecting **Add descriptive tags**. A neat feature is that tags already used for other pictures will appear as drop-down options and can be quickly reused with this one. You can add place names, activities and other descriptions of what's happening in the frame. Directly tagging people in the picture can be more fun; clicking **Tag someone** changes the cursor to a cross-

To highlight a continuous block of pictures, select the first then hold down SHIFT while selecting the last picture. All the pictures between the two will be selected. To select or deselect individual pictures together, hold down CTRL while clicking on them. This doesn't just work for photos, it'll work for any type of file anywhere within Windows.

Photos, videos and blogging

People tags

Tag someone

That's me!

Descriptive tags

Add descriptive tags

Caption

Add caption

Information

Filename:	CIMG1790.JPG
Date taken:	08/02/2009
	1:19 PM
Size:	4.06 MB
Dimensions:	2304 x 3072
Rating:	☆☆☆☆☆
Camera:	EX-Z70
Author:	Add an author
Exposure:	1/13 sec
Aperture:	f/4.0
Focal length:	10.4 mm
ISO:	Unavailable

Windows Live Photo Gallery can help organize your video with tags. It doesn't actually offer any facilities to edit the video, though; for that use Windows Live Movie Maker, described a little later in this chapter. To tag yourself in a picture select That's me! from the right pane, then draw a box around yourself in the photo.

> **Tip:** Windows Live Photo Gallery will automatically organize all the photos it finds in ascending name order, but by clicking Arrange by auto and selecting Date a very simple chronological view of pictures can be achieved.

hair allowing a box to be drawn around the person (or just their face). It can automatically link that individual to anyone in your Live! Contacts, or you can click **Add new person** to type in the name of someone who's not already in your contacts list.

Fixing photos

If a photo doesn't look quite right (perhaps the colour is wrong, it's not straight or someone has red eye) Live Photo Gallery can help you correct it. Highlight the problem picture, click **Fix** on the toolbar to open it and make some changes; a pane appears on the right with some interesting-looking tools in it.

Auto adjust is a useful tool for altering photos quickly, automatically changing colour balance, contrast, shadows, highlights, tints, saturations and other technical photographic settings. It'll also attempt to automatically straighten out any tilt on the photo if, for example, the camera was at a bit of angle when it was taken.

> **Tip:** If a fix has been applied that doesn't look quite right there are undo (and redo) buttons at the bottom of the Fix panel.

Fix red eye is another tool that does what it says. It provides a small grey dot to place over any red eyes on a photo, often totally removing the demonic look that can be caused by a camera flash.

Black and white effects offer the opportunity to turn any photo into an arty masterpiece, while **crop** can remove all but the best bit of a photo.

To save the changes click **Back to Gallery** and a prompt to save or abandon changes will appear.

Publishing photos

Where Windows Live Photo Gallery comes into its own is in publishing and sharing photos with friends and family via the Internet. The **Publish** button is the gateway to just that. The simplest option will use Windows Live Photos, Microsoft's photo-sharing site, to publish a photo album online.

Much like a real-life photo album, any number of pictures can be added. Select the ones you want to add by highlighting them and checking the tick box that appears to the top left of the thumbnail, then click **Publish > Online album**. Give the album a name and select who can see it from your Live Contacts. **My Network** is basically your Windows Live Messenger contacts, and **Public** is anyone on the planet.

There are two more default options for publishing to Live. **Publish > Group album** will publish to a Live group, such as any of the groups in your Windows Live Messenger. Or you can publish to event page on **events.live.com** with **Publish >**

> **Tip:** It's also possible to publish to photo-sharing services like flickr.com **or to** facebook.com**. A** connector for flickr is built in by default but connectors to Facebook and other sites can be obtained by selecting Publish > More services > Add a plug-in and downloading one.
>
> Another excellent Facebook add-in allows the people in a photo to be tagged from your Facebook friends list. The photo can then be uploaded to Face-book for sharing.

Any album can be shared online with people you know or people you don't, and you have up to 5gb of space to play with. Select Publish > Online album to get started.

127

Tip: Ratings are best changed on an individual photo-by-photo basis. Open a photo and find the Rating property in the info panel, then simply click the number of stars to rate the picture.

Tip: Windows Live Photo Gallery will automatically upload photos in a smaller (but still good quality) Web-optimized size. Change the size to Original in the publishing wizard to upload the exact file without shrinking it down. That way the copy uploaded to Windows Live Photos will be an exact backup of the one on your PC.

Event album. Events is a feature of Live! that helps plan a party or something similar and add photos, calendar reminders and other cool stuff.

Another quick way to share a selected photo is to click the **E-mail** button. An e-mail will be created with the selected snaps already embedded in it. Then simply address it to someone and hit send!

Other cool things to do with photos

Stitching a group of photos together to create a panoramic view can have a dramatic effect. Highlight two or more photos you've taken of a scene and select **Make > Create panoramic photo**. The program will examine the photos, find reference points in each and stitch them together into one panoramic image. It's surprisingly effective!

Similarly the **Make** button is a simple way to create a slide show of pictures on DVD that can be played in any DVD player, another cool way to show people your pictures.

Another very, very neat addition is a Microsoft technology called **PhotoSynth**. It has to be seen to be believed! Much like creating a panoramic photo, it selects points within lots of slightly different photos of the same place and stitches them together. The result is a very accurate 3D model that can be walked through and explored almost as if you are there. The National Geographic synth of the Sphinx in Egypt is stunning! **Extras > Create a PhotoSynth** will kick the process off for you, including getting the PhotoSynth software installed. Find the Sphinx onilne at **photosynth.net**.

Making movies

Windows Live Movie Maker is a simple editing program for movies and home videos. Its features are quite limited but it does allow for creating a simple movie from clips, pictures and soundtracks. It's also possible to perform basic editing such as trimming unwanted bits out of a video clip.

Creating a basic montage

The program can be opened from **Start > All Programs > Windows Live > Windows Live Movie Maker.** From there the best way to get familiar with it is to start adding some clips. There's a toolbar known as a "ribbon" for navigation, which is divided into sections. Click the **Add** button in the Videos and Photos section. The video will appear as a thumbnail in the right-hand pane of the window and in the preview pane to the left when selected. Video and pictures can be added in any order and then arranged into the desired play sequence in the right-hand panel.

The soundtrack works slightly differently. It can be any MP3 or WAV file (two common music file formats), but you can only use one, which will span the whole movie.

To create simple videos with Windows Live Movie Maker is easy. Add some video clips, transition them together, overlay a soundtrack, add the titles and you have your movie. It can't do everything a professional package can but it does produce fun results.

Moving between video clips and pictures

Some simple effects to transition between one clip or photo and another are available from the **Visual Effects** tab at the top of the ribbon interface. Transitions allow the next clip to do things like "drop" in or for the clips and photos to fade into one another.

Also included are some simple colourization filters that can turn a colour video or photo into black and white or into what looks like an old-fashioned film negative.

Editing

Use the Trim feature to remove the unwanted parts of a video, select the video, click **Trim** and use the sliders to set the start and end position for the clip. This keeps the portion of video between the sliders and removes the rest.

You can trim a video clip and keep just the good bit. Highlight the video and click **Trim** from the Video section of the ribbon. Beneath the video preview you'll see two start and stop bars that can be dragged to cut the video to the segment you want to keep. When finished, click **Save and close**, but note that the original video clip will be cut! If you change your mind just click **Cancel**. Videos can also be muted to silence their original soundtrack.

Photos only have one edit option, which is to set the length of time they appear on screen in seconds. There are no soundtrack edit options.

Any photo or video can have text placed onto it, such as credits or opening titles. But each photo or video has to have text added to it individually. So if you want to have, say, a message on screen throughout the whole movie, the message would have to be added to each separate video clip.

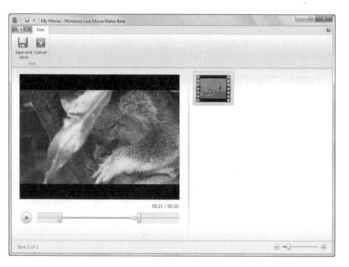

Sharing

Sharing videos with friends is easy thanks to the built-in publishing options. Clicking the **Publish** button on the Home tab of the ribbon will automatically upload the video to Microsoft Soap Box on MSN video (the Microsoft version of YouTube). Once you've entered your Live account details the process is almost automatic, except for giving the video a name, providing some tags to describe it and marking it as hidden or public. If it's hidden then your audience will need to be pointed to it with an e-mailed link.

Saving

Saving your edited movie is a case of clicking **Save** on the ribbon. Two options are available; the default creates DVD-quality movie files. It doesn't actually create a DVD though; see the Windows DVD Maker section below to learn how to do that. Windows Media portable device creates a smaller, lower quality file that is perfectly watchable on the Internet and portable devices.

Making a DVD

Windows 7 includes an application to turn any collection of photos or videos into a DVD that can be played on any player. Windows DVD Maker will automatically convert the videos and make a fancy DVD menu in four simple steps!

Launch the program from **Start > All Programs > Windows DVD Maker** and insert a blank DVD into the DVD +/- RW drive. Click **Add** to select the videos that will appear on the DVD. Each video will be its own chapter, and you can get them in the right order with the up and down arrow buttons. You can see how much space there is left on the DVD at the bottom of the window, and there's an area for adding a title there too. Click **Next** to move on.

> **Tip:** More popular sharing sites, like YouTube and Facebook, can be added by clicking the drop-down arrow under Publish **and selecting** Add a plug-in**. This will launch a website where plug-ins for sharing with more popular websites can be found. Installation is simple and well explained.

> **Tip:** Watch the DVD to be sure it works before sending it to friends!

Adding videos is a simple process of selection.

Creating a menu is as simple as selecting a template from the list on the right-hand side. If a menu template isn't selected a menu will be created with a frame from the first chapter used for a background. It's also possible to create a custom slide show menu using the **Slide show** button on the toolbar.

Finally click the **Burn** button to produce the DVD.

Blogging

Blogging is a way for anyone to publish information about their life, hobbies or interests for anyone else to read. It's sort of like printing a newsletter and putting it on a lamppost. It's easy to start a blog, and there are lots of services available for free. Blogs make it simple to get information out without having to mess about creating new webpages; the focus can be on the content. A blog is made up of a series of chronologically ordered blog posts. There's a simple Web-based editor to allow content to be created and published quickly. It's a great way to take your family newsletter online.

Windows Live Writer makes blogging even easier. The advantages of using software on the PC rather than just on the Web are the same as for e-mail. It's possible to write without an Internet connection and do more powerful things such as quickly edit images. The only thing that requires an Internet connection is publishing the post. LIke the other LIve Essentials, Live Writer can be found in the Start menu at **Start > All Programs > Windows Live > Windows Live Writer**.

Setting up a blog

The first thing you'll need is a blog to post to. Live Writer will hide much of the complex detail about connecting to a blogging service, especially for the well-known ones. If the blogging service is not listed on the first page (Live Spaces is really the only one that would be) then select **Other blog service**. On the next page of the wizard, after entering the address of the blog (for example **mygeekout.com**), it will try to work out which service it is con-

Write blog posts about anything that interests you or that you have an opinion about. It's a quick and easy way to get information out there, even if it's just letting your extended family know what's happening at home.

Tip: Getting a blog is easy. wordpress.com is a very powerful blogging platform and has many advanced features whilst remaining simple to use. typepad.com is a similar service and also has a large community surrounding it. The community around a blog is often where lots of the visitors come from. There are plenty of other blogging services available but Microsoft's own spaces.microsoft.com integrates well with all things Microsoft.

Tip: Remember to stay secure whilst you blog. It can be easy to release private details about where you live or your habits that could be useful to someone looking to steal your identity. Be careful and don't reveal anything that you wouldn't want people to know.

necting to. In most cases it will be able to, but sometimes it will need to know the address of the "XML-RPC" service of the blog. The blogging service will have this information on their website in the help pages.

One useful thing is that it can handle more than one blog; set up new ones by going to **Blogs > Add blog account**. To switch between blogs a drop-down will appear to the top right of the window, or you can do this from the **Blogs** menu.

Writing a post

To start writing a post, click **New** on the toolbar. Writing a post is just like writing in a word processor or e-mail; all the same formatting can be used. The style of the blog, which defines the fonts, colours and background, should have been detected by Live Writer. If the style has been detected everything should look just right; if not, go to **Blogs > Edit blog settings**, select the **Editing** tab and click the **Refresh theme** button.

If you have pictures inserted, select one and you can apply some handy effects to it from a bar to the right. You can change the colours, rotate pictures and frame them. The flow of text around a picture can also be changed.

Previewing a post

Before publishing a post it's a good plan to see what it'll look like, and to proofread it for mistakes. Clicking the **Preview** tab at the bottom of the writing pane shows how the post will appear once it's been published.

The **Source** tab allows for more technical editing of the HTML code (the language of the Web) that supports the post. It's possible to make all the tweaks you need to get it just right.

Publishing

To publish to your blog, simply hit the **Publish** button on the tool-bar. A Web browser will open showing your published post. A useful option is to be able to set a post to publish at some point in the future, for example to publish a thank you post the day after a birthday. The **Set publish date** option in the bottom left of the window allows this to be changed. You can directly enter the date and time you want to publish, or select it by clicking the little calendar.

Categories are a way of tagging blog posts so that people can find stuff that interests them, and can be set at the bottom of the window. You can select a category from the list of ones already used in the blog or just type a new one in.

Tip: Windows Live Writer can cleverly insert all kinds of content, and add-ins are available to make this even easier. gallery.live.com is where you'll find add-ins that can quickly pull photos from Flickr or video from YouTube, insert signatures or change photos into Polaroid-style pictures.

Putting pictures onto a digital photo frame

Digital photo frames have become very popular for showing off a selection of photos to friends. Basically they consist of an LCD screen set into a photo frame. You can load your pictures onto it and have them change at regular intervals.

The simple way

One way to get photos onto a frame is to copy them onto a storage device that the frame can read. Some frames plug directly into the PC using a USB cable. Most will support either an SD card or USB memory stick. If your frame connects to the PC it may also have some drivers on a CD that you'll need to install on the PC first. If there's no CD, have a look at Chapter 3 for where to find drivers for devices.

If your frame takes a USB key or SD card then things are simple. The best thing to do is to use Windows Live Photo Gallery and cre-

When buying a digital photo frame some things to look out for are:

▶ Does it look nice in my home? – the most important thing.
▶ Will my pictures look good? – get the highest resolution you can afford. A higher resolution means a clearer, sharper image. It's just like selecting a monitor. Also try to get a good contrast ratio (it will look like 1000:1); the higher the first number the more black blacks appear and the brighter colours look. The best test, though, despite any specifications, is to look at the screen and decide if you like the way the picture looks!
▶ Try to get wireless – it's just more fun and you'll find you use it more if you don't have to keep going backwards and forwards with memory cards to get new pictures into the frame.

ate a folder of just the photos you want to display. Select these from the gallery and move them to the folder. First, create a new folder by right clicking one from the left pane (My Pictures is the best bet) and selecting **Create new folder**. Next copy the pictures into the folder by selecting the pictures (use the tick box in the top left of each thumbnail to select more than one at a time) and selecting **File > Copy** (or **CTRL + C**), then select the new folder and click **File > Paste** (or **CTRL + V**). Finally, make sure they're all the right way up by using the rotation tool at the bottom of the window.

You can then copy the contents of the folder over the SD card or USB key, pop it in the frame and off you go.

The clever way

An even better way is to use a photo frame that supports wireless. First follow the instructions to set up the frame on your wireless network; if you don't have a wireless network see Chapter 21. Most frames that support wireless also support pulling frames from an RSS feed. This is just the same kind of feed that Internet Explorer, Firefox and Windows Live Mail support, except that instead of delivering news stories it delivers pictures.

The question is how do you get an RSS feed of all your pictures? The answer lies in using a service like Flickr (**flickr.com**), which lets you share your photos with people, or just use their space to store your pictures privately. After signing up for an account pictures that you want to appear on the frame can be uploaded to Flickr with Windows Live Photo Gallery, creating an album. The Flickr website will provide an RSS feed that the digital photo frame can be pointed to. Now all you need to do to add extra photos to the frame is just to upload them; there's no need to mess around with memory cards. The final bonus is that because everything is stored online rather than on the frame or a memory card there's virtually no limit to how many photos the frame can display in a slide show.

Other things to do on the Internet

The Internet isn't just made up of webpages; there are lots of other things going on. There are easy ways to share files with lots of other people. There are legal and not so legal ways to download music and movies. It's also possible to share videos and photos with friends or anyone else for that matter; to find out more check out Chapter 23.

RSS Feeds

Feeds have really taken off in recent years and seem like they're here to stay. What they do is distribute regular updates about a website, a blog or something similar. News websites are a good example; whenever they publish a bit of news their feed is updated.

Subscribing to a feed means it's not necessary to keep checking back on the website every five minutes. The software to read feeds is known as a feed reader or (less obviously) an aggregator.

The two main ways to read feeds in Windows 7 are via Internet Explorer 8 and the Desktop RSS gadget.

You can also read RSS feeds with Windows Live Essentials; have a look at Chapter 11 to find out how.

Other things to do on the Internet

Tip: There are lots of on-line feed readers too. Google reader (google.com/reader) is one of the best. It can even recommend new feeds based on existing subscriptions, and includes options for sharing feeds with friends. NewsGator (newsgator.com) is another very good online feed reader.

Anywhere this icon appears there's a feed that can be subscribed to; once subscribed the information from it flows in effortlessly.

Internet Explorer

Internet Explorer is the easiest way to find feeds. When viewing a site with a feed associated with it the feed icon will light up orange on the taskbar. Click it and the feed will open up and display each story in an easy-to-read format. To the right is a bar to search, sort and filter the feed to help sift information from it. At the top of the page you'll see a yellow box that summarizes the feed, what it's about and who publishes it. Simply click the **Subscribe to this feed** link at the bottom of the yellow box and you're all set. Once you're subscribed, IE8 will automatically update the feed. You can find your subscribed feed in the Favourites pane under the feed tab. Anything that's been updated since the last time you saw it will be highlighted in bold.

The Desktop

The Feed Headlines gadget can be added to the Desktop to give a quick view of any updates. Right click the Desktop and select Gadgets and drag the Feed Headlines gadget to the Desktop. The gadget automatically updates with any feeds subscribed to in Internet Explorer.

Create your own website

These days everyone has their own website, from companies to celebrities, even your best friend or that local restaurant. If you have money to spend and want it to look great you can go to a professional, or with a little effort you can build one yourself.

If you are expecting to make money from your website it really is a must to track down a "hosting" company. Just do a search for "website hosting" and find something in the right price bracket. But if you're just looking for a free and easy way to share stuff with your friends, check out **google.com/sites** for a simple free service that really helps you to get a website up and running quickly. There's not even any need for tools to do the basics.

To create a higher standard of webpage you'll need an HTML editor. Windows 7 doesn't come with one, but you can find one easily online. CoffeeCup is a good package that's available for just a few dollars for the full version (**coffeecup.com**). Kompozer (**kompozer. net**) is a simple-to-use, yet powerful and completely free editor. Microsoft Word also includes the ability to do Web design but it's very limited and best avoided. At the more expensive but feature-rich professional end of the spectrum there's Expressions Web from Microsoft (**microsoft.com**) and Adobe Dreamweaver (**adobe.com**).

FTP

FTP or File Transfer Protocol is a way to transfer files over the Internet. You'll most likely come across it when setting up a website with a free or paid-for hosting service. A hosting service provides a website on the Internet that is run from their systems, so your PC doesn't need to be left on.

Windows 7 has built-in ability to access FTP sites. You can set this up from **Start > Computer**, right click anywhere in the blank space on the right side of the window and select **Add a Network Location**. This starts a wizard that walks you through obtaining the information required, such as the name of the FTP site (it will need to have **ftp://** before it and not **http://** as a webpage would). You'll also need the username and password used to access the FTP site.

Once added, the network folder for the FTP site will always appear in the Computer window.

P2P file sharing

P2P (peer-to-peer) file sharing is widely used as an illegal way of obtaining copyrighted movies, games, software and music. It works like this: lots of people around the world each have a copy of

Tip: Lifehacker.com is a great site to subscribe to for inside tricks on how to use a PC, as well as much more. They publish information about handy software, great ways to get things done and manage your time as well as lots of other useful stuff.

Adding FTP locations for quick access makes it easy to keep your website up to date. Be sure to enter "ftp://" so that Windows knows that it's an FTP site and not a different kind of shared location, such as another PC on your network.

Other things to do on the Internet

Tip: GoDaddy.com is a great place to get website hosting. They offer competitive rates and a good service and can help with domain name reg- istration. Many ISPs (Internet Service Providers; the company that provides your connection to the Internet) offer free Web space included in the monthly fee for your Internet connec- tion; to find out more check out the website of the ISP provid- ing your service.

Tip: The most popular Bit Tor- rent client is called uTorrent and is available from uTorrent. com. The software is very cus- tomizable, even allowing for download scheduling. Another client that's gaining popular- ity is Vuze (azureus.sourceforge. net). But remember: if you use these programs to download copyrighted material, you are breaking the law.

the same file and they all make it available to be shared with other people. The technology and software that enables this sharing is not illegal but the sharing of copyrighted materials is. It's basically theft to download copyrighted music, video and software without the permission of the publisher. For the legal methods of down- load music and video take a look at Chapter 18.

The most commonly used P2P technology used for file sharing is Bit Torrent. The technology delivers very fast download speeds because in the background only a very small amount of a file is downloaded from each person in the peer-to-peer group. There are many legal uses for Bit Torrent; in fact it's used in the massively popular game *World of Warcraft*, to distribute software updates.

Bit Torrent works by allowing the user to download a **.torrent** file to their PC. A small application called a Bit Torrent client uses the information in that file to set up connections to other users' computers where copies of the file they are after reside; every- one downloads different small parts of the file and then "seeds", or shares these parts with other users while downloading other parts from them, creating a cloud of sharing. The bigger the cloud, the faster the download. Bit Torrent is the name of the company that develops Bit Torrent technology; their own client is available for download at **bittorrent.com**.

Windows Live Family Safety

Windows 7 already includes a number of features to keep families more in control of what kids can do on the PC. Windows Live Fam- ily Safety adds to these features and provides some of the missing pieces of the puzzle. It includes components to filter which web- sites kids can access and keeps a record of activity that the head of the family can access. Chapter 26 covers this in more detail.

Having fun

Windows Media Player

Windows Media Player is an evolved and capable application that can play back a wide variety of different media, from music to video and recorded TV. It's also a very accomplished media manager or jukebox, storing and organizing huge collections of music and video on the PC, and can even stream the media stored on your PC to other PCs and media devices around the home. It can even stream to a stereo system if the stereo system supports it – just like sending your own radio signal (although it's not something a standard radio can receive).

Starting Media Player for the first time

The first time Windows Media Player is started a wizard will walk you through the set up process, asking about your preferences for things like how much information it should get from the Internet. It also asks if information about your watching and listening habits should be sent to Microsoft and other content providers. The **Recommended settings** option will send information to Microsoft but not to other content providers. It's also possible to select **Custom settings**, which lets you view the privacy statements that govern what any information provided will be used for. The wizard offers the option of making Windows Media Player the default for open-

Windows Media Player

An introduction to media in Windows 7

Windows 7 excels at helping you enjoy your movies, music, pictures and other media, but to get the most out of these a few different programs are needed. Two media players are built in to Windows 7: Windows Media Player and Windows Media Center.

Windows Media Player is a jukebox program that catalogues all the media on the PC and its related information (for example the band, artist and cover art for music) into a Library. It's best suited to using the PC "up close", just as you would for any other purpose.

Windows Media Center is a different kind of animal altogether. It's designed primarily to be used at a more TV-like distance from the screen; everything is bigger and easier to see from further away and it can be operated with a remote control. It still has the same kind of media Library functionality, but because it's designed to be used on a big screen, Microsoft have also built in fantastic TV-watching and TV-recording capabilities.

If you have a portable music device, such as an iPod or a Zune, then you'll probably need somw kind of third-party media software too – something designed specifically to work with all the features that the device supports. In the chapters that follow, you'll find details about iTunes, the software used in conjunction with iPods and also the Zune software, which is used with Zune players (pictured); both applications make a superb addition to any PC and give you an easy way to discover new media.

For the full story on using iPods and iTunes on a Windows PC, purchase a copy of *The Rough Guide to iPods & iTunes*.

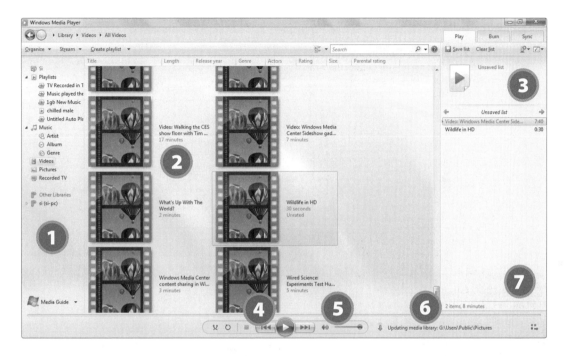

1 **Library Pane** – shows all media available to play on the PC and any other devices on the network that are sharing media.

2 **Media Pane** – more detail about the item selected in the Library pane.

3 **Playlist, Burnlist and Synclist pane** – holds a list of files to be played, burnt or synced to a portable device. Files can be dragged here from the media pane. Play, Burn or Sync are selected from tabs at the top.

4 **Media Controls** – large play button surrounded by previous (to the left) and next (to the right) buttons. To the far left are the shuffle and repeat buttons.

5 **Volume and Mute** – adjusts the playback volume of any music or video and can mute the output completely.

6 **Current status** – shows what Windows Media Player is currently doing.

7 **Now Playing** – switches to the Now Playing view; for music this will be a visualization (a pretty pattern in time to the music), for videos it will be the video itself. A similar button in the Now Playing view switches back.

When starting Windows Media Player for the first time you'll need to decide how to have it set up. Most of the time the Recommended settings are fine for getting the most from it but if you know what you're doing then go for the Custom settings.

Tip: Using Windows Media Player as the default player for specific file types can be changed at any time. Go to Control Panel > All Control Panel Items > Default Programs > Set Default Programs, select Windows Media Player then select Choose Defaults for this program. From here there will be a very long list of file types that can be associated with the program. Check the ones you want to use Windows Media Player for and uncheck the rest.

ing all media files, or for you to choose specifically which types it'll play. Finally Windows Media Player asks which online store to buy media from.

For most people the **Recommended settings** option is the best to choose; it's far simpler and though it does provide some information to Microsoft, that information is governed by a privacy policy.

The Music Library

At the core of Windows Media Player is its Library function. The first time it's started it searches the PC for any media it can find. Normally media is stored in the Libraries for Music, Video and Pictures and if possible it's best to stick to using these locations as Media Player watches them and knows automatically when they've been updated. Libraries in Windows

7 and in Windows Media Player are not quite the same thing, however; in Media Player the Libraries store more information about the media, such as artist names and album covers, stuff which a Windows 7 Library doesn't bother itself with.

Once media is found on the PC it'll automatically seek out information for each item from the Internet (if the information isn't already "embedded" in a file). The Library in Windows Media Player is made up of the different sorts of media on the PC but it's divided into separate views for Music, Video, Pictures, and Recorded TV. The music view there is also broken down into separate views for Artist, Album and Genre. When Media Player first opens it displays the contents of the Library and opens to the last view of the Library that was used.

There are three panels in Windows Media Player 12. The left panel shows the individual views of the Library and the centre panel shows the contents. The right panel has three tabs at the top called Play, Burn, and Sync.

The Play tab shows the queue of items that are currently playing, the Burn tab creates a list of files for burning to CD or DVD and the Sync tab is used to build a list of media files to sync with an MP3 player or similar device. The panels work together, and playing anything is a three-step process:

1 Select the Library and the type of media in the left panel.
2 Select which specific media to use from the centre panel, then either press play or drag them to the right panel.
3 Change the order if necessary and decide whether to play, burn or sync the tracks.

Playing media

At the bottom of the Media Player window is a bar that contains the playback controls. There's the usual Play, Pause, Next, Previous,

Tip: Media Files, like MP3s, have extra bits of information in them called metadata which can include, in the case of an MP3, the name of the artist, the name of the band, song name, album name and much more. This information is "embedded", or stored as part of the file. This isn't just limited to MP3 files; WMV and some other media formats do the same. A problem when building up a good Library is that certain other file types (MPEG1, for example) don't store this kind of data. So Windows Media Player Library stores information about these files in its own database. To make things run a bit quicker it also copies the embedded metadata in an MP3 file (or similar) into its database. This database is the Library: a complete record of all the media files on your PC and details about what's in them.

Windows Media Player

Tip: Clicking the Switch to Now Playing button on the control bar will go into the Now Playing view and start the visualization (a display of pretty patterns in time to the audio). To set a visualization, right click the Now Playing window and select one; *Alchemy* is pretty mesmerizing.

Stop and volume controls but there are also buttons to shuffle the current playlist (in the right-hand panel) and repeat the current track. When repeat is on the file playing will repeat infinitely until Stop is pressed or repeat is turned off. When a video, picture or recorded TV file is played the view will change to the **Now Playing** view; only when listening to music will the Library remain visible. To get back to the Library view from the playback view, hit the **Switch to Library** button.

Adding new media to the Library

Any media placed into the various Windows 7 Libraries will automatically be imported into the Windows Media Player Library, making for a very straightforward way of adding stuff into Windows Media Player.

Windows Media Player comes with the ability to copy a CD to the Library and to store it on your hard drive; this is called ripping, so when an audio CD is inserted into your CD drive Auto Play will appear asking what to do with the CD. One of these options should be **Rip with Windows Media Player**; selecting this will rip the album and copy it directly into the Windows Media Player Library.

Tip: When audio is ripped from a CD it's converted into a format that can be saved on the hard disk; to save space files are generally compressed. Compression effectively removes the parts of a track you can't hear to make the file smaller; usually it isn't noticeable. Audiophiles can sometimes tell the difference, so if you're fastidious about sound quality you can rip to a "lossless" format to keep the whole track intact. WMA lossless or WAV are the two options available; they use up drastically more disk space but do sound a bit better.

There's another way to rip the CD to the Library if the Auto Play option doesn't appear. In Windows Media Player the left panel that will display either the name of the album that's been inserted or "Unknown Album". As soon as a CD is inserted, Windows Media Player uses the number of tracks on the CD and the length of those tracks to look up the CD on the Internet. If it finds the right details it displays the album name, track names, sleeve art and tons of other information. To rip the CD to the Library click **Rip CD** on the toolbar.

The **Rip Settings** button gives you a few options to change the way music is ripped, including the format and quality (how good it sounds). By default Windows Media Player will rip music to WMA (Windows Media Audio) format, and for most purposes this format is fine. MP3 is more compatible with other devices though, so if you plan on using Windows Media Player to rip music and also plan on using an iPod it's better to rip to MP3. Besides compatibility, quality is the other important factor to bear in mind. Quality is expressed in "kbps"; essentially the higher the number of "kbps" the higher the quality of the audio but the more disk space is used. For most ears, 192 kbps is generally accepted as being good enough, but experiment to find out what you enjoy the most.

Playlists

A playlist is a selection of media that Windows Media Player will play in sequence. You can get quite creative with playlists: a selection of music for a dinner party, all with a specific theme, or a compilation of music to get you in the mood for going out on the town. You can also use playlists to cue up groups of videos that need to be watched in a certain order, like a TV series. The playlist in Windows Media Player lives in the right-hand window; dump anything here and Windows Media Player will play it back in that order. Like the good old days of making a mixtape, it's possible to spend hours creating the right playlist that evokes just the perfect mood, so it's good to be able to save your efforts. At the top of the right panel with the **Play** tab active there's a **Save List** button; click that and the title of your list will become editable. Tap in a name for the list, like "romantic", and hit **Enter** to save it. To change the order of items just drag and drop them up and down the list.

Now whenever you're in a romantic mood you have a playlist to suit. From the left panel select **Playlist,** then drag a saved list from the middle panel to the right panel and it'll start playing.

There are also Auto Playlists, which differ from standard playlists in that they're rule-based rather than based on chosen media files. For example an Auto Playlist might include any music added in the last thirty days, or any music with a five-star rating. Auto

Tip: Sometimes Windows Media Player struggles to find information about a CD, but that's not the end of the world. Right-click on either the album or one of its tracks and select Find album info. It will go looking for the album information again and if it can't find it this time it offers the opportunity to enter the name of the album manually and search again using that. Most of the time it'll find the details; if it's still confused a list of different albums will appear and you can pick the right one.

Tip: Playlists can be dragged to the Burn or Sync tab to either burn a CD of all the tracks on the playlist or sync them to a compatible device.

Tip: To make sure a device will sync with Windows Media Player make sure it has the Windows 7 certified logo.

Playlists are a flexible way to listen to new music, and are brilliant for syncing with devices that aren't large enough to hold your entire Library. To create one click the drop-down next to **Create Playlist**, then select **Create Auto Playlist**. For each type of media included in the Auto Playlist a criteria can be set. Criteria vary by media type, but they basically limit which items go into the playlist in one way or another. Restrictions around number of items, total size and duration apply to the whole playlist and give even more control.

Burning and syncing

It's great having a massive music collection but sometimes it's nice to have a good old-fashioned CD, say for playing in the car on a road trip, or giving to a friend as a kind of mix tape. Click the Burn tab on the top of the right-hand side panel. From here you can drag any album or number of tracks over to the burn list. A progress bar indicates when the combined size of the tracks is up to (or has exceeded) the size of a CD.

Windows Media Player includes support for syncing tracks with portable media devices and USB keys. Some media devices will be big enough to hold a copy of your entire Library, in which case there are very few choices that need to be made. Some devices don't have that much capacity so the best thing to do is to select specific tracks and playlists that will be synced. Auto playlists come in handy here!

Windows Media Player remembers each different device that's been plugged in and it's possible to sync more than one device on the same PC. Syncing works in much the same way as burning a CD; just drag the media or playlists to the Sync list (the right pane with the Sync tab selected). Do this once for a device and whenever the device is inserted everything in the playlist will sync automatically.

Network Media

Windows Media Player is actually a very powerful DLNA-compliant network media server and receiver. DLNA (Digital Living Network Alliance) is a standard developed outside of Microsoft that ensures technology designed for the home works well together. This means that the media stored in the Windows Media Player Library can easily be shared with other PCs on a home network, and media from other shared Libraries can easily be played. DLNA compliance is a new thing in Windows 7, and it means that music can be shared not only with other Windows devices but with other DLNA-compatible devices. The list of DLNA-compliant devices is massive; it's an industry standard encompassing TVs, hi-fis and home cinema systems.

Tip: A very long list of DLNA-compatible devices is available at dlna.org, but devices with the Windows 7 certified logo will also work.

Media sharing allows other devices on the network, like DLNA-certified network music players or other Windows PCs, to stream music from your PC, playing music and video files from your PC without having to copy them across the network first.

To use Windows 7 as a network media server the feature needs to be turned on from **Control Panel > All Control Panel Items > Network and Sharing Center > Share with media devices**. Make sure the other devices to share media with are turned on and connected and they'll appear in the **Share with media devices** window. For each device select whether to **Block** or **Allow** access; to allow all devices on the network to access media on the PC click **Allow All**. **Block All** obviously does the opposite.

Windows Media Player automatically listens out for devices on the network that are sharing

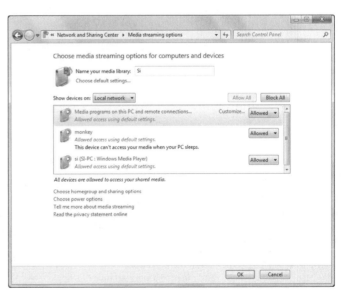

Windows Media Player

media; these will appear as an extra Library in the left panel. You can browse this Library and play things just as if it were on the PC. When something is played it's actually left on the original device that's sharing it – it's a process called streaming. As the music is being streamed there's virtually no wait till it starts playing because whole files don't have to be copied across the network. This also means that because it's not on the local PC it can't be synced to a portable media device or USB key or burned to a CD.

Windows 7 is a powerful whole-house media remote; with the right hardware or with other Windows 7 PCs music and video playback can be remotely controlled. Just right click a file in Windows Explorer or in Windows Media Player and select Play to, then select the destination device and the media will start on it.

Play To

A cool new feature of Windows 7 is something called Play To; it's part of the DLNA compliance and works with media on the nework. There are two aspects to it; the first is just like a remote control for networked media devices. Right click on any media in Windows Media Player (or actually on a media file anywhere in Windows 7) and one of the options available, if there's another DLNA device on the network, will be **Play To**. The **Play To** menu will show a list of DLNA devices on the network, and selecting a device will start to play the media on it! A window will pop up allowing the playback to be controlled.

What's cool about this feature is that as long as the receiving device can understand something of a similar format, media formatted (aka encoded) in any way can be played on it; this is called "transcoding". So, let's say the device is a network radio and can play only WMA files, but the file we want to play is an M4A. Windows 7 will automatically convert the file to WMA and stream it straight to the device.

Another cool thing is that Windows 7 PCs can also be on the receiving end of this process! So if there are two Windows 7 PCs on the network, one in the office and one in the kitchen, the kitchen could be used to control music in the office! To turn the feature on, go into Windows Media Player and select **Share > Receive media on your network**. Music, video, TV or pictures can then be played to a PC from other PCs in the home.

Setting up other devices will require following the instructions for each; nothing needs to be done on Windows 7 apart from making it listen out for devices, as described above. As long as it has a DLNA logo, everything will work.

> **Tip:** See later in this section for how to make the Xbox 360 into a Play To compatible device, by using it to extend Windows Media Center into other rooms of the house.

Windows Media Center

Tip: Windows Media Center has a very enthusiastic following. More than two million people use it to watch TV regularly. There are some great online resources:

thedigitallifestyle.com is where a handful of experts produce fantastic videos, blogs, how-to's and where there's a great community of people to help. Ian's weekly podcast is well worth a subscription.

thegreenbutton.com is a very active community site; everyone is keen to help and lots of new add-in software gets released there.

microsoft.com/windows/windows-media-center is a Microsoft's own site and includes some great demos.

Windows includes an advanced but easy-to-use application that can bring the PC into the center of the living room. It's particularly handy for students in dorm rooms too. Windows Media Center plays music, shows videos and displays pictures. What makes it different is that it is designed to work beautifully on a TV screen. With a TV tuner inside the PC it turns into an advanced and adaptable DVR or Digital Video Recorder, like a hard disk TV recorder on steroids!

The user interface is designed to be used at a distance from the screen, so everything is big and clear. Remote controls are available too; in fact it's quite possible that a remote control came bundled with your PC. The big buttons and user-friendly screen make it a perfect media player to control using touch if the PC has a multi-touch-enabled screen. The media that's accessible through Windows Media Player is also available through Media Center, and the two programs coexist nicely.

Easy to install "add-ins" for Windows Media Center also provide extra functionality like weather updates, movie guides and Internet TV channels.

With very little effort it can become the center of your home. Imagine watching a film on the TV downstairs and because you're

1 **Back button and Start menu** – the back button always returns to the previous screen; the Start menu button will pull up the Media Center Start menu at any time.

2 **Time** – the current time; this vanishes after a couple of seconds and reappears when touching the screen, moving the mouse or using the remote.

3 **Seek bar** – shows progress through the current video and can be clicked anywhere along the timeline to jump to that point.

4 **Media controls** – for controlling playback and volume as well as starting recordings quickly.

tired, pause it, then go upstairs and continue watching where you left off in the bedroom. That's a reality right now with Windows Media Center and Windows 7.

The wizard that runs the first time you start Windows Media Center shows off exactly what it can do for you. If you're new to Windows Media Center it's worth spending two minutes exploring it.

Setting up Media Center

Click the green orb to get started; you'll find it at **Start** > **All Programs** > **Windows Media Center**, or on a Media Center remote if you have one. The first time you start Media Center a flashy wizard appears to help you configure your PC. Press the left and right arrow keys on the keyboard or remote for a quick walk through of the program and its main features. Clicking **Continue** will start the set-up process. As with all set-ups there's an **Express** option which will be fine for most uses and a **Custom** option to let you get into more of the detail. There's also a **Learn more** option that'll trigger a demonstration video.

The **Custom** option provides control over whether to pass information about your usage experience to Microsoft and whether or not to download information about music, video, DVDs and the like (metadata). Next the TV tuners, TV guide, speakers and Media Libraries are set up. If you don't have a TV adapter in your computer, check out the side box on TV tuners for more information on what to buy. The **Set up my speakers** option makes sure all the speakers are connected correctly with the right sound coming from each. **The Set up my Media Libraries** option allows specific folders to be identified for storing music, pictures and video and recorded TV shows. **Optimize how Windows Media Center looks on my display** allows the screen to be customized; this one is a must if you have a TV connected, as screen sizes and types vary.

The **Express** option sets everything up for you to a basic level but it won't configure TV tuners for you. If you have one installed when using the set-up wizard it's best to choose **Custom**. Alternately you can set up your tuner at a later point by going to the **TV** option and moving to the right with the remote or keyboard to **Set up TV Signal**.

To run the wizard all over again go to **Tasks > Settings > General > Windows Media Center Setup > Run Setup Again**.

Configuring TV tuners

Setting up TV tuners is the same process whether you're installing from the wizard that starts the first time Media Center runs or from **Tasks > Settings > General > Windows Me-**

Buying TV tuners

No matter where you are or what type of TV signal you want to receive it should be possible with Windows Media Center. Make sure that whatever you buy has a Windows 7 logo on it, or failing that most hardware that has the Windows Vista logo on should also work. It's well worth doing some research before choosing a tuner. Some of the top manufacturers are Hauppage (hauppauge.com), ATI (ATI. com), Pinnacle (pinnaclesys.com), Silicon Dust (silicondust. com) and BlackGold (shop.blackgold.tv). Any TV tuner will need drivers, and these are usually provided on CD by the tuner's manufacturer.

Tuners are available for:
- ▶ Analog broadcast (Careful! It'll be no use when everything moves over to digital)
- ▶ Cable
- ▶ Satellite
- ▶ Digital Terrestrial Broadcast (DVB-T)

Many new tuners also support HD-quality broadcasts. Analog tuners can be used to help connect to a set-top box (STB), as provided by a cable company or satellite broadcaster. Analog cards normally include a coaxial TV wire connection (the Aerial) and an SVideo connection; either of these can be used to connect to the STB.

Connecting TV tuners varies by device but it's usually either via USB, an internal card or over a network. Silicon Dust make a great tuner that can be used over a network and shared between PCs.

A cool feature of Windows 7 is that tuners can be mixed and matched. Up to two of each type can be added, so it's possible to have two cable and two digital terrestrial tuners. If the same channels are available on each, then Media Center can be told which ones to prefer. Check out thedigitallifestyle.com or thegreenbutton.com to find out just how much can be done.

dia Center Setup > Set up TV signal. You'll need to have installed the TV tuner card and the drivers for it onto your computer already.

Install the TV tuner and drivers according to the instructions that come with it. In most cases this just means plugging it in and popping a CD into the drive. If you're running the wizard and haven't yet installed the drivers close the Media Center window and do that bit first; the wizard will run again next time you open Media Center.

Once the tuner and its drivers are installed, start Windows Media Center, and if you haven't yet completed the set-up wizard it will run again, or you can start the process manually from **TV > Set up TV tuner**.

Where you are in the world is important; it will be used to help locate TV signals and find the right program guide. The wizard will ask for confirmation of location, and may also ask for your postal code. There are specific terms of service for the TV guide data and for premium (pay per view) content. If you don't read and agree to it then you'll still be able to watch TV but won't be able to schedule recordings or know what programs are coming up. Once everything is agreed a download of guide data and signal information starts.

A few minutes later the wizard will offer up some idea of the type of signal it's found; if this seems correct hit **Yes**, if not then obviously say **No** and it'll try again. Downloading the guide data will start (this will automatically get updated every day in the background). Finally a scan will begin finding the actual channels available. When it's done just click **Finish**, and go watch some TV!

Connecting to a TV screen

Windows Media Center is designed for use on a big screen so it's easy to connect to a TV. The TV can be either the main or secondary display, depending upon what hardware your PC has. Most laptops come with a second VGA connection so that an external screen can

Tip: It's possible for IR emitters (sometimes called "blasters") to interfere with each other. To stop that it can be worth covering them and the rest of the IR receiver on a set-top box with a bit of thick tape.

be attached to them; some come with a TV out or HDMI too. Desktops often come with VGA or DVI and some come with TV out or HDMI. There's no right or wrong way to connect a big-screen display; it simply depends on what connections you have and what you want to do. The sidebar explains the various types of connections.

The screens themselves are configured outside of Windows Media Center by right clicking on the Desktop and selecting **Screen Resolution**.

Remote control

Being ten feet away from the screen, and probably the computer, makes it neces-

Types of video connection

VGA is the standard output from most PCs, and many new LCD TVs or HDTVs come with a VGA connector, sometimes called RGB. A VGA-to-VGA cable is all that's needed.

 TV Out is standard definition output (meaning it's not HD). PCs often come with this, especially if they have been designed for home theatre use. This is often the only connection found on older TVs and it's compatible with SCART in Europe.

DVI is a High Definition (HD) output, and it's often found on new desktop PCs. DVI can be converted to HDMI, which is found on new HDTVs.

 HDMI is the new universal standard format for audio and video cables. All new High Definition TVs come with HDMI connections.

sary for Media Center to have some remote control options. Many PCs, including laptops, which are designed for entertainment and Windows 7, will come with a Windows Media Center remote control included. There are two components to the remote control: the thing you hold in your hand with the buttons on it, and the receiver. The receiver will either be built into the PC (as is the case with laptops generally) or will be a USB device that will need to be plugged in. If it's the latter make sure it's possible to aim the remote control at the receiver; it needs a "line of sight" to work properly.

There should also be some "IR emitters" that came with the receiver. They are long wires with a little "widget" at the end that sit on top of the infrared sensor of a set-top box (such as your digital receiver) and make it so that the one remote can control everything necessary to change channels on a TV setup. For more information on how to set up set-top boxes, take a look at **clubhouse.**

Tip: On the remote control there are quick-access buttons for Live TV, Recorded TV, Music and Pictures. When Windows Media Center is running they can be used to switch between activities. When it's not running, pressing these buttons actually starts Windows Media Center and then goes directly to that activity.

microsoft.com or one of the sites mentioned in the box at the beginning of this chapter.

A first look at Media Center

The interface is far flashier, bigger and quite unlike any other program in Windows. That's because it's designed to work when viewed from a distance or up close with touch screens. The main screen is a carousel of options, each designed around a specific type of media. This is the Windows Media Center Start menu, and despite the name it's not actually the same as the Windows Start menu. In this section we'll just call it the Start menu.

Getting around

Use the arrow keys on the keyboard or remote control, the mouse, or a finger stroke up or down on a touch screen to select any of the options. Each option has a further menu of sub-options, so for example **Music** has: **Music Library**, **play Favorites**, **Radio** and

Search. To select one of these, use the left and right arrows on either the remote or the keyboard or simply click one with the mouse. If you're using touch, simply prod it.

Having gone into one of the screens – **Picture Library**, for example – there are a couple of ways to get back to the main screen. From the keyboard hit the **backspace** key, or with a mouse or touch press the back arrow in the top left of the screen. Next to that back arrow is a green orb. That green orb will go right back to the Windows Media Center Start menu. The cool thing about using the green orb is that if a video is playing, pressing it will bring up an overlay of the Start menu, while video remains watchable. The green orb on the screen and the green button on your remote perform the same function: taking you back to the Media Center Start menu. The one on the remote can also be used to start Media Center if it isn't already running.

The Windows Media Center Start menu provides access to everything that the application can do. Scroll up and down using the arrow keys, touch screen or mouse, then scroll left and right to select the required activity (recorded TV or the Guide, for example).

Exploring media

The sections for Music, Video + Pictures, TV and Movies are all different but follow a similar theme. Each section has a number of different views that show the media different ways. Recorded TV, for example, has **date recorded**, **title** and **shared** options; these different views make it easier to find things. With a mouse or touch just select the one to view. To select them with the remote press the **up** button and the title of the current view will highlight and grow in size; use the left and right buttons to select a different view.

The **shared** view is common to all sections and shows content that is shared with the HomeGroup from any other PC on the network. So in a house with two Windows 7 PCs it'll automatically show the pictures, videos and recorded TV on both PCs. To learn more about HomeGroups and sharing see Chapter 22.

Tip: Don't bother to add media from other Windows 7 PCs using Manage Libraries. Instead, make sure all the Windows 7 PCs are part of the same Home-Group and all the media that they are sharing will appear in the shared view within each type of media.

Managing Libraries

From the Start menu going to any of the options for Music, Video, Movies or Recorded TV will open a Library of that type of media. From there the easiest way to add media is to press the **info** button on the remote or right click with the mouse and select **Media Libraries**. By default the Library will include any media of that type in the Windows Library. So Music will show any content in your Windows Music Library. It's also possible to add media from other folders on the PC, or in fact from other PCs on the network. Go into **Manage Libraries** and select **Add folder to monitor** then choose where you want to add your folder from (including shared locations on other networked computers). Of the four options most work in the same way: just browse for the folder to add. **Manually add a shared folder** lets you add a folder from another computer on the network by typing their details in. Once the extra media has been added it will be available in the Library.

Removing media from Libraries

Sometimes you might want to remove media stored in a specific place from a Library; perhaps the PC it's shared from has been replaced or the files deleted to save space. To remove media go to **Tasks > Settings > Manage Libraries** and select the type of Library to manage. Then select the **Stop monitoring a folder** option and uncheck the box next to the location that you no longer wish to monitor.

Tip: It's also possible to listen to digital radio channels available over digital satellite or digital terrestrial TV. The radio channels appear in the Guide within TV. Sadly there's currently no way to listen to DAB radio in the UK.

Pictures + Video

Two Libraries are represented by this section of the Start menu. The Picture Library lets pictures on the PC or the network be shown in full screen glory. The Video Library does the same for video; it's a great way to get family movies onto the big screen. Another option from within this tab is play Favorites, a fantastic way to view photos. Play Favorites selects all the photos tagged as three stars or higher (tagging is possible with Windows Live Gallery; see Chapter 14). Each picture is beautifully displayed as a printed photo with a white border.

Unleashing your photo collection onto the TV is great, but all of a sudden you're in a position to potentially show all your pictures to your friends. It's a good idea to make sure that your Favorites are things you actually want to share. What goes into the Favorites view can be controlled in **Settings > Pictures > Favorite Pictures**.

Viewing albums on a big screen with Windows Media Center is a great way to explore a music collection. You can view by albums, artists, genres, individual song titles, playlists, composers and album artists (which displays every album you have for a specific artist).

Music

The Music section has four subsections, but most of your actual music can be found under Music Library. The Play Favorites option is much like the Favorites option in Pictures + Video. It plays all the songs in the Library that are rated three stars or higher. The Radio option will play Internet radio channels and will also list FM radio channels if there's an FM tuner in the PC. Search allows you to find things in your music collection; it's an intelligent search, though, and will look at all the information associated with a track.

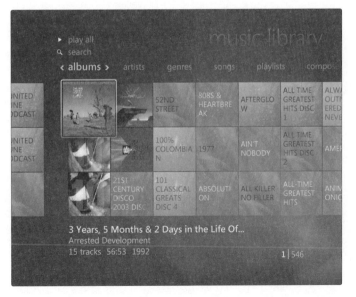

Windows Media Center

Tip: To get an even more interesting visual display when listening to music select Visualize. This will display a series of pretty patterns on screen in time to the music. Try not to get hypnotized by it! (Don't worry, there isn't a risk really.) To get even more visualizations go to wmplugins.com.

Music Library is where the music on your PC and network can be found. As with other parts of the program there are different views that make it easier to get to music in different ways. The default view is **albums** and lists all albums in alphabetical order. It builds a grid of album covers that looks nice on a big screen. Navigating around is done in the usual way, with the left and right buttons, a swipe with the fingers or a click of the mouse.

Of the other views, one of the most useful is **album artist**, which lists all the artists in your music collection and their albums. When thinking about music you may often think of the name of the artist first, and then the name of the album (if we can remember the name of the album at all!). So this may be your preferred view.

Going into an album reveals various options; for playing the whole album just hit **play album**. Individual tracks can also be played if you highlight them with the remote, or click them with the mouse and then hit **play**. You may prefer to queue something up rather than playing it immediately, and hitting **add to now playing** will add the album, or an individual track, to the queue. Everything in the queue plays in turn, or you can press the **Shuffle** button to mix it up.

When something's playing the cover art is displayed in front of a background made up of the cover art for other albums. At the bottom right of the screen are a group of media controls – play, pause, next, back etc – that can be triggered with a mouse or touch. If you're using a remote just use the media controls on the remote. Selecting **View Song List** shows the queue of music that's playing; things can be moved up and down in a rather obvious fashion.

Playing music with a big screen to browse through your collection is a surprisingly addictive experience, especially when you do it with friends.

Movie Library

Where Windows Media Center really comes into its own is showing things off on the big screen. And what better to show off than a massive collection of movies! The movies can be in a number of formats, too; see the sidebar for those supported. Just as you can have a Library of all of your music, the same thing is possible with movies, all stored on the hard drive and ready to play in an instant.

Movies have all the usual controls for play, pause etc, and as always they are found in the bottom right-hand corner.

TV

Watching TV on the PC is where Windows Media Center excels. With the addition of a tuner card it becomes a powerful video recorder. The main options under the TV section of the menu are live TV, the guide and recorded TV.

Live TV

Just watching what's currently on TV is easy: just go to **Live TV** from within the **TV** section or press the **Live TV** button on your remote. Live TV will start up, and is just like using any normal TV. The number pad on your remote and the channel up and down buttons (or keyboard up and down) let you change channels.

Now for the cool bit. The pause button will do just that: pause live TV. There's no need to set the program to record, no need to have loaded a VHS tape and gotten things ready or anything like that. Simply hit **pause** and the TV pauses, it'll stay paused for about half an hour or until the end of the programme. Not only that; did you just miss that bit of important dialogue in your favourite soap?

Supported video formats

- VOB (DVD)
- M2TS (Blu-ray)
- WTV (Recorded TV)
- DVR-MS (Microsoft's old recorded TV format)
- AVI (DIVX)
- WMV
- MOV
- MKV
- FLV (Flash)
- MPG
- MP4

Windows Media Center

Tip: If you're watching TV that you've either recorded or if you've just rewound live TV or paused it for a while, you can avoid watching the adverts. Press the skip button on the remote, or in the bottom right of the screen, to skip forward in ten-second jumps.

Hit the **rewind** button! Again, nothing to set up, just rewind. Once it's rewound to where you want, press **play**. When you've caught up you can press **fast forward** to get back to where you were. If you want to record and save a programme for future viewing press the **record** button on either the remote or in the bottom right of the screen.

Want to know what it is you're watching? Press the **information** button or the left or right buttons. Wondering what's on next? Press the **up** or **down** buttons to display a mini-guide. It's all very fast and looks much nicer than the menus on your normal TV.

The guide

Press the **Guide** button on the remote or select **Guide** from the **TV** menu and a guide will pop up showing all the upcoming TV shows for the channels you can receive.

The guide is split into three sections. To the right are all the programs that are on TV for the next fourteen days; those highlighted with white text are what's currently being broadcast. Navigate through them with the arrow keys on either the remote or keyboard, or you can use mouse or touch. Scroll through the channels with the up and down buttons, pressing and holding to "turbo scroll" through the list. Any programme in the guide can be recorded, even entire series, so you'll never miss an episode.

To set a single episode of a show to be recorded, highlight it and hit the record button on the remote, or right-click it with the mouse and select **Record**. To record an entire series press the **info** button, or again right click with the mouse and select **Record Series**. Highlighting a show and pressing **OK** or hitting the **Enter** key brings up details about that programme; it can be set to record from here too.

The centre column of the guide lists all the available TV channels by name. Selecting a channel and pressing **OK** will focus on just that channel and shows all the forthcoming programmes in a vertical list.

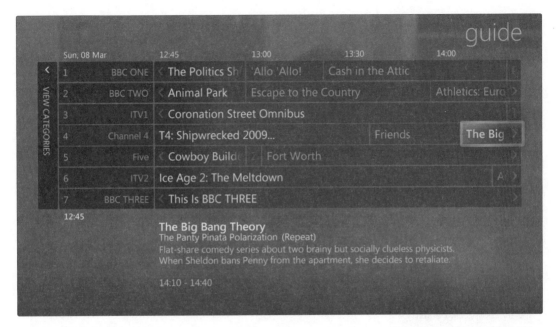

The guide in Windows Media Center appears when a TV tuner has been installed and is just like any other TV guide except that you can use it to record programmes. Entire series can even be set to record if you like.

The left-hand side column allows programmes to be filtered by type, such as movies, game shows or drama.

Recorded TV

Once you've recorded some TV you'll find it in the **Recorded TV** section. This can be found through the **TV** menu or with the button on the remote. It works just like the Movie Library or the Music Library. You can list shows by date or title.

When quite a few shows have been recorded a message will pop up offering a "List" view.

Windows Media Center

Any programmes that are recorded show up in recorded TV along with a thumbnail taken from the programme itself.

> **Tip:** Adverts can be a serious waste of time. As well as using the skip button to bypass them it's also possible to automate removing commercials from recorded TV. The two best tools are DVRMS Toolbox (babgvant. com) and LifExtender (lifextend-er.com). They take a little time to set up but they are brilliant and will save literally hours of your life!

From here any recorded shows can be played back with the usual controls for play, pause etc. Two other useful options worth mentioning are:

▶ add recording – reveals a couple of other ways to set programmes up to record. From here it's possible to search for the name of a show, or keywords within a show's description. It's also possible to record a specific channel at a specific time. Careful, though; if the broadcaster changes their time slots the guide will get updated, but timed recordings won't.

▶ view scheduled – does what it says on the tin: it reveals a list of everything that's set to record and when.

You can also access List view, by right clicking (or pressing **info**) and selecting **View List** from the pop-up menu.

Extras

The Extras option reveals a Library of extras that includes the games that are installed with Windows 7. Most of them work well in full-screen mode and can be controlled with the remote or the mouse.

There's much more to the Extras Library than meets the eye. Windows Media Center is a platform for which people have created some fantastic add-ons. There are weather guides, movie information programmes and others. The sidebar lists some of the best. Many are community projects and don't come with much support.

The **explore** option within **Extras** lists quite a few interactive TV channels that can be fun to use.

IPTV

Within Windows Media Center there is support for IPTV channels (channels that are available over the Internet). This is limited by geographic location because of restrictions placed around the content by the broadcasters. If you're in the US then there's a lot here to play with.

IPTV channels are located in sensible places throughout Media Center, so within Movies there are **movie trailers**, and within Music there are **live concerts**. Pictures + Videos has **viral videos** which are interesting short movies not unlike those you might find on YouTube. There are also IPTV channels from broadcasters including ABC, FOX and other networks, and these are listed in the guide. If there's a TV tuner installed the IPTV channels are found either side of the TV tuner's channels.

Tip: Unfortunately there is no one "best place" to go to for add-ons. However, the community sites do a very good job of letting people know what's new. Try thegreenbutton.com and thedigitallifestyle.com for some great reviews and how-tos. A couple to look into are:

▸ Heatwave – tells you about the current weather and the forecast (thegreenbutton.com/forums/post/276418.aspx).

▸ Media Browser – a fantastic replacement for the Movie Library function with even more features and a beautiful interface! (mediabrowser.tv).

Tasks

The tasks menu contains all the settings for Media Center, but there are a couple of other useful things here.

Burning a DVD or CD

Just like Windows Media Player can burn a CD or DVD for you, so can Media Center. The advantage is that with Media Center there's no need to leave the big-screen view; it can still be done from the couch. Just pop in a blank CD or DVD and it's like falling off a log: select the media to put on the CD or DVD from your Library and it'll do the rest for you.

Sync a portable media player

It's also possible to sync media to a USB drive or portable music player from the tasks menu. The syncing is based on auto playlists like those created with Windows Media Player; to find out how to create auto playlists, see Chapter 16. The **Add More** button selects which playlists are synced, and there are a number of special Media Center playlists already set up for you. To remove a list, just select the **X** to the right of it. The lists are synced in order, so if the top playlist fills the device the rest won't sync.

Advanced Setup

For times when it's necessary to tweak the setup of Media Center, head to **Tasks > Settings**. Its possible to control almost all aspects of Media Center from this menu. The **general** button includes options for how the program starts up, sounds that are made when moving around and what information is shared with third parties. A couple of the settings here require a specific mention:

Tip: Using Media Center to burn a CD or DVD or even to sync to a device doesn't stop you from being able to do other things, like watching TV. The burning and syncing happens in the background, leaving you to enjoy your media. It'll notify you when it's done, but if you want to check on progress just go back into burn CD/DVD or sync.

▸ Parental Controls – To stop kids watching something they shouldn't, either on TV or DVDs, this option lets you set a four-digit pin before anything rated for adults will play.

▸ Optimization – If you intend to leave Windows Media Center running all the time, as you might if it's your main TV, then enabling optimization will make the application restart occasionally when you aren't using it, helping things run smoothly and preventing minor problems accumulating within the software..

Back in the main settings menu the **TV** option lets you fiddle with the location that's used for recorded TV on the hard disk and allows the amount of hard disk used for storing recorded TV to be controlled. By default the hard disk is allowed to fill up completely with TV recordings, so you may want to set this to something more conservative. The **Guide** option allows the guide to be customized; you can manage a list of favourite channels or change their order.

Extending to other rooms

Connecting a TV to the PC gives a great experience, but it's not always possible to put the TV and the PC close together. That's where extenders come in. An extender is a small box that performs just the Windows Media Center functions of the PC. It can run over a wired or wireless network and can access the live and recorded TV and all the Libraries on the PC running Windows Media Center. The user interface that appears is exactly that of Windows Media Center.

Extenders are made by a few companies as dedicated boxes, about the size of a DVD player. Up to five extenders can run from a single PC, so it's a great way to get a very consistent TV experience all over your home. With very little set up (and for no subscription costs) you can have your cable TV in every room of the home.

Microsoft's Xbox 360 includes everything necessary for it to be used as an extender, and with the optional WiFi card that's available

> **Tip:** There isn't currently a wireless N network adapter available for Xbox so it won't stream HD content over wireless. Homeplug adapters make a great alternative for setting up a home network, and the newer versions are capable of very high speeds needed for streaming HD video. Have a look at Chapter 21 on networking to find out what to do.

> **Tip:** The Xbox is one of the best extenders available, but it doesn't come with a normal remote control. Although the Xbox controller can be used as a remote, there is a remote control available for the Xbox for about $40. What's cool about it is that it's also a universal remote, so it can be used to turn the TV and cinema system on and off too!

it can stream standard definition TV just fine, so it could be worth considering buying one just for use as an extender.

Once set up, using the extender is exactly the same as using Windows Media Center with a remote.

Setup

To set up a device as an extender you first have to run setup on the device itself. This is very easy to do and wizard-based; it will deliver an eight digit number. Take this number to the PC and from within Media Center go to **Tasks > Settings > Extender > Add Extender**. Enter the number and you're basically done. If UAC is on then click **Yes** to the request to allow the process to continue.

Using an Xbox 360 as a Media Center extender is an excellent way to move media around the home. It includes a useful tool to show the quality of content the network can handle. In this case top quality hi-def content can be shared easily.

Checking performance

To make sure your network is up to streaming HD content around your home, the Media Center should either be connected to the extender over a wire, or if using a wireless network it should be at least wireless N standard.

There is a performance tool to double check this from the extender. Go to **Tasks > Settings > Extender** and select **Tune Network**. This will launch a wizard to determine how fast the link is between the extender and the PC and will be able to show the results as a bar graph.

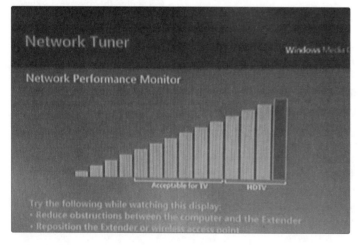

iTunes and Zunes

18

iTunes

If you want to use an iPod with Windows the obvious way to do it is to install iTunes (itunes.com), Apple's own jukebox software. There are other ways to manage an iPod, but few have the same features or support from Apple. It's free to download and works just like it did in previous versions of Windows.

Much like Windows Media Player, iTunes is a media Library or jukebox, managing the audio and video on your PC. Installation is simple; just download and then follow the install wizard.

Setting up

When you start iTunes for the first time, a wizard walks you through making adjustments to your system. First it asks which music files to add into the iTunes Library; MP3, AAC (Apple's proprietary format) and WMA are selected by default. The next step is important if you're planning to use iTunes with other Libraries like Windows Media Player or Windows Media Center: it'll ask you if you want it to keep your iTunes music folder organized. If you choose **Yes, keep my iTunes Music Folder organized**, iTunes will move the media on your PC around into its own folder system, and other applica-

> **Tip:** Often something called DRM or Digital Rights Management comes embedded in music or video downloads. It's a mechanism to protect the copyright owners from theft or illegal copying of their material. It also happens to be very annoying from a consumer's point of view because it makes moving that media collection around difficult. iTunes is now doing away with DRM, and anything marked as "iTunes plus" is DRM free. To save future hassles try to get DRM free media where possible.

tions won't be able to find it, so if you're unsure pick **No, I'll change the file and folder names myself**.

iTunes will try to connect to the iTunes store and associate with an account. An iTunes account is needed for downloading music from iTunes and also for getting media information and cover art, but it's not mandatory.

Shopping online with iTunes

iTunes' online music store is considered by many to be the best on the Internet. Virtually any music tracks can be downloaded, for a price, with new releases often hitting iTunes before they're even available in the shops on CD.

A credit card can be set up within an account on iTunes and used to buy tracks, TV shows or movie rentals. Alternatively you can buy a prepaid iTunes card from almost anywhere that sells music. They come in various denominations and make great gifts.

One of the reasons iTunes gets installed on so many machines is it enables iPod functionality. Once it's installed you can simply plug in the iPod and iTunes will detect the device and start to sync with it. iTunes won't allow the iPod to be synchronized with any other PCs, so it will break any previous synchronization partnerships.

The Zune

Microsoft makes an alternative to the iPod which also requires its own software to get the best out of it. The Zune software is available from zune.net. Even if you don't own a Zune the software is lots of fun and worth a look.

Zune is currently only available in the US and Canada, but there are plenty of people selling Zunes (the actual player) on eBay. Finally, just like iTunes, Zune has its own music store, the Zune marketplace.

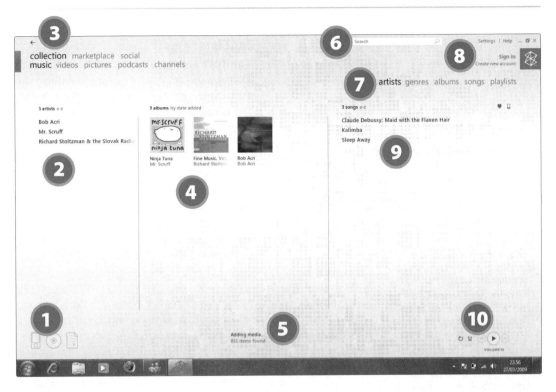

1 **Devices** – shows if a Zune is connected, or if a CD is in the drive; dragging music or video here syncs it to the device or burns it to CD.

2 **Artists** – selecting an artist shows only the albums and songs by that artist in the artist and album panes.

3 **Navigation** – move through the types of media in your collection, go to the marketplace to get new music or swap tracks with friends in social.

4 **Albums** – shows the albums for the selected artist. If no artist is selected, as is the case here, then all albums in your collection appear.

5 **Status** – lets you know what's happening at any time.

6 **Search** – quickly find specific music in your collection.

7 **Views** – organize your music in different ways.

8 **User info** – shows the User Account used to buy music and videos in the marketplace and to swap music experiences in social.

9 **Songs** – shows individual tracks for the selected artists or albums.

10 **Media controls** – the usual play, pause, next and previous buttons along with repeat, shuffle and volume controls.

iTunes and Zunes

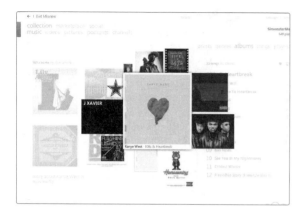

Anywhere you see the mix view icon, click it to find albums that are in some way related. These could be previous collaborations for an artist or even other musicians who influenced their style. It's a great way to discover new music.

Setup

The first thing to do is not connect the Zune to the computer before installing the software. Just start the installation; if the PC has an Internet connection the latest version of the software will be downloaded before setup runs.

The first time you run the Zune software you're presented with two choices. The usual "do it all for me" option is **go right to my collection**. The second option, **customize my settings first**, is the one that lets you get more involved with how Zune is set up, allowing the locations for music, pictures, videos and podcasts to be changed. Each can be kept in more than one location either on a hard drive or on the network; your Window 7 Libraries are included automatically. The file types (like MP3, WMA etc) that will open with Zune can also be changed, as can the options to participate, or not, in the "Customer Experience Program" (basically sending usage data to Microsoft).

Collection and Devices

The Zune software is divided into four sections. **Collection** is your personal collection of music, video, podcasts and pictures. **Devices** looks almost the same but it's the Library that's actually on the Zune device. These two sections have a number of subsections for each type of media that Zune looks after. Essentially click on anything, and use the media controls at the bottom right of the window to start it playing.

Tip: The Zune device comes in 4gb, 8gb, 80gb and 120gb versions, with older 30gb versions still available. A couple of clever features set it apart from the iPod. The first is buy from FM. There's a built-in FM tuner that identifies the songs being played on a radio station; the Zune then lets you choose to buy the song there and then. The second feature is the ability to share music with other Zune owners wirelessly; any music or video can be shared and played three times on another device. The built-in WiFi can also be used to sync with the Zune software without having to plug it in.

Social and marketplace

Finding new music is what Zune is really all about. The software makes this possible through the Zune marketplace and Zune social. The marketplace is Microsoft's online store; it'll look at your existing music collection and what you've listened to recently and select recommendations for you. Zune social adds social networking functionality; it'll suggest other people with similar music or movie tastes. Having like-minded listening buddies is a great way to find new music.

One of the most addictive features of the Zune software is mixview. Pressing the mixview button takes the album you've selected and works out what other albums are similar, the idea being that if you like "Run DMC – Best of" then you will probably like "Grand Master Flash". Recommendations come from the marketplace so it's possible to listen to samples or buy them.

Syncing with a Zune

Connect a Zune and it will sync almost automatically. There are a couple of things you may have to do. First, define whether this PC is the main computer that the Zune will connect to. Zunes can connect to more than one PC, but will behave as a guest on others. Each Zune will need to be given a name, because more than one Zune can be used with the same PC. It's also useful to associate a Zune tag with a Zune. A Zune tag identifies the individual who uses the Zune, keeping track of what they listen to just like the software does, allowing you to get more recommendations from mixview as described above.

If the Zune can't store your whole collection, you'll have to make some decisions about what to put on it. A small image of the Zune will appear in the bottom left of the window. Drag any media to it to sync it with the Zune. Alternatively, right-click on some media and select **Sync with <your Zune's name here> Zune**.

Tip: The Zune software offers another way to discover new music, called a Zune pass. For $14 per month as many tracks as you like can be downloaded and kept for as long as your subscription runs. Ten tracks per month can be added to your permanent collection and kept even if you cancel your subscription, but you lose access to the rest. The tracks can be copied to three PCs and three Zunes. It's an interesting deal, but only available to US credit card holders.

Tip: To get even better recommendations that match your music taste, don't forget to rate things as you listen and watch. The rating system on Zune deals in hearts: an empty heart is neutral, a full heart means you love it and a broken heart means if makes your ears bleed (But not in a good way!).

Games

Windows is the most popular gaming platform in the world; more people choose to play games on Windows than on any other system, including games consoles. It's no surprise then that parts of Windows have been built specifically for playing games. The content and type of games varies drastically and every type of game imaginable is represented in Windows, from racing, adventure, strategy and role play games to games like chess, card games and board games. Games are becoming more and more immersive, transporting the player to a new reality.

Games are not just something that one plays alone anymore; playing online with friends is now built into more and more games. In fact the number of players able to play in a single game is increasing all the time with "MMORPG" or Massively Multi-player Online Role Playing Games becoming increasingly popular.

There are different categories of gamer out there. This chapter is aimed at the casual gamer, people who don't take games too seriously, but who play occasionally for fun. The opposite end of the spectrum is the serious gamer; for them playing games is a major hobby or pastime.

Content varies considerably from game to game and generally determines the age range of the players. Some games contain language or scenes that are only suitable for adults. Rating systems for these are explained later this chapter.

Not all games need to be installed on Windows to play them; there are many available purely online through a webpage. Windows 7 ships with a number of games included, all of which are suitable for family use and are resource-friendly enough be played on virtually any system. There are updated takes on the games that have become an integral part of Windows over the years; Minesweeper, Solitaire and FreeCell alongside some great new Internet games. One of the primary reasons for including games with Windows has always been to help people to improve their mouse skills – Solitaire is particularly good for this. As well as the games that come with Windows 7, many others exist that you can buy either from a gaming shop on the high street or from online stores.

For compatibility, look out for the Games for Windows logo on the game's box. This indicates that the game meets specific requirements, basically telling you it will install and play easily.

> **Fact:** Games have been part of Windows since Windows 1.0. The first ever game for Windows was Reversi, a strategy game based on the game Othello, where the intention was to make as many of the counters on the games board coloured in your playing colour.

What you'll need to play games

The hardware that's needed to play games varies according to the content. Most games will list the minimum and recommended system requirements on their website or on the DVD or CD case. There will also be minimum software requirements; but by using Windows 7 everything you need for playing games should be built in. To play Internet games, however, you'll often need to install a plugin for your browser.

Hardware

The minimum requirement for most modern games is around an Intel P4 or AMD processor running at about 3Ghz, 1.5Gb RAM and 128mb graphics card. That might sound like utter gibberish, but luckily Windows can help that make sense. The higher specification your hardware is, the faster and smoother a game will run and the more detailed the graphics will be.

To find out what's inside your PC go to **Start > Control Panel > All Control Panel Items > System**. Here the specific information about your system will be listed; look for **Processor** and **RAM**. Video performance is not listed here, but it's easy enough to find by going to **Start > Control Panel > All Control Panel Items > Display > Screen Resolution** and selecting **Advanced Settings**. The window that appears will tell you all about your graphics card, including how much memory is available; look for **Total Available Graphics Memory**.

Windows makes it even easier to understand what the PC is capable of with the Windows Experience Index Rating. This index gives an indication of your PC's ability to process resource-hungry tasks such as playing high-definition video or playing games. A higher rating indicates a more powerful PC, so the more capable of running games it will be. If you go to **Start > Control Panel > All Control Panel Items > System**, the Experience Index will be listed next to **Rating**. If it says **System rating is not available** then click **Rate this computer** to see what your PC is capable of.

If you go to Start > Control Panel > All Control Panel Items > System and the Windows Experience Index isn't listed, click the System rating not available link to have Windows work it out for you.

From a rating point of view the thing to look out for are 3.0 scores, in particular in the subcategories of memory (RAM), graphics and gaming graphics. The overall score is determined by the lowest subscore. If the PC reaches or exceeds a 3.0 score overall and in the above subcategories then it should be fine, but the higher the better. Look to Chapter 33 to find out how to improve scores.

> **Tip:** If you plan to use your PC for playing games then it might be worth considering a dedicated gaming PC. Most manufacturers make PCs designed for hardcore gamers where everything has been pushed to maximum. Some even involve water-cooling components to make them faster (because silicon chips are more efficient at lower temperatures) and quieter.
>
> Dell's XPS (del.com/xps) is a range of striking looking PCs with high-spec components tweaked to work as fast as possible. Alienware produce computers with similar performance considerations and which are some of the coolest looking PCs available (alienware.com).

Controllers

The controllers used to play games on PCs vary according to the type of game being played. The keyboard and mouse are the most obvious; in fact they can be the best controllers for a lot of games. First-person shooters, where you play as a character and look out through their eyes or over their shoulder, are often best with a keyboard and mouse combination. The mouse gives you intuitive access to aim weapons and the keyboard gives good control over character movement and direction. There are hundreds of keyboards and mice designed specifically for gaming, in all shapes and sizes with extra buttons all over the place.

Among the plethora of other controllers available are joysticks for flight simulators, steering wheels for racing games and joy-pad controllers for general game use. Many games that bear the Games for Windows branding are compatible with the popular Xbox 360 wireless controller. As well as the wireless controller you'll need to fork out for an Xbox 360 wireless gaming receiver for Windows in order to use it with your PC.

Many online games include the ability to talk to the

Game controllers in Control Panel lists any controllers you have installed. The Advanced and Properties buttons allow settings to be changed for specific controllers.

Game controllers

Some of the most popular game controllers are made by Logitech (logitech.com). Their range includes optical mice with extra high quality lasers to make them faster and more accurate, and keyboards with back-lit keys so that they're visible when playing in the dark. They even make a complete driving cockpit that includes steering wheel and gear stick!

Microsoft also makes hardware for games (microsoft.com/hardware), including the incredibly popular SideWinder range.

Tip: Managing game controllers can be done from Start > Control Panel > All Control Panel Items > Game Controllers. And a more friendly interface can be found in Start > Control Panel > All Control Panel Items > Devices and Printers.

players. For this it's best to use a headset microphone, just like those used with Windows Live Messenger or Skype. They enhance the game tremendously, and if you're playing a team game they are invaluable.

Software

The main software that's needed to play games is **DirectX**. You don't need to worry about that since the current standard is built into Windows 7.

Where software does become a concern, and only a minor one, is for Web-based games. Adobe Flash will probably be required by your Internet browser; it's practically essential for using the Internet at all these days. You can get it from **get. adobe.com/flashplayer**.

Games for Windows

Microsoft and a number of other top game manufacturers got together to create a set of standards called Games for Windows so that anyone buying a game knows it'll meet certain requirements of quality, compatibility, safety and ease of play. Any game that meets the standard will have the Games for Windows logo on the box.

The quality standard ensures that the game isn't riddled with bugs that make it crash. Compatibility ensures it'll play well on the Windows version it's intended for. Safety means it's content-rated and that the Parental Controls in Windows protect access based on those ratings. Games are also guaranteed to install to the Games Explorer, making them much easier to find and start playing. For more information about these standards and a list of games that support them check **gamesforwindows.com**.

Games for Windows compatible games are not the only ones that'll play on Windows. Anything that says PC CD-ROM on the box will probably still play fine, but there's no guarantee they'll install to the Games explorer and be compatible with Parental Controls.

Tip: If you play games on both Windows and Xbox you only need one Gamertag. Your Gamerscore is increased whichever platform you're using. You can even put your Gamertag on your website or blog, or customize it at xboxlive.com.

Games for Windows – Live

Many of the compatible games are playable online with friends through Games for Windows – Live. You can even play against people who are playing the same game on Xbox. It's also possible to buy games or extend them with new levels, maps and achievements with Live marketplace.

Gamertags

Everyone who holds an account on Games for Windows – Live or Xbox Live has a Gamertag – this is information about your playing habits – and a Gamerscore which reflects your playing skills and is increased by completing achievements in a game. Most games that support Live also support achievements, which are basically milestones within the game.

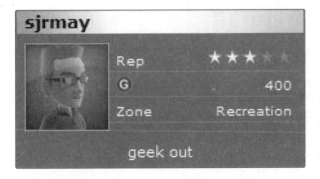

A Gamertag rates your gaming skills. Details behind the tag are specific to the games you play such as how many achievements you have in a particular game. The Gamerscore, represented by a G to the left, shows overall proficiency. 400 is actually quite poor!

Tip: Essentially 80 points is $1. The number of points available on a prepaid card varies by country to make both the price and points a round number.

Live marketplace

The Live marketplace is where you can buy new games and extensions to ones you already own. Many games now have add-ons that extend the life of a game – for example, extra models of cars in a racing game, or extra levels, maps or new characters in an adventure. The client that enables all of this can be downloaded from **gamesforwindows.com**. Once it's installed it's easy to get updates for games, download demos and watch video previews of unreleased games.

Microsoft points

Kids play a lot games but generally don't have credit cards, for obvious reasons. That's partly why Microsoft uses points to allow purchases on Live (and on Xbox Live and the Zune marketplace). Points are purchased in advanced and can be given just like gift vouchers. Points can be purchased from **points.microsoft.com**, or if you can tear yourself away from your computer, on the high street in the form of prepaid cards (any branded as Xbox Live or Zune can be used).

Installing games

Every game comes with its own installation program. It's just like installing any other application; first you'll need to tell it where to install the game to, which in most cases will be a location on the C: drive. The installer may also need to connect to the Internet in order to download updates. Much like any other software, games have occasional updates to fix problems or plug security holes in the original release, so it's always worth staying up to date.

Games for Windows logoed games will install shortcuts into the

Games Explorer and can be accessed from **Start > Games**. Non-compatible games that don't hold the logo will just install into the regular Start menu.

The Games Explorer

Any game that carries the Games for Windows logo will be installed here by default, and other games that aren't installed here can be added by dragging their shortcuts into the Games Explorer window. This'll keep everything ordered in one place, and make finding your games a lot easier than if they were peppered about on your Desktop and Start menu.

The window is organized into two sections: Game Providers, where links to the makers of games can be found, and games, which are links to the games themselves. Selecting a games provider displays recent news from that provider, including any available game updates. Start a game by double clicking its icon. Double clicking on a Game Provider will take you to their website.

The right-hand side of the window contains some useful data about each game. The first tab gives some general information about the game, including its content rating. The

Tip: Removing games is the same as removing any other application from your PC. Select Control Panel > All Control Panel Items > Programs and Features, highlight the game to remove and select Uninstall.

Games for Windows certified games will install to the Games Explorer, making them easy to find and quick to launch. Scores appear in the right-hand panel once games have been played.

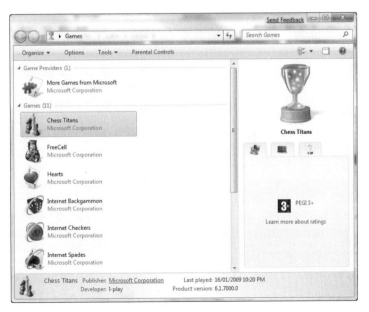

Tip: The Microsoft Game Provider link will take you to lots more free games from Microsoft. Many of these integrate with Windows Live Messenger and can be played over the Internet with friends.

second tab gives an idea of how well the game will play, showing the PC's current Windows Experience Index and the indices that are **Required** and **Recommended** for the game. Another tab will appear once a game has been played (as long as the game supports it), displaying statistics about your playing skills. All the games included with Windows support this; it's a handy place to look to see how good you are at chess.

The toolbar at the top allows access to some game settings and allows you to configure the Games Explorer. The **Organize** button changes the layout, while the **Options** button changes update settings and what information gets displayed. The **Tools** button provides fast access to some of the common control panel items that might need tweaking to play specific games, and **Parental Controls** lets you set access levels for your family.

Getting games updates

Click the **Options** button and you'll be able to set games to update automatically or for you to decide when to do it yourself. Generally it's worth leaving it set to automatic.

Highlighting a Game Provider will show any updates that are available for any of that manufacturer's games. You can also see available updates from an **Update Available** notification under the title of each game in the Games window.

When an update is available, highlight the game and click the **Download Now** button that appears in the right-hand pane. A progress bar will appear to show how much of your update is downloaded, followed by an **Install Now** button once it's complete.

Unfortunately this functionality is only available to games that are programmed to take advantage of the feature. To get updates for other games, check the game maker's website.

Parental Controls

Games often contain content that's only suitable for certain age ranges. Some games contain extreme violence, language or other things that kids of certain ages shouldn't see or hear. Luckily Windows 7 supports parental control and content-rating standards that make it easy to manage which games your kids can get access to. This is all done from the **Parental Controls** button.

In order for this to be effective, each person who uses the PC really needs their own User Account (see Chapter 8 for more detail on creating accounts). Select the account you wish to control and a settings window will appear; ensure that Parental Controls are turned on. Then select **Games** and another window will appear.

In this window, games can be turned on or off completely. Access to games can also be allowed based on the rating or the name of the game. Clicking **Set game rating** allows the maximum (the rating that includes the most extreme content) to be set for the user. Specific types of content, such as "fear" or "comic violence", can also be blocked. Selecting **Block or Allow specific games** displays a list of all the games that are installed, and each can be turned off or on individually. Parental Controls are covered in more detail in Chapter 26.

A word of warning: only games that the Games Explorer knows about will be guarded, so some games, especially very old ones, might not be protected.

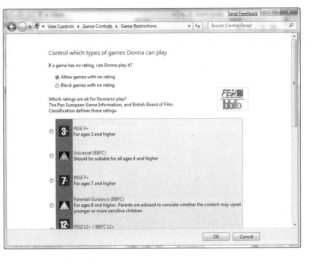

Games Explorer shows game ratings from your country's content-rating organization, helping you determine whether the game is suitable for your children.

Devices and printers

Device Stage is a single program to manage all the settings for devices used with the PC: printers, PDAs, mobile phones, webcams, CD/DVD drives, portable media players and so on. If there's anything you need to know about the devices connected to the PC then this is where to look first.

It's accessible from **Start > Devices and Printers** or from **Start > Control Panel > Hardware and Sound > Devices and Printers**. To manage a device just double click it. From here you'll see either the manufacturer's own interface or a more generic **Properties** window. Connecting a mobile phone, for example, provides options to play music from the phone, download new applications to it, import photos from it or visit the manufacturer's website.

There are activities available for almost any device attached to the PC; right click its icon and activities will appear at the top of the menu. Activities include such things as ejecting CDs, browsing files on a USB key or accessing the music on an MP3 player.

If a device isn't listed, check to see if it's physically connected to the PC. If it's wireless then make sure it's turned on and if it still doesn't appear click Add a device to force Windows to check for it. If it still doesn't appear then use the wizard to help Windows find it.

Printers

You can also manage printers from Device Stage; every printer connected to the PC, either physically or over the network, will be displayed here. You'll also notice a couple of extra printers; "Microsoft XPS Document Writer", the default printer (useful if you're on the move a lot (see the sidebar for what it can do) and "Fax". Fax makes it easy to use an attached scanner as a fax machine, assuming the PC is connected to a phone line via a modem.

Connecting printers

Printers should be connected according to the manufacturer's instructions but for most this just means plugging in a USB cable. Some older printers will have a larger "Parallel" cable interface. Windows 7 includes drivers for a vast array of printers, and there are more available from the Internet. When connecting a printer, a window will appear asking if you want to install additional software from the bundled CD. It's not always necessary but can be helpful in order to access more advanced functions.

Adding a local printer

If the printer isn't detected, or if it's connected to a parallel printer port, it might be necessary to force Windows to realize it's there. On the toolbar in the Devices and Printers window click **Add a printer**, then in the wizard that appears select **Add a local printer**. You'll then need to identify the make and model and give it a name. Windows will install it and ask if you want to share the printer with other people on your network, to set it as the default printer (the one that's used automatically) and to print a test page.

Tip: The Microsoft XPS Document Writer is a handy printer to keep around, especially if you're away from a printer for a while. It doesn't produce a printed piece of paper; it actually saves anything that can be printed as a file, which can then be printed out later using a real printer. Anything that's printed to it is saved exactly as it would have been printed, so it's useful for record keeping too. It works in just the same way as any other printer; just click Print in whatever application to use it, and select where to save the file when prompted. Later just double click the file to open it or use Start > All Programs > XPS Viewer to open and print it on a real printer.

Devices and printers

If the printer you've added is attached to another PC, it's unlikely you'll be asked to provide drivers, but if it's networked via wireless or Bluetooth, Windows will ask for drivers if it doesn't already have them.

Tip: Before trying to add a printer, make sure it's turned on. It's the number one reason that people can't add their printer!

Adding a network printer

Shared printers on a HomeGroup (see chapter 22) will be added automatically. But to manually add a network printer click **Add a printer** and select **Add a network, wireless, or Bluetooth printer**. Windows will search the networks it's connected to, along with any Bluetooth devices. If it finds nothing you can **Search again** (but go check the device is turned on first) or click **The printer that I want isn't listed**. This second option gives you the ability to:

▶ Browse the network for the printer.
▶ Add its address in the form of a share name.
▶ Use the IP address of the printer, if it's directly connected to the network (which a wireless printer might be).
▶ Add it as a Bluetooth printer. You might be asked to trust a network printer before the software for it is installed; generally it's fine, but check the details in the message first to be sure.

Managing printers

Double click on a printer to reveal the tasks that are available. This window also shows the printer's status, how many documents are waiting to print and what type of paper is inserted. The tasks listed will vary slightly by printer, but the standard ones are:

▶ See what's printing – shows what's currently in the print queue and allows you to pause it by going to **Printer > Pause Printing**. You can then select a document you don't want to print and select **Document > Cancel**. To get the printer going again select **Printer > Pause printing** again.
▶ Customize your printer – from here you can change the printer's name, sharing settings and how it connects to the PC.
▶ Adjust print options – changes paper types, size, orientation and print quality. It's also where to find tasks like aligning ink cartridges.

Connecting up the home

Networking your home

These days it's not uncommon for a family to have more than one computer in their home. Mum and Dad might each have a laptop for work, there might be a family PC in the living room and the kids may have their own computers too. It makes things easier if those PCs are connected together, and to the Internet, by some sort of network. Connecting PCs together makes it far easier to share the connection to the Internet or to share documents and media around the home.

Typically there are some complexities to setting up a network at home; this chapter should help alleviate some of them. The good news is that Windows 7 makes setting up and running a home network far easier than it ever has been. It also makes it possible to do more than ever before with that network.

Wired or wireless?

The traditional way to create a network was to run cables between each PC. These types of networks can be cumbersome to install physically, especially in a home. Thankfully things have moved on a little and we now have the flexibility of wireless to help us out. That said, there's still a place in the home for wired networks, and both have their distinct advantages. Fortunately they can be mixed and matched to get the best of both worlds.

A standard Ethernet cable, also known as a Cat5 cable (left) is used to connect up the computers in a wired network. For wireless networks you'll need a wireless router (right), which come in a variety of shapes and sizes.

Wired networks

Modern wired networks typically don't run from computer to computer. Each computer generally runs back to a device called a "router". The router is in charge of the network and knows where each computer is. It's responsible for relaying (or routing) information between each machine.

Each computer connects to the router via a cable, the most common being an Ethernet cable, also known as a "patch" or "cat5" cable. Using a wired network in the home normally means either having the computers located physically close together or having long cables running through the walls. If it's the latter it really needs to be professionally installed.

An easier option for running a wired network around the home which doesn't require making holes in the walls is something called a "Homeplug". This ingenious system can run a wired network using the electrical wiring of your home. You'll need to buy some extra hardware to set it up. See p.199 for a guide on how to install this kind of network.

The main disadvantage of wired networks is a lack of flexibility. So what's the upside? There are a few:

▶ Security – no one can get on to your wired network without physically plugging in somewhere in your house.

▶ Reliability – there's less to go wrong than with a wireless network. There's not really any need for encryption for the reason above, and far less chance of interference.

▶ Speed – depending upon the hardware used (the router and the computers) wired networks can be blazingly fast. That makes sharing things like high definition video (HD) very easy.

> **Tip:** Even if you decide to go for a wireless network you'll probably still need the occasional cable. One should be included with your router. If not you can get one from a local computer shop, for only a few dollars. An Ethernet cable is invaluable when troubleshooting problems with a wireless network; never throw them out. For information on troubleshooting and fixing network problems, head over to Chapter 31.

Wireless networks

The most flexible way to set up a network is to use wireless. Just like a wired network, the main piece of kit that runs the show is the router. There are a few different standards of wireless network, each signifying the speeds at which the wireless router is capable of transferring data. The sidebar explains these standards in more detail.

Wireless is built into almost every new PC, and most come

Wireless standards
There are a few wireless standards, but equipment that supports the newer standards normally supports the old standards too. Look for the WiFi symbol to indicate which standard is supported by your hardware. The fastest is currently N, with G next, and B the slowest that you're likely to find. Some manufacturers like Linksys (linksys.com) have enhanced the technology further; their "Dual-Band Wireless-N" offers more speed and reliability. Other manufacturers have similar products, but for compatibility stick to N, G or B. Most built-in wireless, such as that found in laptops, runs up to the G standard (with newer models starting to support the N standard).

Networking your home

Tip: Most wireless routers also include a few wired ports too. So wireless and wired networks can be combined. If your router is next to a desktop PC, that can be connected by an Ethernet cable, while the kids' laptops in their bedrooms can work over wireless. This allows the PC to have the fastest possible connection while the laptops have the most flexible.

equipped with 802.11g. Normally with wireless everything is backwards compatible. So a device capable of 802.11g is probably also capable of 802.11b and will quite happily run on an older, slower wireless network.

Security is a massive concern with wireless networks, and some serious attention needs to be paid to making yours secure. The most common way to do this is with encryption. Encryption scrambles everything that computers transmit to each other using a specific code (a public key). Only other computers that know this code can unscramble the message, making it difficult for anyone without the code to listen in. The stronger (i.e. the longer and more complicated) a code the harder it is to crack. In fact, it takes someone very determined to break in to your network. Keeping secure is covered in more detail in Chapter 24.

Wireless networks can struggle with the construction of some buildings. Thick concrete absorbs the wireless signal, meaning less signal gets through. And as a wireless signal gets weaker it typically gets slower.

The good things about wireless networks are:
- ▶ **Security** – by taking control of security and using encryption you can actually make them more secure than a wired network.
- ▶ **Flexibility** – the lack of wires is a big plus; it means the laptop you have can be used in any room of the house with little fuss. It also means you don't have to drill holes in the walls of the house to put cables in.

Connecting your home network to the Internet

One of the main reasons for having a home network is to be able to share one Internet connection between multiple computers. Often the operator, the phone or cable company will supply the router and in some cases configure it for you. Windows assumes that sharing the Internet is a primary concern for you; it also assumes that the Internet is always available, and so uses it to help diagnose faults with things like network connections.

Typically the broadband provider will provide some type of modem to convert their broadband signal into something the router can understand. The modem socket built into your PCs is used for a dial-up connection and is not the same thing as a broadband modem.

Some routers come with a broadband modem built in; caution is recommended when buying one of these, though, as different kinds of modem are required for different types of connection. Check with your internet service provider (ISP) which type you need before buying a combined router and modem.

If you have a router that is separate to your broadband modem then the two will need to be connected with an Ethernet cable. You probably have one that shipped with your router. There's a specific port on the back of the router that the modem can be plugged into; sometimes it's called an uplink port. Refer to the

Choosing an Internet connection

Two main deciding factors when choosing an Internet connection are price and availability. What the service provider actually allows you to do with the connection also comes into it, but normally that just increases the price. Do some research before choosing an ISP, and look out for:

▶ The speed of the connection. A slow connection is anything less than 512kbps; dial-up is about 54kbps. 512kbps is good for Web surfing; 2mbps is enough for downloading music quickly; 10mbps is great for watching Internet video. If you're a keen gamer, then head to something even faster.

▶ How much the ISP will let you download in a billing period. 1GB is the basic level. Anything less than that and it can feel restrictive, but 1GB is fine for just surfing. If you intend to download lots of music and video head for the higher end of the price spectrum.

▶ Is it available in your area? Cable and telephone ISPs make it fairly obvious that they are available in your area; they probably mail leaflets to you at regular intervals. Mobile broadband might well vary in availability, so double check before you subscribe. If you're in a remote location then dial-up might seem like the only way to go, but consider satellite as another option.

▶ A special note about mobile broadband. Speeds and signal strength vary; check first that your home is covered by the carrier. Mobile broadband can be very flexible, and there are now special routers that take the adapters. The fastest speed currently is HSUPA, then running down it's: HSDPA & EVDO, 3G, EDGE and GPRS, which is about the same as dial-up.

Wireless routers like this one from Cisco come in all shapes and sizes; many newer routers have a button for Wireless Protected Setup. In Windows, start to connect to the network, then push the button on the router and voila! – all connected with no need for a password.

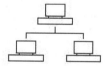

This indicates a local area network connection; connect a cable between the socket in your PC with an icon like this and one on the router with a similar symbol and…instant network!

documentation for your router if you're unsure which port to use.

Some broadband providers require a code called a MAC address from the router (or from one PC) in order to enable the modem to talk with it. MAC addresses are formed of letters and numbers in a pattern of **xx:xx:xx:xx:xx:xx**. You'll probably find this on a sticker on the router itself. This is a unique number that identifies the router, who manufactured it etc, and doesn't identify much about you.

Generally, all that's needed is to connect the modem to the phone socket and the router to the modem.

Setting up a wired network

Wired networks are far easier to set up than wireless ones; there's basically very little you have to do before being able to get stuck in and use it. Typically everything is "plug and play"; all that's needed is to:

▸ Plug the router in, and turn it on.
▸ Plug an Ethernet cable into one of the LAN ports on the router. The documentation that came with your router will explain this, and will show which ports they are. They are also often marked with the network symbol, which looks like three little computers in a triangle.
▸ Plug the other end of that Ethernet cable into the Ethernet port on the PC; again it's probably marked with the network symbol.

To help here make sure that everything is up and running properly; you'll find a simple map of the network by going to **Start > Control Panel > Network and Internet > Network and Sharing Center**. This map shows three icons from left to right, representing your PC, then the router, and then the Internet. The lines between the icons should be green. If there's a problem with one of the connections the relevant line will have a red X through it and the item that can't be "reached" is greyed out.

If it turns out there is a problem then select **Fix a network problem** at the bottom of the **Network and Sharing Center** window. Windows will try to help figure out what the problem is and how to fix it. For more about troubleshooting network connections see Chapter 31.

Powerline networking

A new technology that's only recently gaining real ground is Powerline networking. Adapters that adhere to the Homeplug standard allow a wired network to be set up using the existing power lines in your home. The Homeplug adapter simply plugs into a power socket and an Ethernet cable then runs from that adapter to the PC. Even though it's plugged into the mains socket it's perfectly safe; there's absolutely no risk of overloading the PC with a power surge. In fact most Homeplug adapters have built-in surge protection.

Anything that has an Ethernet port will work with a Powerline network. So in Windows 7 there's no setup to do and Windows doesn't even need to be aware that a Powerline adapter is being used. Powerline networks have all the advantages of a wired network plus increased flexibility; every power outlet becomes a network port! It's not quite as flexible as wireless in that sense; there's still a wire running back to the outlet (and no, it's not combined with the power cord for the PC).

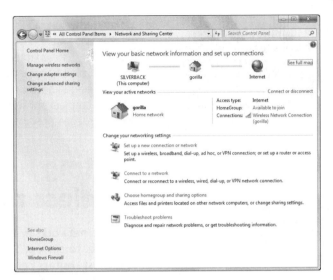

Manage your network settings from the Network and Sharing Center in Control Panel. A handy diagram at the top indicates good connections with green lines and bad ones crossed through with a red X.

Powerline networking hardware

The main thing to look out for with Powerline networking hardware is that it's Homeplug compatible. It should be possible to mix and match Powerline adapters if they are. Amazon (amazon.com) have a good selection. Linksys, Netgear and ZyXEL are the best-known manufacturers, although more are coming out all the time. For the best future proofing go for the 200mbps standard.

Powerline adapaters are a cheap and easy network solution. They run up to speeds of 200mbps over the existing power cabling of the house. Connect a network cable to the PC and you're set to go.

Some Powerline adapters even use encryption, but that's probably overkill. To set up a Powerline network a minimum of two adapters are needed. One adapter connects to the PC and one to the router and both plug into the mains power. A router is still required as the Powerline adapters don't perform that function. However, only one Ethernet connection is needed from the router to the power cabling. See the sidebar for suggestions on hardware to buy.

Setting up a wireless network

Wireless networks are slightly more complicated than wired networks to set up. That said, it's still very straightforward, and most routers come with comprehensive instructions to help get you started.

The bulk of the work in getting a wireless network set up comes from making sure it's secure. If it's not secure there are two things that can happen: first, anyone walking by can just hop on your wireless connection and use it. If you have a monthly bandwidth limit on how much data can be downloaded that could be very bad news. Second, if someone wanted access to your private data they could easily access your PCs and take whatever they like. An unsecured wireless network is like leaving your front door unlocked. When it's secured it's like locking the door.

So how do you keep it secure? First by encrypting the signal; once this is done everything that connects to the wireless network will need a password to gain access. Normally that password only has to be entered once per PC. Pick a long and random password, with lots of letters, numbers and special characters, not something that's simple or easy to remember.

You'll also need a second password for the Web configuration interface of the router. Without a good password anyone who can access the network can access the Web configuration interface and change anything they like. The router will come with a default password in place, but you should always change this to something else as they're published on the Internet by the manufacturers so that customers can look them up when they lose them.

Changing the router password, and making any of the security changes suggested on the next couple of pages, is done through the Web configuration for your router. Check the instructions for how to connect to this, but generally if you point your Web browser to **http://192.168.1.1** all these settings will be found within the "security" or "wireless" options in the Web interface.

Some notes on encryption

There are a few wireless security standards about. WEP, or Wireless Encryption Protocol, is the old standard and as such it's most useful if you have some very old devices that won't work with the newer WPA standards. WPA or Wireless Protected Access is more secure and harder to crack than WEP. More secure still is WPA2. Within the WPA2 standard there are two algorithms (basically how the information gets jumbled) called TKIP and AES. Where possible use AES as TKIP has been cracked, so some determined individual could spend the week or so it would take to break into your network. The risk is small, but if you have the option to use AES (only WPA2 supports it, not WPA) it makes sense to go with that.

So use WPA2-AES encryption where available. The configuration for this will need to be done on your router, and the instruction manual will guide you through the procedure for your specific device. If the password is ever changed every device that connects to the wireless network will need to be updated with the new password.

Hiding the name of your network

Another sensible security measure is to hide the name of your network; essentially this makes it anonymous. Your wireless network will have a name, sometimes called an SSID. This name can be anything you want it to be but choose carefully. If you decide not to hide your SSID anyone will be able to read it, so calling it "Johnson house" is probably a bad plan if your name is Mr Johnson. Why? Well simply because someone will know exactly where the router is.

Once the SSID is hidden it can make setting things up slightly more difficult because your computers won't be able to find the network; they'll need to be told it's there. So it's easiest to hide the name once all the PCs on the network have been set up.

The draconian approach

To be even more strict about which devices can connect to your network use MAC address filtering. This prevents any devices that aren't on a router's guest list from joining the party. MAC addresses are explained earlier in this chapter. Every network device has a MAC address.

Through the router software a list of allowed addresses can be defined, and anything that doesn't match can't talk with the network. It's a very secure approach. Without first setting the device up on the router it can't connect. See your router's instructions for details on how to configure MAC address filtering.

Connecting to WiFi with Windows 7

Windows 7 has a few tricks up its sleeve when it comes to connecting to wireless networks. There have been some massive improvements over previous versions of Windows in this area. It's now possible to securely set up wireless access with the press of a button. When a network has been connected to once, Windows will normally remember it and connect automatically in the future. If for some reason it doesn't automatically connect, then finding the network is the next step.

Finding wireless networks

To make it easy to find wireless networks there's an icon in the system tray; it looks like a small bar graph which acts as a wireless signal indicator. The more white bars, the stronger the signal. When no wireless network is connected, but one has been detected, a yellow star will appear over the icon to let you know.

Clicking the graph icon pops up a list of all wireless networks within range, and indicates how strong the signal is for each. A yellow shield above the icon indicates that a network is unsecured. Unsecured networks should be treated with caution because there are no restrictions as to who can connect and what they can do. You'll be perfectly safe with Windows 7's public profile settings, though; just don't go selecting the **Home** profile for an unsecured network.

The pop-up list refreshes automatically, but to force it there's a refresh icon in the top right. When connected to a network, either wireless or wired, the refresh icon appears at the top of the list. At the bottom, the **Open Network and Sharing Center** link opens the Control Panel items for networking configuration.

Networking your home

The network that's connected is shown at the top, under "Currently connected to", and the icon (a house, office block, or park bench) indicates the home, work or public profile applied to the connection.

When connecting to a secured network you'll need to enter the password. If there's a Wireless Protected Setup button on the router then press it at this point and the password won't be required.

Each item in the list can be selected; doing so will reveal a button for connecting or disconnecting. It's only possible to connect to one wireless network at a time.

Connecting to a secured network

Any network that is shown with no shield symbol above the bar graph icon is a secured network. To connect, just highlight it and click the **Connect** button. If the PC has connected to this network before and knows the password then it'll connect straight away. If not you'll be prompted for the relevant security information.

Entering a network key

The most obvious way to enter the security key is to just type it in. It'll appear as clear text as you type, but if someone is looking over your shoulder check **Hide Characters**. A slightly easier way to enter your network key to avoid typing the wrong characters in is to use one of the following methods.

Pressing a button or using a USB key

Windows 7 supports something called Wireless Protected Setup (WPS), which simplifies setting up wireless networks. Check your router's manual to see if it supports WPS. Whilst Windows is showing the **Connect to a Network** dialogue for the password to be entered, press the WPS button on the router and bingo! The PC will be on the network, without the need to enter a long password. It's still secure because it requires physical access to both the router and the PC; it's like you just plugged it into the network.

Another simple way is to use a USB key to copy the code from the router or another PC. The router's manual will explain how to create a network code from the router. To create one on another Windows 7 PC:

> **Tip:** The USB key method can be a quick way to set up lots of PCs around the home with your wireless broadband. Once a key has been created with the wireless configuration it can be used on as many PCs as you like.

▶ Go to **Start > Control Panel > All Control Panel Items > Network and Sharing Center**.

▶ Select **Manage Wireless Networks** from the left-hand side.

▶ Highlight the network to copy the settings from, then **right click** and select **Properties**.

▶ Finally select **Copy this network profile to a USB flash drive**; a wizard will check that a USB key is inserted and copy everything over. It takes just seconds.

Now simply insert this USB key into the Windows 7 PC you want to add to the network and one of the autoplay options will be **Wireless Network Setup Wizard**. It will ask if the network should be added; say **Yes** and the network will be configured and Windows will connect to it.

Securing your PC on the network

Windows 7 includes a clever network profile tool that helps to secure the PC on the network. Different networks might require

Tip: A firewall is an application that runs in the background constantly looking at what's coming in over the network. It's like having someone looking at all the post coming to your house to see if it's something you want. If that postman doesn't like the look of what's come in, he'll send it back, based on the rules he's been told. The firewall works in much the same way; if something doesn't match its rules it gets sent back (actually it just gets lost in the post!). Firewalls protect the PC from attack. Find out more about security in Chapter 24.

different levels of sharing. For example, in a coffee shop, on a public wireless network do you really want everyone around to be able to access your shared documents?

The network profiles provide three basic levels of control; these were discussed briefly at the beginning of the book when setting up Windows. The first level, **Home**, enables something called HomeGroup, which basically shares all your media and documents around your home. The **Work** profile only leaves your files and documents shared and disables HomeGroup. The idea of these two profiles is that home and work are places you trust, but that at work you don't want to be sharing your music with your colleagues, but you do want to share your documents.

The **Public** profile is the one to use in places you don't trust, like a public WiFi location. It shares nothing, and secures your PC. The profiles don't just affect sharing, they also affect the firewall on the PC: for Home and Work the shields are down (but still selectively), and for Public the shields are up. Everything is a one-way street; you can browse the Web, but no one can connect to your PC.

Connecting to a secured network that you can't see

If you have chosen to hide the SSID or name of your network then it will appear in the list as "Other Network". To connect click the **Connect** button and it'll ask for the name of the network. Essentially the name becomes a secret that you need to reveal to gain access. From this point on it's just the same as if connecting to a network where the name is visible; it will ask for the password and then try to connect.

Connecting to an unsecured network

Connecting to an unsecured network requires no password, or associated button presses or USB keys. Hopefully you aren't doing this at home; if you are it's strongly recommended you secure your home network.

Doing this in a public WiFi location is fairly normal, although many places still protect their network to ensure that only patrons get access.

Connecting to an unsecured network puts your PC at higher risk, because anyone can get onto your network. Be sure to select the **Public** profile when you are prompted; it will prevent any sharing of the information on your PC. Also be sure that your firewall is working.

Connecting to a public WiFi network

Public wireless networks, especially those in hotels, often require you to sign in to a webpage to provide a special account password or token. It will be the only website that can be opened until a token is provided and should automatically open up when your Internet browser is launched.

Hotels often give these passwords out at check-in, or if they charge for Internet access there'll be a website to go to in order to purchase a token for some period of time. Wireless carriers, like T-Mobile and AT&T, also run schemes that allow tokens to be purchased as part of a mobile phone plan.

Tip: If you are going to use public wireless a lot it's a good idea to know where it's free. Two good sites are wififreespot.com and myhotspots.co.uk. Also internationally McDonalds have free hotspots as long you like it with a burger.

Sharing files at home

It's important to understand sharing, especially if you intend to use a work laptop at home and still want to be able to access all the content on your home PCs from it. Whilst Internet access is generally the most common thing to share, it's also useful to be able to share documents and media. Windows 7 makes this easy with a number of systems that allow anything to be shared safely around the house.

HomeGroup

The biggest sharing feature of Windows 7 is HomeGroup, a simple-to-use facility wherein all the Windows 7 computers in the home can talk to each other and share things with very little configuration. HomeGroup makes one big assumption about your network; that everyone on the network is an equal. This means that if an item is shared with the HomeGroup then anyone in that HomeGroup can access it. It also means that no one person needs to manage the network, so it's not a burden on anyone.

Do you want to create a homegroup?

There is currently no homegroup on your network.

A homegroup links computers on your home network so that you can share pictures, music, videos, documents, and printers. The homegroup is protected with a password, and you'll always be able to choose what you share with the group.

Tell me more about homegroups

Change advanced sharing settings

Create now   Cancel

Joining or creating a HomeGroup lets you share music, videos, pictures, documents and printers around the house. It's simple to set up; create the group on the first PC and use the password that it provides on every other PC so that they can join.

What gets shared with the HomeGroup is up to the individuals who join it. By default, media like photos, video and music become shared along with printers and some other hardware, but documents aren't included. This can all be tweaked to taste during setup or at any point further down the line.

Tip: HomeGroup only works between Windows 7 PCs. If you have PCs that are running older operating systems, like Vista or XP, then you'll need a different approach, described later in this chapter.

Setup

Setting up or joining a HomeGroup can be done during the installation of Windows 7 or at any point later by going to **Start > Control Panel > All Control Panel Items > HomeGroup**. The first computer on the network sets up the HomeGroup and others join it as they're added.

If your computer is the first one on the network you'll get a message saying **There is currently no HomeGroup on your network** accompanied by a **Create Now** button. A window appears allowing you to select which Libraries and devices to share with the HomeGroup. Clicking **Create Now** again will set up your HomeGroup and generate a password. If you have a printer attached, click

> **Tip:** Using the automatically generated password might seem more difficult to remember than one of your own choosing. People tend to gravitate towards using one or two passwords mainly because they're memorable; however, remembering this password isn't necessary. At any time you can check to see what it is through Start > Control Panel > All Control Panel Items > Home-Group. If you do set something memorable and then share that with someone else in the house, the chances are you just told them one of your usual passwords, so now they could have access to anything else protected by that password.

the **Print password and instructions** button or if not just write it down somewhere safe or copy it to a Notepad file. You won't be able to change the password at this initial stage, but it is possible to find it and change it later.

That's the first part done. The HomeGroup is now established, but it's not much use if only one computer can access it. So the next step is to get other PCs joined up.

Joining

To join another PC to your new HomeGroup go to the same starting place: **Start > Control Panel > All Control Panel Items > HomeGroup**. This time it'll say that someone has already created a home group. Click the **Join now** button.

Again it will ask what to share with the HomeGroup from this PC and user, and again document sharing will be deselected by default. Select the different Libraries and devices to share and click **Join now**. Now you'll need to enter that password that was generated when the group was set up, and click **Join now** for the third time. The PC will then join the HomeGroup. If you've mislaid the back of the envelope that you scribbled the password onto, all is not lost! On any PC that is already a member of the group go to **Start > Control Panel > All Control Panel Items > HomeGroup** and select **View or print the HomeGroup password**.

The computers on your home network are now connected and able to access each other's shared media and documents as if they were their own.

Using

Okay, you're all set up using HomeGroup, but how do you access all those shared videos and pictures? It's actually quite simple. Everything shared through HomeGroup can be found through Windows Explorer. Open it from the Library icon on the taskbar, or by going to **Start > Computer**. On the left-hand side, **HomeGroup** will be shown as an option, and below it a list of the other PCs in the HomeGroup. Note that the actual computer you're using isn't listed there, in much the same way when you look out the window of your house you can see all the other houses in your street but not your own.

Libraries and devices that are shared with the HomeGroup are only available when the PC is turned on since everything is still stored on the individual PCs that are sharing them. For that reason if a PC is off or not connected to the network it won't appear in the HomeGroup.

Everything in the HomeGroup folder is available to use just as if it were located on the PC you're using. So to open a video, just double click it and watch as normal. The same goes for any other type of file.

> **Tip:** When an extra folder is added to a Windows Library it isn't automatically shared with the HomeGroup, even if the Library itself is shared. To share it, first add the new folder location to the Library, then highlight the folder within the Library and select Share with > HomeGroup (Read) **or** Share with > HomeGroup (Read/Write).

Share with ▼
- 🔒 Nobody
- 🔒 Homegroup (Read)
- 🔒 Homegroup (Read/Write)
- 🔒 Specific people...

Sharing with people in the HomeGroup is easy; wherever the Share with button appears, click it and select who to share with. To give only some people access select Specific people and choose them from the list.

Sharing more

The contents of Libraries can be shared from the HomeGroup Control Panel, but that doesn't include everything on the PC that it might be useful to share. Any other folder can be shared easily with the HomeGroup from within Windows Explorer. In the folder to share, click the **Share with** button on the toolbar; it'll drop down to reveal more options:

Sharing files at home

Any folders that are shared will appear with a small "two heads" icon to the bottom left of the main folder icon; the same goes for printers or other devices that are shared.

▶ Nobody – This might seem like a strange option, but choosing this actually stops the sharing of a folder. So if you are sharing something with the HomeGroup and decide you no longer want to, select **Share with > Nobody**.

▶ HomeGroup (Read) – If there's something that you want people in the HomeGroup to have access to but don't want them to be able to make changes to it, select **Share with > HomeGroup (Read).**

▶ HomeGroup (Read/Write) – Allows anyone who has access to the HomeGroup to be able to open files and update them, put new files in the directory or even delete them. Select **Share with > HomeGroup (Read/Write).**

▶ Specific People – To select only specific individuals in your HomeGroup to share with. The people you want to share with will either need a User Account on the PC or a linked ID (see p.65 for information on setting up linked IDs). If they're not listed just type in their name or e-mail address. Click the drop-down arrow under **Permission Level** to select what level of access (either read or write) they should have.

Stop sharing

There are a couple of ways to stop sharing. The first is to stop sharing entire Libraries or all devices by going to **Start > Control Panel > All Control Panel Items > HomeGroup** and unchecking them.

It's also possible to stop sharing individual folders within a Library. Select the folder then click **Share with > Nobody** and immediately that folder will no longer be available to other people in the HomeGroup.

Managing the HomeGroup

Even though HomeGroup is designed to require very little management there are still some tasks that might be required from time to time. This is done from within **Start > Control Panel > All**

Control Panel Items > HomeGroup. The HomeGroup settings page does much more than just turn sharing on or off; it also manages everything else about the HomeGroup, such as joining and leaving, passwords and more advanced settings.

Sharing media with devices

You can have HomeGroup share videos, pictures and music with various devices on your network. Devices can include stereo systems, TVs, digital photo frames or mobile phones, in fact anything that implements a set of standards created by the Digital Living Network Alliance or DLNA (there'll be a logo on it if it does). When media is shared with devices in this way it's fed to them one bit at a time as a stream, and their access is read-only.

Your PC basically becomes a media server for these devices, which allows them to access your media without having to worry about storing it themselves. Other PCs on the network with Windows Media Player can also receive media like this. Unless you plan to use the PC as a media server it's probably best to leave it disabled. To enable or disable, tick the box next to **Share my pictures, music, and videos with devices on my home network**.

Finding the HomeGroup password again

Any computer that's a member of the HomeGroup has access to view the password. Select **View or print the HomeGroup password**; nothing but viewing or printing of the password is possible from this window.

Change homegroup settings

This computer belongs to a homegroup.

Share libraries and printers

☑ Pictures   ☑ Music   ☑ Videos

☑ Documents   ☑ Printers

How do I share additional libraries?   How do I exclude files and folders?

Share media with devices

☑ Stream my pictures, music, and videos to all devices on my home network
Choose media streaming options...
Note: Shared media is not secure. Anyone connected to your network can receive your shared media.

Other homegroup actions

View or print the homegroup password
Change the password...
Leave the homegroup...
Change advanced sharing settings...
Start the HomeGroup troubleshooter

Each HomeGroup member is only responsible for managing what they share within the group. The one and only exception to this is the Home-Group password; when it's changed it affects every other member of the group as the password must then be changed on each PC. Changing the password is effectively a way of kicking everyone out!

Tip: After sharing media with devices the shared media will appear in Windows Media Player in the left-hand panel as a new Library, or through Windows Media Center in the Shared view of any of the media Libraries.

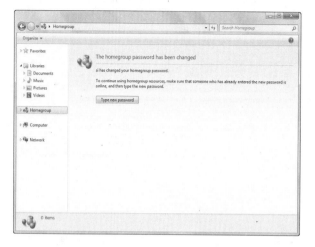

Changing the HomeGroup password

Not only can any computer view the password, it can also change it. From the Home-Group settings page select **Change the password**. A window will appear with a new password; if it's too complex or doesn't appeal you can change it to something you like. Print or write it down so you have it to hand when joining other PCs to the HomeGroup.

Next you'll need to visit every PC in the HomeGroup and enter the new password for each. Open Windows Explorer and go to the HomeGroup section. There'll be a message telling you the password has been changed and who changed it. To update to the new password click **Type new password**. Until it's set, anyone who tries to access the HomeGroup will get a message requesting the new password.

Leaving

When you select **Leave the HomeGroup**, it will ask for confirmation that leaving is all you want to do, and that you don't just need to stop sharing specific files or devices. Once you've left, you can rejoin again at any time.

Advanced

Settings within **Change advanced sharing settings** allow for even more control over what's shared by toggling various elements on or off. In the main, there's no need to change these settings as the **Home**, **Work** and **Public** network profiles are designed to manage this for you. Changing these settings actually changes those profiles.

Other ways to share

Sharing Public folders is an alternative to using HomeGroup and is the best way to share with older PCs not running Windows 7, since only Windows 7 PCs can participate in a HomeGroup.

Setting up shared folders can be more complicated than using HomeGroup and is a little more time consuming, so if all the computers in your home are running Windows 7, then using HomeGroup is by far the easier option.

What to share

Some folders are created by default for sharing on the PC; these are known as Public folders and serve two purposes for sharing. The first is to allow different users on the same PC to share anything they like. Anything placed into the Public folders can be accessed by anyone logged onto the PC with a different User Account. They can be found by browsing to **C:\users\public** using Windows Explorer. The Public folders are included within Libraries and have equivalents for each Library type; for example, the contents of **C:\users\public\music** appears in the Music Library.

The second purpose is enabled by sharing the Public folders and is intended to create a location on the PC where files can be shared with anyone else on the network.

Sharing Public folders

Sharing Public folders allows anyone on the network to access them. To share the folders go to **Start > Control Panel > All Control Panel Items > Network and Sharing Center** and select **Change advanced sharing settings** from the left panel. Within **Advanced Sharing Settings** find the **Public Folder Sharing** options and select one of the very descriptively named options.

Tip: If at some point you want to see who's connected to the shares on your PC, then go to Start and type Task Manager or right click the taskbar and select Start Task Manager. When Task Manager opens go to the Users tab where everyone connected will be listed. From here you can also kill their connection, stopping them from accessing your shared files, by clicking the Disconnect button, although they can always reconnect!

Sharing files at home

Public shared folders can be controlled easily and provide a simple way to share with older operating systems. Using Public folders keeps everything in one place so it's easier for you to manage what others can access.

Any folder can be shared on the network by right-clicking and selecting Properties, then from the Sharing tab clicking the Share button. Select who can access the folder and how much access they have, and you're done.

Sharing any folder

Any files on your PC can be shared, not just the Public folders. To share a folder, first open Windows Explorer and navigate to the folder to share. Open the folder and right click on some white space and select **Properties**. Another way to do this is to right click on the folder itself and select **Properties**.

A tabbed window appears; the second tab is **Sharing**. Select this tab to reveal the sharing options. There are two ways to share folders; the simple one is much like HomeGroup. The advanced approach gives more control but is probably overkill for most home networks.

The easy way is to click the **Share** button. All that's needed then is to select who to share the folder with from the drop-down list. Any User Accounts that exist on the PC can be used as credentials to access the share over the network; linked ID names (often an e-mail address) can be used. One special entry in the list is **Everyone**, which gives literally everyone access to the folder. Clicking **Add** includes the person on the allowed list, and permissions (read or write) can be set under **Permission Level**.

The **Share** button completes the process. The folder name will be used to name the share.

The **Advanced** button allows the share to be customized further. Comments can be added so that people browsing over the network know what the share is for, and extra share names can be set up. It's possible for a folder to be shared more than once with different names. The **Permissions** button allows the permissions to be tweaked and it's also possible to block specific people from accessing folders this way. Most of the time, on a home network the **Advanced** button isn't needed.

Accessing shares from other PCs

There are a few ways to access shares from another PC. The first and easiest is by browsing the network. Open Windows Explorer and find "Network" or "Network Neighbourhood". From there it's possible to browse to the PC that the files are shared on. Listed under each PC will be the shares on that PC and within those shares will be the files.

Another option is to type the path to the share (or just to the computer if the share name is unknown) into the **Start > Run** or **Start > Search** box. Effectively this just shortcuts the process above.

Another way is to "map" a network drive. To do this in Windows 7 open Windows Explorer and select the **Computer** entry in the left panel, then **right click** and select **Map network drive**. Finally select a drive letter and type in the path to the computer and share you want to map to. Mapping a network drive will result in a new drive appearing under **Computer** in Windows Explorer that contains all the information that the share contains. It's not like other drives, though, and is only available if the other PC is available over the network. There are

It's possible to make a network share appear as if it's a hard drive attached to the PC by mapping it as a network drive. If there's one location you need to access often this can be a handy way to create a shortcut to it.

Tip: The location of a shared folder is expressed as a path, so called because it provides the computer with a path to the share. The first part is the computer name, the second is the share name, the third is any subfolders within that share. To signify the start of the path two back slashes are used, then to split each leg of the path a single back slash is used. The end result looks like this: \\my-computer\my-share\my-folder.

two tick boxes; the first, **Reconnect at logon**, will cause the drive to be mapped whenever the PC is logged into, as long as the PC that's hosting the share is turned on. The second tick box, **Connect using different credentials**, is useful if the same User Account or linked ID isn't present on both PCs.

Managing shares

The easiest way to manage shares is to look at them as they appear on the network. Open Windows Explorer and select **Network** from the left panel, then select the name of your PC to reveal all the shares (it will be listed under **Network**). From here simply right click and select **Properties** to change the share settings; it's just the same process as adding a share. Everything that can be changed when sharing a folder can also be changed later.

Turning a share off

To stop sharing a folder, go to **Properties** of a shared folder and from the **Sharing** tab click **Advanced Sharing**; finally, remove the tick from **Share this folder** and click **OK**. The folder will stop sharing immediately.

Sharing printers

Printers can be shared too, either manually or through Home-Group. Setting this up through HomeGroup is by far the simpler option. When joining a HomeGroup make sure Printers is checked in the list of Libraries and devices to share, or later go to Start > Control Panel > All Control Panel Items > HomeGroup and check Printers. This option automatically shares any printers installed on the PC and adds them as available printers to all the other members of the HomeGroup, so that anyone can use any printer. Even PCs that are not part of the HomeGroup (like those running XP) can access the printer; just follow the instructions for adding a network printer below.

Manually sharing a printer

To share a printer so that other PCs can use it, but without the need for HomeGroup, go to **Start > Control Panel > Hardware and Sound > Devices and Printers**. Select the printer to share, right click it and select **Printer properties** then the **Sharing** tab. If the printer is already shared it will be listed here; if not, click **Change Sharing Options**, then check **Share this printer**, then **OK**, and you're ready to roll.

To add a network printer on Windows 7, go to **Start > Control Panel > Hardware and Sound > Devices and Printers** and click the **Add a printer** button on the toolbar. The Add Printer wizard appears: select **Add a network, wireless or Bluetooth printer**. The wizard will then search for the printer and display it as an option. If it can't find it then there's the option to manually go looking for it, just like browsing for a shared folder.

Once added, a network printer works in just the same way as a local printer, except that the PC that's sharing the printer needs to be turned on for it to work.

It doesn't matter how a printer connects to the PC; any printer that is attached can be shared with other PCs on the network. To make the process as simple as possible, after the printer driver has been installed on one PC other PCs that want to use the printer can copy the drivers from the first one, so there's no need to run around installing the printer drivers on every machine!

23 Sharing files outside the home

Sharing files with people at home is useful, but sometimes you'll need to share with people outside of your household, such as wider family members, friends or colleagues. Luckily there are some fantastic, and generally free, technologies that make this easy and that integrate well with Windows 7.

Of course, it's fine to share the presentation you've created for that sales meeting at work with your colleagues, but it's another thing to start sharing copyright material; that can land you in trouble. Copyrighted material means that the creator of that material has the exclusive right to use it over a certain number of years, including where it's published, how it's distributed and how it is adapted. The best way to stay on the right side of copyright law is to not share materials like music or video outside of your house. Whilst the law is a little grey on what constitutes making backups for personal use, it becomes decidedly black and white when you share (or distribute) materials that are under copyright without paying the copyright holder!

Sharing files using USB keys and hard drives

One of the simplest ways to share and move data outside of the home is to copy the files onto a USB key or a USB hard drive. The drive or key can then be given to another person, and all they need to do is copy the files onto their own PC.

Windows 7 will recognize almost any USB hard disk or key when it's inserted into the PC and will make it available for use as an additional drive listed under **Computer** in Windows Explorer. Working with files on a USB key or drive is just like working with files on your PC.

There are two options for putting files onto a removable drive. Copying the files will do exactly that; it will place a second copy of every file on the removable drive. Moving the files, on the other hand, will delete the original file off the PC, leaving the only copy on the USB drive or key. By default, if you drag and drop files to a removable drive they'll be copied rather than moved, but if you **Cut** and **Paste** the files or use the **CTRL + X** and **CTRL + V** keyboard shortcuts then the original will be deleted.

It's important to remove a USB key or drive in the right way in order to prevent data loss. When files are written to a removable drive there are lots of background disk processes that go on and some take a while. To make sure everything is written to the drive and nothing is lost after copying, go to **Start > Devices and Printers,** select the USB key (it will have a drive icon) then right click it and select **Safely Remove**. A message will pop up from the notification area to say that it's now okay to remove the drive and you can be confident that no data is missing from it.

It's very easy to lose a USB key or hard drive, so it's probably a good idea not to put "sensitive" materials such as your bank details

Tip: USB keys come in all shapes and sizes; they can take the form of a simple black stick, the shape of a favourite cartoon character or include heavy-duty padding and protection from the elements (and falling out of your pocket!). It's not just files that can be stored on them; you can also store entire suites of applications, so you can take your Firefox browser or your instant messaging program with you and use it on any machine. Check out portableapps.com for more information on how to do just that.

To make sure you don't lose any data from your USB key it's best to remove them correctly.

Tip: There are some other good options out there for storing files online besides Microsoft. Dropbox is a very popular way to share files online (getdropbox.com). They have accounts available for free that can store up to 2GB of files; above 2GB they charge either an annual or monthly fee but provide a massive 50GB of storage. Livedrive (livedrive.com) is another similar service that offers unlimited storage and synchronization options.

onto one. A good way to protect yourself from the potential consequences of losing sensitive data on a portable storage device is to use disk encryption. Disk encryption scrambles the removable device to ensure that it can only be used by someone with the right password; take a look at Chapter 24 to find out how to encrypt a removable drive.

Sharing files over the Internet

Of course, messing about with USB keys and drives can be cumbersome. There's the question of how the other person physically gets the device, especially if they're a long distance away. Using the Internet to share those files is probably an easier solution, and there are plenty of services out there to help.

Windows Live Skydrive

One service that integrates well with Windows (especially if you're using Windows Live Essentials) is Windows Live Skydrive, a sharing service from Microsoft. It's just like having a hard drive located on the Internet; it's completely free and it provides 25GB of space to store your files. If you're using Windows Live Gallery then you'll already have a Skydrive account, because Windows Live Gallery uses Skydrive to store your uploaded photos.

You can share up to 20GB of files with people all over the world using Windows Live Skydrive. Go to skydrive.com and upload, then select who you want to share with.

If you don't have an account, getting one is as hassle free as getting access to any other Live service and the same log-on details can be used; **skydrive.live.com** is the place to sign up.

Uploading files

To upload files to the service go to **skydrive.live.com**; there are two obviously placed links for **Create Folder** and **Add files**. Like working with files on a local hard drive, it's best to store them in folders to keep them in order, so first use **Create Folder** and give the folder a name when prompted. Next you can configure who should have access to the folder.

Access works just like in any of the Windows Live Essentials programs. **Everyone** is literally everyone on the Internet. **My Network** is anyone in your Windows Live network (which is not the same thing as a HomeGroup); **Just Me** is rather self-explanatory; and **Select people** lets you enter any e-mail address registered as a Live ID (if they don't already have a Live ID they'll have to sign up for one to get access).

The next stage is to upload the files that you want to share; just click **Browse**, find the files on your PC and click **Upload**. Once the files are uploaded, there's an option to alert the people that you shared the folder with by sending them an e-mail. Any folder containing just pictures will be automatically converted into a photo gallery.

Windows Live Mesh

Windows Live Mesh is a similar service to Windows Live Skydrive, but is more advanced in its capabilities. It integrates with your PC and can create a folder on another PC that is an exact mirror of the one on yours, keeping the two in perfect synchronization. So if a file is added on the other PC, magically the same file appears in the same folder on your PC, and vice versa. Sharing files like this

Sharing files outside the home

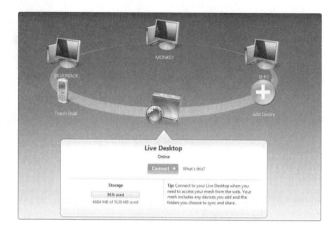

Whilst Windows Live Mesh is very stable, and Microsoft is taking great pains to safeguard your data, (far more than almost any other provider of Internet-based storage), the service is still considered to be "Beta" software. That means that it's not quite finished yet and things are likely to change with the software and the service, so it's a good idea to keep an eye on the Live Mesh blog, blogs.msdn.com/livemesh, to keep up with developments.

can take all the hassle out of sharing files over the Internet.

Signing up

To start using Windows Live Mesh it's necessary to first sign up at **mesh.com** and download a piece of software to your PC. After signing up, which is the same simple process as for Windows Live, you'll need to install the client on the PC. Select the large orange orb with the + sign on it and a drop-down will appear, allowing you to choose either the Windows 7 32 bit or 64 bit option, depending on which version you're running. Click the orange **Install** button and the software will download and install to your PC. (If you're not sure which version of Windows 7 you're running, you can find out by going to **Start > Control Panel > All Control Panel items > System.**)

Once the software has been installed, log in using the Live ID that you used to sign up. Any folder on your PC can be shared over the Internet with anyone else who has Windows Live Mesh installed, as long as you've granted them access.

Live Desktop

The Desktop on your PC is essentially where all your folders and applications are accessed from. Live Mesh has its own Desktop online, which can be accessed from your web browser.

The Windows Desktop and your Live Mesh Desktop are linked together, so anything placed on the Live Mesh Desktop will automatically appear on your Windows Desktop. It's assumed that if something is placed on the Live Mesh Desktop you want it synchronized. The inverse is not true, though, so folders, icons or files placed on your Windows Desktop don't automatically sync to Live Mesh. To sync them, all you need to do is right click and select **Add to Live Mesh.**

It will take a while to run out of space on Windows Live Mesh since it includes 5GB of free storage space.

Mesh folders

Windows Live Mesh can also synchronize a folder shared between two PCs, so the contents of the folder on both computer are "mirrored" (kept idential). Synchronizing folders with another PC is a two-stage process. The folder needs to be configured on the computer where the files already exist, and then a folder needs to be created on the second PC.

To add a folder to "the mesh" right click it and select **Add to Live Mesh**; it must be a folder that's selected and not a Library. The Add Folder window will appear, and towards the bottom you'll see a drop-down arrow labelled **Show synchronization options**. Click it to reveal details about what the folder will sync with. There are a few options for synchronization, but the two you're most likely to use are **Never with this device** (which prevents sync) and **When files are added or modified** (which enables sync). By default the PC and Live Desktop will be set to **When files are added or modified**, meaning that the folder will be created on the Live Desktop and synchronized with.

If you have two computers in your home, download and install the Live Mesh client on the second PC and log in with the same ID as for the first PC. When the same ID is used on both, any

Anything added to Windows Live Mesh can be synchronized with other PCs. Select the Show synchronization options **drop-down** to select which devices to sync with.

Add Folder

Add folder to Live Mesh

This folder will be synchronized with this computer in the following location:

Name: Podcasts

Location: C:\Users\si\Documents\Podcasts   Browse...

Show synchronization options   OK   Cancel

Sharing files outside the home

Tip: Windows Live Mesh can be set to NOT synchronize with the Live Desktop, which means that files aren't stored online and are only accessible if the PC is turned on. Not synchronizing also means that more than 5GB of files can be synchronized between two computers. If the two PCs being synchronized are on the same network then the files don't even go over the Internet connection. So it's a handy way to keep your documents in order on all the PCs around the home without running up your Internet bandwidth usage.

folder added to the mesh on the first PC will then automatically appear on the Desktop of the second PC. Those folders will just sit there unsynced until you double click on one and the synchronization settings appear. Select the drop-down for **Show synchronization options** to reveal details about the synced PCs. To have the folder sync with this PC (the second PC) set the drop-down next to the PC's name to **When files are added or modified**, or, to prevent the folder synchronizing and to have it vanish from the Desktop, select **Never with this device**. Once done that folder will stay in sync across your local network, not having to traverse the entire Internet just to get from one room in your house to another.

Inviting others

To allow other people access to a folder, right click it on the PC you shared it from and select **Live Mesh Options > Invite Members** from the pop-up menu. Enter their e-mail address (if they have a Live ID already it's best to use that), select OK and they'll get an invite and instructions on how to join the folder. They'll then be able to see the folder through **mesh.com** and can install the Windows Live Mesh software on their PC. By changing the synchronization settings to **When files are added or modified** the folder will stay in sync on your PC, their PC and the Live Desktop.

Security and safety

Keeping your PC secure

Going online to surf the Internet is like walking down the street – it's generally safe to do but you need to be aware of potential risks to your safety. Using the Internet brings potential threats to the security of your PC, but knowing how to mitigate those threats should give you the confidence to proceed. The main security issues are:

▶ Viruses – small programs that wreak havoc on the PC or unlock access to some part of it so people can get to your information. Viruses have the ability to replicate and spread themselves, just like a real-world virus, and many can also mutate to avoid detection.

▶ Spyware (aka "malware") – watches what you do and reports it back to someone (thus spying on you). These reports might include sensitive information that you might not want to share, such as your address or bank details.

▶ Network attacks (aka "hacking") – where someone tries to break into your PC from the outside by exploiting known weak spots in the software running on the PC.

▶ Phishing – where a website, e-mail, instant message or chat room pretends to be something or someone it's not in order to dupe

Tip: If you have a virus or bothersome spyware and need to know how to remove it, see Chapter 29.

you into giving information (normally sensitive) that you might not otherwise give.

▶ Adware – not strictly a threat (apart from to your own sanity)! This type of software bombards you with constant adverts, often from dubious sources with adult content.

This chapter will take you through the applications that help prevent infection and protect the PC and your information, helping you make choices about which to use.

Antivirus

Antivirus software attempts to detect, identify and remove a virus once installed on the PC or, preferably, before it even gets that far. Antivirus software is very complicated, and as a result it's often built and sold by specialist companies, and in a competitive market they all have to carve out their own niche. Many antivirus products aren't just capable of protecting the PC against viruses; they are in fact "security suites" that have extra components such as anti-spyware, firewalls and anti-phishing programs, each adding another layer of complexity.

What that means for you is there will be some antivirus software that suits you perfectly and some that gets in the way of what you want to do. If it starts to annoy you constantly with popups, nagging messages or questions then there's a good chance that you'll be thinking, "I'd rather have a virus!". In contrast, if the software never communicates what it's doing you'll be thinking, "Is it working? Was it worth the money?". Windows 7 doesn't come with antivirus software, so unless the PC vendor installed it there's a choice to be made.

What to look for in antivirus software

The first thing when deciding which software to choose is to decide what you actually need. There are some key attributes to look for when comparing the products:

▶ How often is the software updated? – Just like humans have characteristics that are unique to them, so do computer viruses. A virus might leave its "signature" code in a file, and antivirus software uses that "signature" to recognize the virus. Once identified it can be killed, but since viruses mutate the signatures need updating regularly to trap all the mutations.

▶ How resource heavy is the software? – Antivirus runs constantly on the PC in order to be able to act the moment there is a threat. Antivirus software that hogs lots of memory (RAM) or a high percentage of the processor effectively limits what's available for the other applications on the PC to use. Sticking to software that uses up less of the computing power of the PC is helpful.

▶ Does it tell you what's going on? – There's a fine balance between needing to know what the antivirus software is doing and wanting to know that there's a problem. A novice user needs some reassurance that the PC is protected; a veteran just wants to know if there's a problem. Most software allows the level of notification to be changed according to preference, but some are better than others so look for software that manages itself.

▶ How much does it cost? – The big question, will it hurt my wallet? Requiring regular updates to catch all those viruses means that it costs the antivirus companies lots of money in research and development to reproduce the signatures. As a result, much antivirus software requires a paid subscription to those updates, but the question is, is it worth paying for? The answer is yes if the antivirus

Places to find antivirus software

▶ Norton (norton.com) – requires a subscription for updates and has many versions.

▶ McAffee (home.mcaffee.com) – requires a subscription for updates and has many versions.

▶ Kaspersky (kaspersky.co.uk) – again, provides many different versions and is famed for requiring few system resources.

▶ Avast! (avast.com) – has both free and subscription versions; the free version provides basic antivirus protection.

▶ AVG (avg.com) – has subscription versions and a free version that provides basic antivirus protection (free.avg.com).

An extensive list of antivirus products is available on Wikipedia: en.wikipedia.org/wiki/List_of_antivirus_software.

software works the right way for you and gives sufficient answers to all the above. However, there are free alternatives available and many of them are very good. The companies that provide free anti-virus software for consumers make their money from big corporate customers who buy their software to secure their businesses.

The decision over which antivirus software to use in Windows 7 is yours; there's no compulsory choice and doing some research is always the best way to decide which to go for (see the sidebar for some recommendations). Read reviews, get personal recom-mendations and then use the free trial period that most come with to make a decision. Don't forget: once you pay for a subscription you're wasting money if you change to different software.

If antivirus software isn't in-stalled or isn't working for some reason it'll be highlighted with a red strip in Action Center.

How Windows 7 handles antivirus software

Windows 7 wants to make sure the PC is secure and, as a result, a near constant nag message appears if there isn't any antivi-rus software installed, or for that matter if there isn't a firewall or if Windows Update is disabled.

These messages all come from Action Center, which can be accessed from **Start > Control Panel > All Control Panel Items > Action Center** (it also has a flag icon in the notification area). Within Action Center there's a drop-down for **Security**, where all security-related notifications such as anti-virus status are stored. Windows makes it very obvious when something's wrong. If you need an antivirus program and don't have one, Windows 7 kindly points you in the right direction by displaying links and ultimately taking you right to the door of anti-virus companies.

Anti-malware

Tip: If there is ever a concern about anything security related in Windows 7, then Action Center is the application to go first. You can launch it quickly by typing Action in the search box on the Start menu.

Anti-malware protects the PC from spyware and unwanted software such as adware. Both can be very annoying and disruptive and generally slow down the PC. Spyware is a particular threat because it can steal information – for example your usage habits (which websites you visit), address or bank details – and send it back to its creators.

Selecting an anti-malware program is similar to selecting antivirus software; in fact, much antivirus software comes with anti-malware software bundled in. Windows 7 actually has its own anti-malware protection in the shape of Windows Defender built in. This is turned on as your default anti-malware solution, but it's still possible to use another product if you wish.

Windows Defender is Windows 7's built-in anti-malware program. It runs in the background and generally keeps the PC clean; check its status at any time from Control Panel.

Windows Defender

As with antivirus software, information about the current status of Windows Defender is available from Action Center. It also has its own Control Panel application that allows settings to be changed and more information to be obtained. Launch it from **Start > Control Panel > All Control Panel Items > Windows Defender**.

The main window highlights any poten-

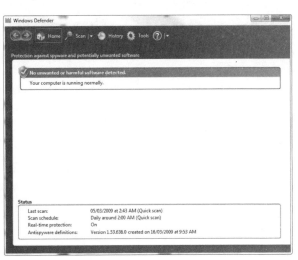

Tip: A free application to check the PC for spyware and adware is Spybot-S&D (search and destroy). It will hunt your hard drive for spyware and destroy anything it finds; it's surprisingly good for free software (safer-networking.org/en/index.html). Another good free malware-removal tool is A-Squared free (emsisoft.com), which scans for both viruses and spyware at the same time.

tial malware that's been detected but it doesn't reveal much detail; to find out more click the **History** button at the top of the window, and then click the **View** button at the bottom of the window to show more information.

Scanning for malware

The **Scan** button will start a scan of the PC to find any spyware that might be hiding away. There are three types of scan:

▸ Quick Scan will check the most common locations for spyware to live.
▸ Full Scan will scan everywhere on the PC where spyware could hide, and can take a very long time!
▸ Custom scan allows specific folders to be scanned.

Generally a quick scan is all that's needed, and when a scan is running an icon will appear in the notification area to let you know.

Changing settings

The **Tools** button reveals options to set how Windows Defender works; there are quite a few choices at this point:

▸ Options contains settings like automatic scanning times (the time of day when a scan of your PC is performed), what happens to any spyware found (whether it's to be deleted or "quarantined" to somewhere safe) and if specific files or folders should be excluded from the scan.
▸ Microsoft SpyNet is used to determine how much information you send to Microsoft about spyware that has been found on the PC.
▸ Quarantined items displays spyware that's been moved to quarantine if the program is set to move spyware to a safe place rather than delete it.
▸ Allowed items allows you to determine that something identified

as spyware is actually a wanted application.

▶ Windows Defender website and Microsoft Malware Protection Center both launch websites with lots of information to digest if you really want to get a great understanding of malware.

Firewalls

A firewall is your primary protection against hacking or network attacks. They can also lock certain information inside your PC or network and stop it from getting to the outside world. In that respect they assist with protection against malware and viruses. By stopping malware from "phoning home" it becomes ineffective (the reason malware exists is to "phone home") and viruses can't spread so easily from inside a firewall.

As with all other security products, firewall options are available from many sources, both free and paid for, and are often bundled with antivirus products. Windows 7 includes its own firewall capable of basic protection and well integrated with other parts of Windows.

Firewalls work by stopping unwanted network traffic coming in from your own network or the Internet whilst allowing wanted network traffic in. They also stop programs on the PC using the network that don't have a good reason to do so. A firewall is only as good as the rules that are set up to allow traffic in or out or applications to use the network or not. Each rule should be seen as a hole. The more holes in the firewall, the more chance of something getting through, so no matter which firewall product is used try to limit what's allowed through. Most firewall software makes this easy for you without requiring any technical knowledge.

Action Center is again your central point of contact to find out the status of any firewall software in Windows 7. But to change the configuration, look to your firewall's own interface.

Tip: If antivirus software is installed that includes malware protection it's a good idea to turn off Windows Defender, since having two scanners doing the same job will slow down the PC. Go to Start > Control Panel > All Control Panel Items > Windows Defender then Tools > Options > Administrator and uncheck Use this program.

Tip: A good alternative to Windows Firewall, and one with a long history and lots of trusting users, is ZoneAlarm (zonealarm.com). It integrates well with Windows and is simple to use, but provides lots of protection. For the advanced user, Comodo is a more configurable free firewall suite, available from comodo.com.

Windows Firewall

Start > Control Panel > All Control Panel Items > Windows Firewall opens settings for the inbuilt Windows Firewall. The first page shows the current status of the firewall. The settings for Windows Firewall can vary depending upon the type of network that the PC is connected to, with different settings possible for public and private networks. The reason for the different types of networks is trust; private networks are more trustworthy than public ones because there's more control over the other users of the network.

Windows Firewall has separate settings for private networks (like Work and Home) and Public networks. It's a good idea not to change any of the settings for the Public network profile as doing so might reduce the protection your PC will have when using it in a public place.

Windows generally manages the firewall for you, but some things do need to be manually dealt with occasionally.

Allowing/blocking specific programs

On the left-hand side of the Windows Firewall Control Panel is a list of activities. The first, **Allow a program or feature through Windows Firewall**, controls the "holes" in the firewall. Without an appropriate hole some programs won't work. Once selected, a list of all the applications that have ever requested a hole is displayed but is greyed out. Clicking **Change Settings** enables the options on this page. Any program can be either allowed (a tick) or blocked (no tick) from using the network, and the **Details** button reveals the location of each program on the hard disk. If a program has not requested access it can still be added to the list with the **Allow another program** button.

Turning the Firewall on, off or changing notifications

Windows Firewall can be turned on or off for each network profile, private and public. The notification that a program has been blocked can also be turned on or off from **Change notification settings** or **Turn Windows Firewall on or off**; both links go to the same settings screen. If you have another firewall installed and running it's better to turn the Windows Firewall off but otherwise you should leave it running at all times.

Extra settings and getting things back

The **Advanced settings** link launches a window that allows more technical things such as IP ports to be managed. It's best not to change any settings here without knowing exactly what needs to be done; consult the Microsoft knowledge base (**support.microsoft.com**) for help. If you do change some settings and things start to behave oddly then the **Restore defaults** option on the left of the Windows Firewall Control Panel is your "get out of jail free" card.

Windows Update

Hackers and viruses exploit flaws in Windows and its associated applications to make their work easier. Reducing the number of flaws is something Microsoft works hard at, but new flaws are often found by the bad guys first and they release that information so that other bad guys can use it (and to publicly warn Microsoft so that they have to produce a fix). When news of a flaw comes out, Microsoft gets to work on fixing it, but sometimes it can take a while (a long while!). Eventually a fix, known as a "patch", comes out, and the faster those patches are applied the less risk there is of being open to attack.

> **Tip:** To test that your firewall is working go to grc.com/intro.htm and run the "ShieldsUp!" firewall tests. This website will run a batch of tests against your firewall and give you a verdict for each; blocked ports and failed connections in this case are a good thing. Taking five minutes to read the background will help your understanding of security greatly.

Windows Update is a service that runs in the background to check if Microsoft has released any new patches (normally they're released on the second Tuesday of the month unless it's particularly serious). When an update is detected, it's downloaded and installed automatically, which works well for most people since it requires no effort.

There are three types of update:

▶ Important –These are security related and are automatically downloaded and installed, but can be turned off.
▶ Recommended – These fix issues with the way that software works and they may or may not be downloaded automatically depending upon the selected setting.
▶ Optional – These add extra functionality and are not automatically downloaded or installed.

Keeping Windows up to date is really important for security. The path of least resistance is to let Windows download and install updates for you automatically.

It's possible to change what Windows Update does and even to disable it altogether, but that's not recommended.

Installing updates

When there are updates ready to be installed the Windows Update Control Panel will let you know. Some of these updates will be installed automatically but you'll have to choose to install optional updates. Simply click the text that says **(N) optional updates are available**, check the ones to install and finally click the **Install Updates** button.

Changing settings

Windows Update is controlled from **Start > Control Panel > All Control Panel Items > Windows Update**. Selecting the **Change settings** link allows alterations to be made.

Getting updates onto Windows is a two-stage process of download and install. Windows Update allows you to decide exactly which combination of downloading and installing to let it do but the obvious option is to let Windows **Install updates automatically**. It's also possible to have updates download automatically and then choose which to install; to have them notify you of their existence and choose whether or not to download or install them; or to do nothing and effectively turn it off. **Install updates automatically** is highly recommended for most people.

Looking at what's been installed

When suddenly encountering problems with the PC for no fathomable reason, it's a good idea to check what updates were recently installed. While Microsoft goes to great pains to test updates, there is no way for them to test every possible combination of hardware and software, so occasionally there can be problems. To find out what's been installed select **View update history** from the Windows Update Control Panel. For more information on troubleshooting problems in Windows take a look at the next section of this book.

Checking for updates

The one task you might want to do is occasionally check what updates are available, which is easily done by clicking **Check for updates**. Windows Update contacts Microsoft and checks if there are any optional updates available that might enhance your PC, so it's worth a look every so often.

Tip: There is another type of important update that will appear in Windows Update from time to time. It's called a Service Pack. During the life of the operating system Microsoft will produce a Service Pack that rolls all the available updates up into one package and often adds extra capabilities. They're quite large and take ages to install, but only happen every couple of years.

Tip: Double click any entry in the installed updates list for more information about that update. Each entry also includes a Web link for even more information about what the update does and what it affects.

Windows Update

Checking for updates...

Most recent check for updates: Today at 00:24
Updates were installed: Today at 00:26. View update history
You receive updates: For Windows and other products from Microsoft Update

Additional Windows Update options are available. View options

239

Updates for other applications

It's not just Windows that needs to be kept up to date; other applications need to be too, particularly applications that work with the Internet such as browsers. Most will have some form of auto update built in; it's important not to disable these as Windows won't update any applications that aren't built to use its update mechanism. As a good rule of thumb, if it's made by Microsoft, Windows Update will do the work; if it's not, then check how the software receives its updates.

User Account Control

Dodgy websites and software often try to install other programs on the PC in order to open up new holes to exploit or cause annoyance through applications like adware. One way Windows combats this is through User Account Control (UAC), which requires that software installations or changes to Windows settings are confirmed by the user. As confirmation is part of Windows, not the installation, there's no way for a program to override what you want to do, putting you in control of what's installed or changed.

Many people are passionate in their hatred for UAC based on how it worked in Windows Vista, but it's much improved in Windows 7 and having it set at the default causes very little aggravation.

UAC is managed on a sliding scale: moving the slider to the top makes UAC more intrusive, causing it to nag you every time you want to change a setting or install a program. Pushing it the other way effectively turns it off, reducing the protection against accidentally making changes or having unexpected programs run.

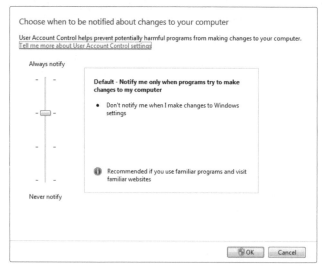

Using UAC

When turned up to its maximum notification setting, every time a change is made to Windows, or when a program attempts to install, UAC will prompt the user to accept the change by dimming the screen and highlighting a UAC dialogue box. To allow the action or installation to take place click **Yes**, but if you didn't start the installation intentionally or didn't intend to make a change then click **No** to stop it happening. Any icon, button or link with a shield next to it will do something that UAC protects but unless UAC is set to **Always notify**, the shield will be all the warning you get.

Changing UAC settings

UAC is very simple to manage, and is handled by Action Center. There's a sliding scale from **Always notify** (some would say annoy) to **Never notify**, which essentially turns UAC off and removes the protection. Between the two extremes are options to only notify for installations by dimming the Desktop, or to only notify for installations by displaying the UAC window and not dimming the Desktop. The default is to dim the Desktop for installations only, which is a good balance between annoying and useful.

Encryption

With all those easy-to-lose USB keys floating around it would be helpful if there were a way to secure them. To that end, Windows 7 comes with BitLocker to Go (if you have the Ultimate or Enterprise editions). BitLocker will encrypt a USB key, basically scrambling all the data on it, so that it can't be opened without a password.

To encrypt a USB key or removable hard drive, open Windows Explorer, select **Computer** from the left panel and then select the

> **Tip:** The UAC settings are themselves protected by UAC; if you try to change its settings you will be asked to confirm the change.

Encryption is the best way to protect data on a removable drive. Windows 7 Ultimate includes BitLocker drive encryption, which can scramble the data on a USB key so that it can only be accessed by a password – more than enough to stop most people accessing the information.

Tip: A great free alternative if you don't have Windows 7 Ultimate is True Crypt (truecrypt.org); it does the same type of thing and is free but is slightly more difficult to use; be sure to read the instructions.

removable disk in the main window. Right click and select **Turn on BitLocker** to configure encryption on the device. A password will be required and the wizard will give the option of saving a recovery key, which can be used to recover the data on the drive if you forget the password. Then hit the **Start encrypting** button. Encryption can take a while, so it's very important to use the **Pause** button if you need to remove the drive before it's finished, otherwise all the data on the drive will be lost. Big drives can take a while, but it's fine to carry on doing other things on the computer whilst it encrypts.

Once encrypted, when the USB key or drive is inserted into a PC a password is required to unlock the files before they can be accessed.

Making backups

A big part of making sure your PC is safe and secure is having a backup for when something goes wrong. It can be useful when just one file has been mistakenly deleted or when the entire PC has been infected by a virus and needs to be restored. Windows 7 has some solutions built in to help deal with both scenarios, and there are also some excellent solutions available online.

Tip: Spend five minutes right now looking at the hard disk on your PC through Windows Explorer, finding all the files you can't live without and making a note of their location. It's a useful exercise to go through every so often to make sure you are backing up the right stuff.

What and when to back up

The question of what to back up and when actually revolves around how much disk space is available, be that space on the PC, on removable drives, somewhere else on the network, or on the Internet. In an ideal world you'd back up everything whenever it changes. Practically speaking, though, that might not be possible as it's unlikely you have unlimited space available.

Everything on a PC can be backed up in some form, including the documents, music, movies, pictures, the way Windows is set up, even your Favorites and personal settings like Desktop wallpaper.

A simple method to create a backup is to copy everything some-

Tip: Invest some money in a device to manage your backups; buy a USB hard drive. A 1TB (that's 1000GB) drive now costs less than $150 and is probably enough to back up your PC many times over. Storage is much cheaper these days and having a backup is just like having insurance.

where else, such as to another PC, the Internet or to a removable drive, but it's not automatic. Having backups that happen automatically without you needing to get involved prevents them from being forgotten.

Windows 7 includes System Protection, which combines two backup systems called **System Restore** and **Previous versions of files**, which create backups on your PC and provide some protection against accidentally deleted files or the software developing some kind of fault.

Backing up to the same PC

Backing up to the same PC is quick and easily available; the only downside is that it doesn't protect against a virus or problem physically affecting the hard disk. In the case of a hardware fault, it might not even be possible to access the backup on the PC, so this method shouldn't be relied on in isolation.

Tip: Mix and match different ways to back up your stuff. If you only back up to your PC, what do you do if your PC has a hardware problem? If you only back up to a USB hard drive, what happens if your PC and USB hard drive are stolen? What happens if your PC corrupts your Internet backup and the copy on your PC? If you have all three – a backup on the PC, another on a USB drive or another PC and a backup on the Internet – then you get maximum protection and it needn't cost the earth.

System Protection

System Protection is a mechanism Windows 7 uses to back itself up. It works by creating system restore points, essentially backups of system data linked to specific points in time. It's configured by going to **Start > Control Panel > All Control Panel Items > System** and selecting the **System Protection** tab. This tab deals with the settings for both System Restore and Previous versions of files. Clicking the **Configure** button will reveal a handful of configuration options.

Complete protection is granted with **Restore system settings** and **previous versions of files**. A portion of the PC's disk space is allocated to System Protection. This space is self-managed, so when it becomes full (to the point that's been allocated, not when the entire hard disk is full), older system restore points are deleted.

Restoring the system to a previous point in time is as easy as going to the advanced system properties window (right) and clicking System Restore, then following the wizard and selecting the restore point to use (below). **Get there from** Control Panel > All Control Panel Items > System > Advanced system settings > System Protection.

There's also the option to manually delete all existing system restore points, something you might want to do if you've just made major changes to the PC that have been successful.

Using restore points

To restore your PC back to how it was at a specific moment in time go to **Start > Control Panel > All Control Panel Items > Recovery** and click **Open System Restore**. This starts a wizard that takes the PC back to an earlier restore point. How far back you can go depends on the amount of disk space available and how many restore points have been created. The process requires a couple of reboots, so make sure all applications are closed.

If after having restored the system the problem still exists, then it's possible to undo the restore by running System Restore again.

Using previous versions of files

To restore a specific file, right click it and select **Restore previous versions**, then select the point to which you'd like to roll back the file. Doing the same thing to a folder allows specific files within that folder to be restored, even deleted ones. In this case a list of restore points

Tip: Consider increasing the amount of space used by System Protection on your PC. More space means more backups so more previous versions will be available. On the System Protection tab click the Configure button and move the slider a little to the right to increase the space.

will be available; select the point to roll back to and click the button to open the previous version of the folder, then just copy or move the files to where you want them.

Backing up externally

Windows Backup is an application which enables you to back files up to another PC or removable drive. It creates an image backup, which is essentially a complete copy of every single file and setting on the PC, unlike a System Restore, which only keeps copies of files that have changed. An image backup has to be on a different drive than the one Windows is installed on.

As a result, Windows Backup can be used to recover from more severe problems because it has a complete copy of everything, so any corruption such as might be caused by a virus can be fixed instantly by going back to a known good version. It can also be used as a restore point for previous versions of files.

Creating a backup with Windows Backup

Launch Windows Backup by going to **Start > Control Panel > All Control Panel Items > Backup and Restore** and clicking **Set up backup**. First set the location where the files will be backed up to; if this is a USB hard disk then it needs to be plugged in (if it doesn't appear, try clicking **Refresh**). You can also store the backup elsewhere on your network. Just click the **Add network location** button and then browse or enter the details of the network location where the backup should be located. Then click **Next**.

The next step is to decide what will be backed up. If all the things you want to keep (remember that prioritized list you made at the beginning of this chapter?) are in their default places, like Libraries, for example, select the **Let Windows Choose** option. If your files are strewn all over the place in custom locations then select **Let me choose**. The second option will force you to go and select everything individually.

Finally there's the option to configure a set time to run this backup; make sure that the backup location is available at that time. For example, is that server in your office available at 3am on a Sunday? When you click the button to **Save settings and create backup**, from this point on your machine will get regular, good-quality backups. As long as there's plenty of space the backup will complete. If backup fails due to lack of space or some other reason it'll provide you with some options to remedy the situation.

If at any point you want to turn off scheduled backups go to **Start > Control Panel > All Control Panel Items > Backup and Restore** and select **Turn off schedule**.

It's also a good idea to create a recovery disk that can help you restore the image backup should anything go wrong. Insert a writable CD or DVD, go to **Start > Control Panel > All Control Panel Items > Backup and Restore**, select **Create a system recovery disk** and then follow the wizard's instructions. To find out how to use this recovery disk to restore the PC go to Chapter 28.

When backing up to a network location there's a security risk you need to think about; can anyone else access that location? If they can, they will also be able to access your backup and therefore all of your files. At home that's probably not an issue, but at work it might better to use a USB hard disk.

Restoring a backup with Windows Backup

To restore from an image backup go to **Start > Control Panel > All Control Panel Items > Backup and Restore** and click **Restore my files**.

Tip: Well-regarded alternatives to Mozy include iDrive (idrive.com) and Elephant Drive (elephantdrive.com).

Backing up to the Internet

While it's not possible to create a full system backup to the Internet, there are some great options for backing up files. Windows Live Mesh can create a synchronized copy of folders from your PC on the Internet (see Chapter 23). The service is limited in size, but it's still a convenient option. What synchronized services like this won't do, however, is help with accidentally deleted files or documents that have been changed in error, as these changes will also be synchronized! Don't try backing up to the Internet unless you have broadband; it'll take forever!

Backing up with Mozy

An interesting backup solution can be found at **Mozy.com**, which offers a 2GB backup facility for free, or $4.99 per year for more space. Configuration is easy. The setup will request the account details that you used when you signed up and ask how strongly you want to encrypt your data (the default is the best option), and will then let you select what files to back up. A network speed test is performed and the backup will then start.

Mozy backup is easy and free; up to 6gb of files can be easily backed up. It integrates well with Windows 7, automatically backing up files when the PC is idle.

You can create more specific backups through **Start > All Programs > MozyHome > MozyHome configuration**. Adjust the setting for when backups happen (the default is when the PC is not doing anything) and the level of notifications that Mozy will give you. The **Restore** tab lets you restore individual files by selecting them and clicking the **Restore** button. To make a one-off backup at any point, go to the notification area, right click the Mozy icon and select **Start Backup**.

Protecting yourself and your family online

If you're new to the Internet or haven't really considered online safety before, now's the time to think about it. The Internet isn't any more dangerous than the real world as long as you follow some simple advice; use common sense and treat things on the Internet just like you would in the real world. It's not any more or less dangerous than it has been in the past but, as with everything else online, the threats change constantly as each new opportunity also gives rise to a new threat.

Think about your family's security too. It's not just a question of what's suitable and safe for you, it's what's suitable for your kids or your brothers or sisters. Technology can help to protect them, but education and understanding can go much further.

Preventing identity theft

The best approach to preventing people getting their hands on your private data is to prevent it being freely available in the first place. But all information has to be stored somewhere, and password protection and encryption are the best ways to prevent stored data from being stolen.

Tip: The certificate source is actually called an authority because that's what it is; an authority on certificates. The authority very quickly checks to make sure the certificate is valid, then confirms that with the browser, which then tells you. The whole process takes fractions of a second. The browser doesn't trust the certificate at face value; it checks it out for you.

Secure sites and certificates

Any organization that requires sensitive information from you should be responsible enough to secure that information and the method used to transmit it. Sites which are secure hold a certificate which authenticates that the website is what it claims to be. When your browser opens a certified site it checks the validity of the certificate with approved sources. In Internet Explorer and Firefox the address bar goes green if a certificate is present and checks out.

Phishing filters

Phishing is the name for scams on the Internet that try to dupe you into providing sensitive data, normally by pretending to be your bank or someone else you'd legitimately give that information to. Internet Explorer includes an anti-phishing filter called SmartScreen that prevents you going to known phishing sites and warns you about suspected ones. It should be switched on already, but you can check by going to **Safety > SmartScreen Filter**. If the menu option **Turn On SmartScreen Filter** appears then it's off – so turn it on! From here it's also possible to run a one-time check or to report what you believe to be a phishing site.

Tip: The SmartScreen phishing filter indicates that a website is unsafe by displaying a very obvious red screen and blocking access but with the option to override it if you believe it's mistaken. A similar red popup will appear if you attempt to download something that is on a list of malware (software that does bad things to your PC such as stealing your information). It's a good idea to have SmartScreen turned on.

Tip: Instead of trying to create your own passwords you can use a random password generator like the one at goodpassword.com. This will generate one for you without you needing to think about it, but make sure that you can remember it!

Passwords

To set a strong password, use a series of letters (both upper and lower case), numbers and symbols that mean something to you, but would mean nothing to someone else. Where possible use more than one word or a minimum of eight random characters.

Wherever possible try not to use the same password repeatedly; people inevitably do this because it's easier to remember. Don't re-use one of your easy-to-remember passwords for something that you might need to disclose to someone else, for example when setting up HomeGroup or your wireless network.

Networks

With wireless networks all over the place it's quite possible that you'll use your laptop on a public wireless connection which any number of other people could be using. Windows 7 should automatically realize you've connected to a new network and display a choice of location: **Home, Work or Public** networks. When using a public connection, always select **Public** as this provides the most protection. You can check this at any time by clicking the bar graph (the network icon) in the notification area. If Windows thinks it's connected to a Home network, a house icon will appear at the top of the window; for Work it's an office block and a Public network is represented by a park bench. If it's set wrong then select the link to **Open network and sharing center**; under **View your active networks** the network location can be changed to Public by clicking the link for **Home network** or **Work network**.

Clearing history

If you use a computer in an Internet café, library or somewhere else public, make sure you wipe your browsing history and any cookies (small packets of information about what you did on a site), passwords or other stored information.

To clear the browsing history in some common browsers:

▸ Internet Explorer 8 – go to **Safety > Delete browsing history** and select what needs to be deleted.

▸ Firefox – go to **Tools > Clear private data**.

▸ Internet Explorer 6 (or earlier versions) – go to **Internet Options > General > Clear History**.

▸ Google Chrome – click the "wrench" icon and select **Clean Browsing History**.

▸ Safari on a Mac – click **Edit > Reset Safari**.

Tip: If you're using someone else's machine, where possible use the private or incognito browsing mode (mainly offered by newer browsers).

Managing sensitive information online

There are many legitimate reasons for revealing specific data online, such as logging into Internet banking or buying goods with a credit card at an online shop. Social networking also encourages us to share more and more information about our daily activities. But it's important to understand the implications of making that information public, and to put measures into place to counteract the risks.

Social networks and blogging

When blogging or using a social networking site it's easy to reveal details that you wouldn't normally want people to know. For example, updating your status on Facebook to say "going away on holiday for two weeks today" could be a little dangerous combined with the knowledge that you're single (also on your profile). Someone could guess that your house is unoccupied for two weeks so it's a good time to break in!

It's important to be careful about what you say, and the pictures you post publicly, any details you share and who you share them with. It might be fun to post photos of you at a raucous party but will your boss see it the same way when you call in sick the day after with "food poisoning"? On social networking sites it's very important to use the built-in controls to limit what other friends or people in your "network" can see.

Tip: Take control of your social networks; create permission levels and categorize your friends. Take special note of the "random" people you meet on the Internet who aren't real-world friends and put them into the most restrictive categories where they only get little snippets of information about you and not the whole picture.

A special note on pictures of children

It's a sad thing to have to say, but be careful about posting pictures of your kids in a school uniform. School uniforms can be unique; the badge on a sweater or blazer can identify the individual school.

There's little to worry about, but make sure the picture is private and can only be seen by the people you want to see it, not the entire Internet.

Shopping

Shopping on the Internet is convenient and easy, and sites such as eBay have become incredibly popular as they facilitate buying and selling between people, not just from established retailers. It does require parting with some financial details, but this is perfectly safe if you follow a few guidelines:

▸ Use an online payment service where you can. Services like **Pay-pal.com** work by providing a trustworthy intermediary to give your banking details to. For example: you buy a product from Rodrigo in Brazil, but you don't really want to give him your credit card number. A payment service like Paypal takes the risk out of your hands; you trust them with your credit card number, they give Rodrigo the money and Juan never gets your financial details.

▸ If you can't use an online payment service get a credit card with a small credit facility. The smaller the facility, the lower the risk. Use credit cards where possible because the financial rules around them often provide more protection than a checking account.

▸ Only provide details over a secure connection to people you have reason to trust. See the section about phishing earlier in this chapter to find out why.

Tip: If you need to print out sensitive information, such as bank statements or medical details, then either file it away in a lockable cabinet or, if you don't need to keep it, shred it with a cross-cut shredder. It's amazing how many people go to all the right lengths to secure their computers and the information on them, but leave their bank statements out on their desk.

Family safety

Deciding upon online activities that are suitable for your kids to do is up to you, but if you aren't careful it will be up to them. Knowing your children (which is easier said than done) is the first step to helping them be safe online. All the information in

Protecting yourself and your family online

Tip: Microsoft has some very sage family safety advice at microsoft.com/uk/protect/family/default.mspx. It's worth fifteen minutes of any parent's time to read and understand the principles there.

this chapter is relevant to kids and adults alike, but in addition to this, kids need supervising and monitoring.

Guidance says that up to about the age of ten most kids' Internet activity should be supervised to make sure they don't accidentally find things that they won't be able to comprehend.

Over the age of eleven it's important to still monitor access but it's probably time to start phasing out the supervising in favour of trust and education about looking after their own safety online.

Mid-to-late teens should have near unrestricted access to the Internet (just try and stop em!). They'll still need support from adults to understand the finer points of not sharing too much.

Content ratings

So how do you know if content is suitable? The Internet changes so rapidly that it's virtually impossible to implement a good content rating system – although some governments keep trying. The best advice here is to look at it yourself and talk to your kids about it.

Movies and computer games are another story; these have content ratings and Parental Controls which Windows 7 uses to help you mediate what kinds of information your children are exposed to.

Controlling access and setting rules

Windows 7 includes Parental Controls which can be found at **Start > Control Panel > Parental Controls**. These give you control over which specific computer games and other programs can be used, and how long the computer itself can be used for. Parental Controls can only be applied to a standard user, so it's important that kids don't have administrator accounts.

Once you've selected whose access to restrict, you'll see the "master switch", where Parental Controls can be turned on and individual settings can be configured. Select **On, enforce current settings** to allow the settings for games, applications and time limits to be changed.

Setting time limits

A grid represents the 24 hours of the day, 7 days a week. During the times selected the restricted user will be blocked from logging on, or forced to log off if they're already logged on when a blocked period begins.

Configuring game options

There is a "master" switch to block users from playing any games whatsoever. It'll prompt you with the question "Can the user play games?". If you answer **No** then that's it, all games are barred. If the answer is **Yes** then additional options are available to set which games are allowed – specific games or those containing types of content can be blocked.

Click on **Set game ratings** and select the maximum rating that the person can play. At the bottom of the screen specific types of content, such as "cartoon violence", can also be blocked.

Set up how testy will use the computer

⚠ Web filtering and activity reporting are not available on this computer. To enable web filtering and activity reporting, you must install additional controls.

Parental Controls:
○ On, enforce current settings
◉ Off

Windows Settings
🕐 Time limits
   Control when testy uses the computer

🏆 Games
   Control games by rating, content, or title

🖥 Allow and block specific programs
   Allow and block any programs on your computer

Current Settings:

testy
Standard user
No Password

Parental Controls: Off

Be careful not to be too restrictive as this will most likely cause most kids to try working around the controls and they could end up doing more damage. Make sure the communication lines stay open at all times.

Specific programs

Allow and block specific programs allows you to build up a list of every application that a person can use; if it's not on the list then it's blocked. It can be quite time consuming to build this list but a very effective control method once in place.

Filtering Web content

Windows 7 needs Windows Live Essentials to be installed for online Parental Controls to work. Go to **fss.live.com** to sign in to Windows Live and download the Family Safety filter. Family Safety can be used to block access to specific websites, monitor which sites kids visit and control who they can talk to with IM

Tip: Game ratings, just like film ratings, are based on what's suitable for a set age range. These vary by country and region, but Windows 7 uses ratings for the region the PC is set up in. If it uses the wrong rating (the logos will be different to the ones on the game box or disk) then the correct one can be selected by going to Start > Control Panel > Parental Controls and clicking Game Rating Systems. From the left select the correct rating system (in the UK it's PEGI and the US it's ESRB).

Protecting yourself and your family online

and e-mail. Because the service is web based you can access it to manage your settings from any computer anywhere in the world, although you will have to set it up on each different PC you want to control.

Log in to **fss.live.com** and click **Add Child** on the website to configure a separate account for everyone in the house whose usage is to be controlled or monitored. If the child already has a Live account, use those details; if not, create them a new one.

There are two preset levels and a custom level to choose from:
▸ Strict – only allows access to websites known to be child friendly.
▸ Basic – blocks only content Microsoft knows to be adult in nature.
▸ Custom – create your own list of allowed or blocked websites.

The **Activity Reporting** button on the left of the webpage will report details of every website or instant messaging conversation that the monitored person has had. The person will know they're being monitored because they need to sign into Family Safety to access the Internet, and it's important to have a conversation with them about why you're doing this.

Once Windows Essentials is installed, you can find it at Start > All Programs > Windows Live > Family Safety. **Each user will need to log in with their Live ID before they can get access to the Internet.**

Contact management can also be selected over on the left and manages the contacts that the person can interact with using Windows Live Messenger, Windows Live Hotmail and on Windows Live Spaces (Microsoft's blogging and social network site).

When someone attempts to visit a blocked site, they will instead be taken to a page where they can request the parents' permission to access the site.

Trouble-
shooting

Help!

When you have an impending deadline, only minutes to spare and just need to get that one thing done, that's often the time that Windows seems to give up the fight and decide to lie down for a while – otherwise known as crashing; at least that's how it feels. This section covers some of the ways to get out of trouble when all seems to be lost and discusses some of the fundamentals needed for working out what's really wrong with the PC.

Windows 7 includes a variety of methods to get to the root cause of a problem as well as some handy clues to help you fix the problem. It also delivers something revolutionary: automatic troubleshooting.

Where to look for problems

The first time you realize there is a problem with your PC is normally when an error message of some sort appears on the screen or you notice that it's behaving differently – often very slowly! But those errors or that slow performance doesn't actually provide much in the way of a clue as to what's gone wrong.

The central place to find any errors that Windows has produced (and you'll find there are many more than you're aware of) is the event viewer, which is located in **Start > All Programs > Administrative Tools > Event Viewer.** The information that it reveals is very technical

Help!

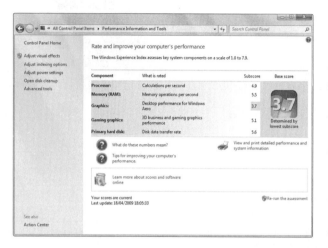

Tools for improving the performance of your PC and solving problems, as well as overall speed ratings are available from the Performance and Information Tools Control Panel.

in nature, but it's possible to get some basic clues without needing to know too much.

Performance and Information tools, found in **Start > Control Panel > All Control Panel Items > Performance Information and Tools**, can help improve performance by identifying problems and can also help with tasks like reducing wasted disk space and fixing power settings.

Action Center will report any problems with security on the PC or any issues with maintenance tasks, such as running backups or spyware scans. It's also a launch pad for troubleshooting, performance applications and changing settings such as how much User Account Control notifies you when something is about to change with the system.

Finding a solution

Automated troubleshooting wizards are all available from **Start > Control Panel > All Control Panel Items > Troubleshooting** and can help with a variety of problems, but these aren't the only way to find solutions.

The Microsoft Knowledge base is available at **support.microsoft. com** and includes thousands of fixes for lots of problems. Something new that Microsoft has added is **Fix it**, which makes it possible to apply a fix right from the website, without having to fiddle with settings and options yourself. The Microsoft site on its own is an amazingly good source of problem-solving information, and is often overlooked; it should really be the first port of call when looking for a way to fix something with Windows. One thing often missing from solutions found on the Internet is any validation of accuracy, but support.microsoft.com is curated by Microsoft so nothing gets in unless it's accurate.

Your second port of call should be Google. It's amazing what searching for an error message will turn up. More often than not you'll find the answer to your problem in the first three or four results and often those answers will come from a very knowledgeable source: the community of people using Windows.

How to solve a problem

Solving problems isn't just about knowledge; it's equally about taking the right steps in the right order and not panicking when something goes wrong. The problem-solving process is generally always the same:

1 Experience the problem.
2 Research fixes for the problem.
3 Try to apply that research to fix the problem.
4 If it didn't work – undo it!
5 Then do more research and try again.
6 Keep going until it's fixed; or…
7 Give up and get someone else to do it!

Remember there's no shame in not being able to fix a problem with your PC; technicians spend years learning the darn things inside-out and then work hard to keep that knowledge updated year on year. There are always experts out there who will be able to help. But before you get to that point, the troubleshooting wizards in Windows 7 are invaluable and much of the time they can fix a problem with virtually no help from outside.

Getting someone else to help

We all know that special someone who can talk to PCs in much the same way as Dr Doolittle could talk to animals. Hopefully they're a friend who doesn't charge by the hour and who's happy to help

Help!

you out. Windows 7 includes something called Windows Remote Assistance, found in **Start > All Programs > Maintenance > Windows Remote Assistance**, that helps people to help each other.

To get someone to help you with Remote Assistance they first need to be invited with one of the following methods:

▶ Send them an e-mail invitation – Select **Invite someone you trust to help you**. The invite can be saved as a file and attached to an e-mail (choose **Save this information as file**) or sent directly as an e-mail (by choosing **Use e-mail to send an invitation**). Both do the same thing but the first option is useful if you use Hotmail or a similar webmail service where Windows can't automatically create e-mail attachments.

▶ Use EasyConnect – The person who's helping needs to open Remote Assistance on their PC and select **Help someone who has invited you**, and at the same time you need to select **Use EasyConnect**.

Once the invitation is sent a password will appear that needs to be given to the helper separately – it's best to do this over the phone. When they open the invite or start EasyConnect they just need to enter the password to get started.

A useful tool when getting help is the Problem Steps Recorder, which lets you record the problem you're having and send a recording of it for someone to look at. Go to **Start**, type **psr**, hit **Enter** and the tool will start. Hit the record button and and do whatever it is that causes the problem. Everything you do will be saved to a file that you can then send to a friend so they can see the exact problem you're having. The file will be a .zip file containing a webpage (don't worry, it's not on the Internet) of everything you did, including screen shots of every step of the process.

Start the Problem Steps Recorder by typing psr into the Start menu. It'll record your problems as they happen and make it easier for someone else to help you out.

Startup problems

There are a lot of reasons why Windows sometimes won't start up properly: a problem from when the PC was last shut down; a piece of failed hardware; or some software that's actually preventing the OS from starting. There are a few ways to diagnose and solve startup and operating system problems with Windows 7, but the first thing to do is work out if it's a problem with the OS or with your actual computer hardware.

If you turn on the PC and hear beeps coming from it and nothing appears on screen then there is a high possibility that the main circuit board (sometimes called main board or motherboard), graphics card or memory are damaged in some way. Of course there is also the possibility that they have somehow come loose from their connection to the rest of the PC. It's probably worth seeking professional help, or call the PC manufacturer (especially if it's in warranty). It's okay to attempt repairs on your own and if you feel comfortable doing that you probably don't need any advice from this book on what to do!

Should Windows not start just after you've plugged something new in, like a USB camera or hard drive, try starting the PC without it; if it works you know where the problem is. Go to the manufacturer's website and check for compatibility with Windows 7.

What does the startup problem look like?
How a problem with startup presents itself is often the clue to how to fix it. If you see the Starting Windows screen, but then everything goes black, that's likely to be a screen resolution problem. If the PC continually reboots then it's likely that a problem with a service or driver is causing Windows to fail; Startup Repair or Safe Mode are the tools to use.

Tip: Make sure you have a backup; it's so simple in Windows 7 that there's no excuse not to. See Chapter 25 for the different ways to set one up.

Startup Repair

Windows Startup Repair is an advanced diagnosis and troubleshooting tool that will automatically analyse Windows and the hardware in the PC to work out what's wrong. Most of the time it gets it right, but sometimes it needs a little help so access is provided to some other useful tools for restoring image backups, going to a restore point, checking the memory, or (for true geeks) opening a command prompt.

If Windows struggles to start on its own you should see the Windows Error Recover screen. There are times when Windows doesn't detect that it's having a problem and doesn't display this screen; for those times press the **F8** key on the keyboard at the point just before the **Starting Windows** screen appears and then select **Start up Repair** using the up and down arrow keys.

The first thing that will appear is a screen asking what you want to do; select **Repair Your Computer** (see later in this chapter for some of the other options), press the **Enter** key and Startup Repair will load a pared-down version of Windows.

Tip: There are some great professional options for getting help with your PC, such as GeekSquad. For a monthly fee they'll provide technical support and help with any serious problems. Have a look at geek-squad.com for information. Also remember to register your warranty; if something goes wrong then for a certain period of time there will be some responsibility on the manufacturer.

▶ If Startup Repair started automatically (i.e., you didn't press F8), it will skip ahead and ask if you would like to use System Restore to load a restore point (see Chapter 25 for more on restore points). If you already know you want to do this then click **Restore**; otherwise click **Cancel** to begin a scan of the software and hardware to find problems.

▶ If you pressed the F8 key during boot you'll be asked to select a language and keyboard layout, then to supply your username and password. You'll then be taken to a window with a choice of options. Select **Startup Repair** to begin.

Startup Repair may automatically reboot the PC a couple of times, the screen may flash or flicker and other weirdness could happen, but don't worry, Startup Repair will take care of it. Eventually it will offer a solution to the problem, or it will suggest using System Restore to restore the PC to an earlier point in time (for more information on configuring System Restore see Chapter 25). Don't worry about your data getting deleted because System Restore is very careful not to touch your files, it just investigates Windows. At the end of the process either accept the solution or to do more select the link to **View advanced options for system recovery and support**; clicking the **Finish** button will shut down the PC.

If Startup Repair can't fix it for you then there are some more options available from here to get the PC working again. If you didn't press F8 to get to Startup Repair then the first time you want to use any option other than System Restore, you'll be asked for a username and password that's valid on the PC.

Go to a restore point

Assuming System Restore is turned on (hopefully it is if you've read Chapter 25), then returning the PC to the state it was in when a restore point was created can be a good idea. A restore point should be automatically created before any software install takes place. This is a particularly good way to "go back a bit" to just before that whizzy application was installed that promised to make life easier but actually messed with your PC. System restore points aren't great for recovering from a virus; they might work but it all depends on the nature of the virus.

The wizard makes everything straightforward; just select the restore point to use. Click **Scan for affected programs** to find out what will be "uninstalled", then click **Next** and **Finish** to restore to that point. Once the restore has happened the PC will reboot and should be usable again. If not, try something else in this chapter like restoring an image backup.

> **Tip:** Searching online is one of the best ways to get help, but if you use Internet help forums to get that help be careful who you listen to. Look out for people who have accumulated lots of kudos or awards on a site as they usually have the best information. Anyone with MVP after their name is usually a community member recognized by Microsoft, and that award is very hard to get.

> **Tip:** A good way to get help on Windows is from newsgroups, available from Windows Live Mail or any other newsreader software. The Microsoft news server (NNTP) news.microsoft.com is the place to ask questions and get quality answers from the community of Microsoft enthusiasts and sometimes even from Microsoft employees.

Startup problems

The System Recover Options **window will appear after choosing the** Repair your Computer **option from the startup screen, or if Startup Repair can't fix the PC automatically. It's a launchpad for other tools to help fix your system.**

Tip: Always switch the PC off before opening it up and messing around with its insides. It's also important to touch your hand to the internal metal chassis to earth any static charge in your body before touching any of the sensitive electronic components.

System Image Recovery

If you took the advice in Chapter 25 and have created an image backup of your PC to a USB drive, DVD or to another computer on the network, then you can restore that backup. When you do, everything goes back to the point in time that the backup was made, and that includes your own files. It's a good way to go back to when you know everything was working fine, but any software that's been installed since the backup won't be available without being reinstalled, and the same goes for any hardware drivers.

This is a pretty extreme option which means losing everything you did on the PC since the backup, so it should only be used in extreme circumstances and almost as a last resort (the ultimate last resort is to install Windows again from scratch!).

To start the process select **System Image Recovery** and the program will hunt for any image backups on drives or DVDs attached to the computer; if it can't find them it'll ask for them to be attached. If the backup is on the network select **Cancel**, which will reveal the option to **Restore a different system image**; click **Next** then **Advanced** and finally **Search for a system image on the network**. Then simply enter the location of the backup, wait for the program to find it and then restore it following the wizard's directions.

Check the memory

A common issue with PCs is that the memory develops a problem which can be caused by such things as power surges or faulty components. The **Windows Memory Diagnostic** will run a check on all the physical RAM memory in your computer to see if there are any issues. When the scan runs, a blue screen appears showing progress

```
                    Windows Memory Diagnostics Tool

Windows is checking for memory problems...
This might take several minutes.

Running test pass  1 of  2: 08% complete
Overall test status: 04% complete



Status:
No problems have been detected yet.

Although the test may appear inactive at times, it is still running. Please
wait until testing is complete...

Windows will restart the computer automatically. Test results will be
displayed again after you log on.




F1=Options                                                ESC=Exit
```

Memory in a PC is divided into groups known as sticks. Working out exactly which stick of the memory has failed is trial-and-error work; start up with one stick removed and see if problems appear, or run a memory check by typing "memory" into the Start search. If that stick is at fault then replace it; if not put it back and try another. Warning: only to be attempted if you feel confident in doing so; otherwise get help.

and eventually (it can take a very long time) the PC will reboot. If the scan has found a memory fault it's likely that you will need to replace some RAM. If the PC is under warranty contact the manufacturer to find out if memory is covered; otherwise check with the manufacturer's website to determine what replacement memory to buy and install.

Open a command prompt

This is quite an advanced option and it's best to seek help with it. Not all the commands that are available on a standard command prompt within Windows will be available. A good guide to follow is available at **bleepingcomputer.com/ tutorials/tutorial147.html**.

Tip: Removing memory (RAM) is fairly straightforward. The hardest part can sometimes be reaching it behind all the cables and computer parts that may be in the way. If you need to remove any cables you can stick numbered tabs on the cables and the things they plug into as an easy way to get everything back where it should be. The RAM sticks themselves will be locked in by little plastic levers at either end. Simply open these outwards and the RAM will ease out of its socket and should be fairly easy to remove. Try to hold it by the edges and not touch any of the circuitry on the stick or you could render it useless. To put it back in make sure the levers are open and push the RAM in the socket evenly and firmly until they clip back to a closed position. A bar in the socket corresponds to a notch in the bottom of the memory stick that'll prevent you putting it in the wrong way around.

Advanced boot options

System Recovery is actually part of the Advanced Boot Options menu in Windows 7. It's slightly different from the other options in that it's started automatically by Windows when it encounters startup problems. There are some other useful options here though which can help even more than System Recovery.

Safe Modes

Windows 7 has three different types of Safe Mode; each is suited to different tasks but all have the underlying factor that they load a very simplified version of Windows 7 which should be able to start without encountering the problem experienced by the full version of Windows. The vanilla Safe Mode loads only original hardware drivers, and no network drivers (so it can't see other computers). It also only loads original Windows programs that came with Windows and loads a stripped-down user interface. This cuts out lots of potential problems immediately, such as bad drivers or services. If Safe Mode won't start at all then it's best to try Safe Mode with Command Prompt.

For even more help using Safe Mode and some of its advanced functions, go to the Microsoft Help and Support site (support.microsoft. com) and search for "Safe Mode".

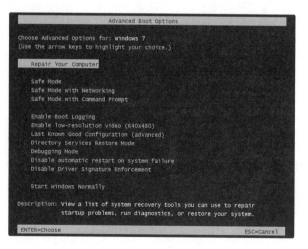

Safe Mode with Command Prompt

This version of Safe Mode only loads a command prompt; it doesn't bother with the Windows user interface and is the most "geeky" option for recovery, so it's best to have some sort of technical knowledge. If this Safe Mode loads when the vanilla Safe Mode won't then the problem is with part of Windows. The best thing to do is use System Recovery and go back to a pre-vious system restore point or use an image backup to restore to.

Safe Mode is a great place to fix problems. Typically it's the best way to fix problems such as when an application that loads at startup crashes Windows or when a device driver does the same. The simplest way to troubleshoot with it is to identify what has been installed since the problem started; remove it all and hopefully Windows will boot again. Then all you need to do is reinstall the applications or devices one at a time, rebooting after each, until you find the problem application or driver.

The tool to do this for applications is **Start > Control Panel > Programs > Programs and Features**. To remove drivers you will need to use Device Manager, so launch that through **Start > Control Panel > All Control Panel Items > Device Manager.** Navigate through the device list, find the device that you installed last, right click it and select **Uninstall**.

Safe Mode looks like a very basic and blocky version of Windows – and that's exactly what it is. Cut down to the bare essentials, it can almost always start even if Windows proper can't. Press F8 before the Windows logo appears at startup and select Safe Mode to activate it.

Safe Mode with Networking

If the vanilla Safe Mode works but you need to get to some resources on the network to help solve the problem, such as needing a file from another PC, then choose the **Safe Mode with Networking** option. This option loads the minimum software required to get the PC on the network, so if this Safe Mode won't load, but the vanilla one does, there's a problem with the network hardware or drivers, so try removing them.

Low res video

One of the most annoying situations that it's possible to get in Windows occurs when changing the display resolution. If it's changed to a mode that the screen doesn't support (normally a very high resolution), nothing appears on screen. Normally Windows will revert back to settings that work, inform you that the settings you wanted to use were no good and then everything will continue as normal. Occasionally, though, a reboot is needed to change resolutions; if that happens and a nonsupported resolution is used, Windows will boot just fine, but you won't be able to see anything!

To sort this out, power the PC down, restart it and press F8 just before the **Starting Windows** message appears, then select **Enable low-resolution video (640x480)**, which will start Windows using a resolution compatible with virtually every screen ever built. Then just change the resolution after the PC has started to something that works (check the screen manufacturer's specs to work out what does) and all will be well again.

Disable automatic restart on failure

Windows 7 automatically reboots when it encounters a major problem, but when it does it very briefly displays an error code on a blue screen that basically points to what went wrong. If that error occurs during the startup process then Windows can get stuck in a cycle of continually rebooting. Interrupting this by pressing F8 just before the **Starting Windows** message and selecting **Disable automatic restart on system failure** will not stop Windows crashing, but it will give you the opportunity to find that error code. Once you have it, do some research on the Web at **support.microsoft. com** or with Google to work out what it means and how to fix it.

Application and virus problems

Sometimes an application you're using will "crash", giving up for no apparent reason or becoming unresponsive. This is less likely in Windows 7 but does still happen occasionally. And getting the PC working without a reboot will save you lots of time.

Odd behaviour from your PC doesn't necessarily mean you have a virus; it could just as easily be an application problem. If you do seem to have a virus, the second part of this chapter will help you remove it, even if you don't have antivirus software installed.

> **Application or process?**
> Applications are programs you use to do something; a process is how an application does that thing. So behind every application are one or more processes.

Application problems

When an application crashes in Windows 7 you'll soon know about it because when the OS detects that something's become "unresponsive" it will dim the window and pop up a message to let you know. It also provides the option to send information about the problem to Microsoft – don't expect to hear anything back, though; they don't respond to individuals.

Windows error reporting and Action Center

Action Center is the single point of contact for security and maintenance alerts and has an important role to play when something has failed. Start it from **Start > Control Panel > System and Security > Action Center**. It can tell you how reliable your PC is, revealing details of every program crash and system event that caused any type of problem; go to the **Maintenance** section and select the **View system history** link.

All the user information Microsoft receives helps them build solutions to common problems, and Action Center can cross-reference the history of problems you've had with Microsoft's fixes to find a fix; from the **Maintenance** section select the **Check for solutions** link. Sometimes the wizard will ask you if it's okay to send more information to Microsoft, which might take a while to gather and send.

Action Center also keeps an eye on fixes being released from Microsoft and if it can't identify a suitable answer immediately, it might be able to at some point in the future. When it finds a fix, a pop-up message will let you know and details will be available from the **Maintenance** section of Action Center as a new message. You can check if any have been found by going to **View archived messages** on the left-hand side. Opening the message will reveal details of how to fix the problem or where to learn more about it.

Action Center makes it obvious when something is wrong. A red stripe next to a message indicates immediate attention is required; amber is just a warning but still worth fixing.

Troubleshooting wizards

Troubleshooting wizards can be launched from **Start > Control Panel > All Control Panel Items > Troubleshooting** (or from within Action Center). There are wizards that help with all manner of problems, many of which will be explored in later chapters, but the **Programs** troubleshooting wizards help with:

- ▶ Internet connections
- ▶ Internet Explorer performance and safety
- ▶ Program compatibility
- ▶ Printer problems
- ▶ Problems with Media Player settings, Libraries and DVD playback

Program compatibility

The main troubleshooting wizard for application problems is program compatibility; launched by right-clicking a program or shortcut that's giving you trouble and selecting **Troubleshoot compatibility**. This wizard can detect any reasons the program won't run on Windows 7. The primary fix for most errant applications is to let them think they're running on an older version of Windows (like XP or Vista).

Running the wizard from the Control Panel presents a list of all the applications installed on the PC. Choose the one that's giving you trouble and it will ask what sorts of problems you're having with it, such as **the program doesn't display correctly**. It'll then ask further questions to clarify the situation and eventually come up with a solution that may involve making changes to Windows or to the way the program runs. Finally it will provide three options:

- ▶ Save these settings for this program.
- ▶ Try again using different settings.
- ▶ Report the problem to Microsoft and check online for a solution.

The troubleshooting tools available from Start > Control Panel > All Control Panel Items > Troubleshooting check online for updates and always have the most accurate information. It's a good idea to leave it set up like this, but if you have trust issues then a tick box at the bottom of the window can be used to prevent those updates.

Removing programs

Sometimes a program will just not work from the get-go, it might develop some sort of problem or you might simply no longer have a use for it. To get rid of it for good, go to **Start > Control Panel > All Control Panel Items > Programs and Features**, select the

Application and virus problems

You can uninstall programs from Start > Control Panel > All Control Panel Items > Programs and Features.

Tip: Another way to change program compatibility settings is to right click a program or shortcut and select Properties, followed by the Compatibility tab; all the settings for starting the applications in different modes can be set without the troubleshooting wizard. The Change settings for all users button should be used with caution; other people who use the PC may not appreciate your tampering.

application from the list and click **Uninstall.** The wizard will guide you through the process of removing it.

Task Manager

Applications sometimes lock up or "freeze" for no apparent reason, causing the PC to slow down and lock up other applications. Task Manager is an age-old solution to this problem; it's always able to close an application down, even when the X in the top right of the program's window can't. As always there are a couple of ways to get to Task Manager, and it's good to know more than one:

▸ Right click the task bar and select **Start Task Manager**.
▸ Press **CTRL + SHIFT + ESC** to launch Task Manager in one step.
▸ The ultimate "get out of jail free" card is to press **CTRL + ALT + DEL** and select **Start Task Manager**; this key combination gets more attention from the PC than anything else, so should always work.

There are various tabs in Task Manager, but to fix application problems you need just two: **Applications** and **Processes**. The **Applications** tab lists everything currently running; you can highlight the misbehaving application and click the **End Task** button, which immediately tells the program to shut down. The **Processes** tab is similar, but can also tell you which process is using the most CPU power, so if you don't know what's crashed, but your PC is running like a lame dog, go to **Task Manager**, then go to the **Process** tab and highlight the heading on the **CPU** column. The offending application will appear at the top. If it's a process called "System Idle Process", this just shows how much CPU power is actually free, so terminate the next one down. If the process hogging all your resources doesn't seem to be listed, click **Show processes from all users** to display processes being used by anyone else logged onto the PC.

Note that when you kill applications like this it's highly unlikely that any work you were doing within the application will be saved.

Viruses and malware

There are lots of annoying and destructive viruses out there and the best ways to protect your PC against them are to have antivirus software installed; to make sure the latest patches are always applied to the PC; and to have a firewall in place. Chapter 24 has some great advice on how to keep your PC secure, but what if it's too late and a virus has already found its way onto the PC?

This wouldn't necessarily be the end of the world, but it would be annoying and there's a very good chance you could lose some data. The first thing to do is disconnect the PC from your home network and other PCs to stop the virus spreading. Then if you do have antivirus software installed, perform an update to get information on the latest viruses and try to clean the PC that way.

If that doesn't get rid of it, or there's no antivirus software installed, it's time to try the following approach.

If you don't have antivirus software

Most antivirus software makers produce a "killer" which can be downloaded from their websites for specific, normally high-profile,

When ending an application, the processes should terminate automatically; however, the reverse isn't necessarily true, so be careful when terminating processes as it can just make the application unstable rather than closing it. Where possible end the application, not the process.

Tip: If you have no antivirus program installed on the PC and suspect a virus, here are three brilliant and free tools for removing specific viruses:

Avast avast.com/eng/avast-virus-cleaner.html
AVG free.avg.com/virus-removal
Avira free-av.com

Tip: Another free malware removal tool is EasyClean from f-secure.com, which provides industrial-strength antivirus and malware tools.

viruses. Look to the makers of your antivirus product first, but if that doesn't work go to another. Lots of free antivirus providers release killers too, and there's a list of some in the sidebar. Killers are specific and target normally only one virus, so you need a general idea which one you'll need. Read the details about each but if nothing sounds appropriate just go for the latest one!

Once you've downloaded the antivirus product for the virus you think you have, run it on the PC and it should find the virus and kill it; if it doesn't then try another until you find one that works. The next thing to do is to get an up-to-date antivirus subscription.

Getting rid of malware

Beyond viruses, spyware and adware are the most disruptive things that can get onto your PC, normally using some specific flaw in Windows to do their worst. Microsoft has a fantastic tool on their website called the malicious software removal tool, available at:

microsoft.com/security/malwareremove/default.mspx. It's updated on the second Tuesday of every month, which is when they release updates for Windows.

It's easy to use and can be a total lifesaver. There's no installation necessary; just run it and it will hunt down and kill any malware on the PC. It has three scanning levels:

▶ **Quick Scan** – which will scan the most likely locations of the PC for malware.
▶ **Full scan** – which scans everywhere.
▶ **Customized scan** – which allows specific folders to be scanned – useful if you know there's a problem somewhere.

Microsoft Windows Malicious Software Removal Tool - March 2009

Scanning your computer

The tool is scanning your computer for prevalent malicious software, and removing any that is found.

After this operation completes, the tool will provide you with a report of the malicious software that was detected and removed.

Currently scanning:
G:\Windows\system32\CLBCatQ.DLL
Files Scanned: 1103
Files Infected: 0
Start time: 17:26
Time elapsed: 00:00:29

< Back   Next >   Cancel

Disk space problems

With everything that's available to download from the Internet today – music, movies, TV shows, videos, applications and a ton of other stuff – it's really easy to fill up that hard drive.

There are plenty of solutions to help you cope with all that bloating, but all require a little caution because you'll be deleting things that you might decide later you wanted to keep. So before you try to create some space, make a backup first; that way you have something to fall back on if you change your mind.

Working out where the space has gone

The first step to reclaiming disk space is working out where it's all gone. There's nothing built in to Windows 7 to make this particularly easy, but there are some great applications available online that can really help. Have a look in the sidebar for a couple of the best. Alternatively, you're stuck with the laborious process in Windows Explorer of looking at the properties for each folder to see how much space it's using.

Tip: Two good hard disk space analysers are available from the sites below; both look at your drives and work out which folders are consuming the most space, displaying the result in an easy-to-follow pie chart.

Xinorbis freshney.org/xinorbis
JDiskReport jgoodies.com/freeware/jdiskreport

What NOT to delete

This isn't an exhaustive list, but steering clear of the temptation to delete any of the following will help you avoid some disastrous situations.

▶ Anything in **C:\Windows** – This is where the Windows operating system lives.

▶ **C:\Windows\Winsxs** – This looks particularly good to remove as it's huge, but don't; it's needed by Windows.

▶ Anything in **C:\Program Files** – Leave everything in this folder alone unless you want your installed applications to stop working.

▶ Anything that **you can't see** – It's possible to turn on viewing hidden files from **Control Panel > Folder Options**, but Windows usually hides files away for a reason.

▶ Whole users from **C:\users** – Even if the user has been removed don't remove their folder.

Making space

The obvious way to make space is to delete files. Using tools like Xinorbis or JDiskReport (see the sidebar on p.277) and the aforementioned rules on what not to delete that should keep this fairly straightforward. There are some other ways to create space that are worth mentioning here: cleaning up temporary files and Internet history is one way; another is to reduce how much space is reserved for backups.

Cleaning up unused files

Using the PC or browsing the Internet causes unwanted files to accumulate over time. An easy way to clean these up is to use Disk Cleanup, found at **Start > All Programs > Accessories > System Tools > Disk Cleanup**. Point it at a drive where space is running short and it'll analyse what's on the disk and return with a list of everything that can be safely deleted. Just tick the files you're happy to delete and click **OK**.

Reducing backups

System Protection keeps a fixed percentage of your total disk space free to use for creating System Restore points (see Chapter 25). It's good to have plenty of these in case anything goes wrong, but to adjust how much space is reserved and delete some redundant restore points, go to **Start > Control Panel > All Control Panel Items > System** and select the **System Protection** link from the left. Highlight the drive that's running short of space and click **Configure**. The slider lets you reduce the amount of allocated space, but remember that by doing so you're reducing how many system backups are made and how long they're kept for. The **Delete** button will delete all the previous restore points.

Adding space

An alternative to deleting everything is to buy another hard drive and add it to your PC. You can use a USB hard drive or network attached hard drive (called a NAS), or if you're comfortable fumbling around inside the computer you can install an extra hard drive internally.

Internal

If you're not comfortable messing about with hardware then this probably isn't the option for you; skip to the next section about external drives.

System Restore is a great way to keep your PC protected should something go wrong, but when running out of disk space the archived backups can be trimmed down. Go to Start > Control Panel > All Control Panel Items > System > System Protection and reduce the space allocated with the slider. But remember, less space equals fewer backups!

Disk space problems

Tip: There are plenty of NAS solutions out there that are simple, hard-drive only setups. For a more comprehensive option that will automatically back up every PC in your home, allow you to access your data remotely and magically collect and centralize all the media in the home, go for a HP Media Smart Server. (hp.com/united-states/campaigns/mediasmart-server). These cost more than most NAS devices, but are worth their weight in gold for their back-up capabilities alone.

To add an internal hard drive the PC needs to be opened up. You'll need a spare drive bay (where the drive physically sits) and the appropriate connection slots and cables. Buy a drive of a similar specification to the current one and connect it as per the instructions that come with it. It's much easier to add an extra disk than it is to completely replace the existing one; when replacing a disk everything on the original will need moving to the new disk, so if you need to do this it's best to get someone skilled to help out.

The next step will be to make sure it's formatted and that Windows can see it, so go to **Start > All Programs > Administrative Tools > Computer Management**, then select **Storage > Disk Management** from the left-hand side. This shows all the disks in your system: the new disk should be listed at the bottom, called something like "Disk 1". It now needs to be made ready for use; right click it and select **Initialize Disk**. Once that's done, highlight the space on the disk (it will have a black bar running across the top), right click again and select **New Simple Volume**. A wizard will begin to make the drive ready for use; generally just keep clicking **Next,** and eventually **Finish**.

External

By far the easiest way to add extra space is to add a USB hard disk or network storage device and just move the files around to create some space. To add a USB hard disk, simply plug it in. It should come ready formatted but if it doesn't go to Windows Explorer, click on **Computer** on the left-hand side and the main part of the window will reveal all the drives on the PC, including your new USB drive. Just right click and select **Format** and choose the default options.

The other option is to add a network attached storage (NAS) device. It's essentially a hard disk drive attached to a tiny computer that's only good at sharing. Windows 7 will see this as just another PC on the network. There's no real setup required in Windows 7 but there might be some listed in the instructions for the NAS.

Network problems

Windows 7 includes some excellent ways to fix network problems without drawing you too deeply into the technicalities of the network or how it works, taking a lot of the frustration out of the process. Of course, there are problems that can occur outside of Windows that affect your network, such as your router going wrong. There's very little Windows can do to help you with these sorts of problems beyond alerting you to them. So it's useful to understand the problems a little, and knowing where to look for solutions helps a lot.

Potential trouble spots with networks are:
- Connections to the local network and how they're made.
- The software and hardware that's running the network.
- The connection to the Internet.

Connections to the local network are normally within your control, especially if you're at home. The same is true of the software that's running the connection, but problems connecting to the Internet might well be beyond your control.

Common connection problems include cables being unplugged or kinked, wireless connections not being made and firewalls block-

Tip: If you're having problems with a wireless network, connect the PC to the router with an Ethernet cable and see if the problem still exists. This one simple step works out if it's a wireless problem or a problem with the router; if it's a router problem then you still won't be able to access the network even when physically plugged in.

ing the connection. Common network problems can be caused by more than one PC with the same name or address and faulty or badly set up hardware. Common Internet problems include the MAC address of the router (a number on the router in the format of xx:xx:xx:xx:xx:xx) not being registered with the Internet service provider (ISP), or the ISP itself having problems that cause your connection to be unavailable or painfully slow.

Working out what's gone wrong

The first approach Windows 7 takes to find out what's wrong is to look at a map of the network and see where the breaks in the connection are. The network map is available from **Start > Control Panel > All Control Panel Items > Network and Sharing Center**, with a more detailed map available by clicking the **See full map** link. Working connections are shown with green lines, while broken connections are displayed with a red X through them.

Using this simple map, problems can be pinpointed and isolated immediately. The network is represented by a symbol (home, office block or park bench), identifying what type it is: Home, Work or Public. A green line between **This computer** and the network indicates that the PC can talk to the local network successfully; a green line from the network icon to the **Internet** indicates that Internet connections are fine. Each can be double checked by clicking its icon. **This computer** launches Windows Explorer to the local drives; **the network** launches Windows Explorer to the **Network** view; and **Internet** launches the default web browser (Internet Explorer usually). Double clicking on the icons is a useful way to double check that everything's working properly; if what appears isn't what you expect or something's missing, then there's probably still a problem.

If there's a red X between **This computer** and the network icon then the problem is local and the computer can't talk to anything else on the network. Things to check are:

The network map tells you what's working and what's not with your network. There should be a green line linking each part: your PC, your network and the Internet. If there's a red X between any of them then that's where your problem is.

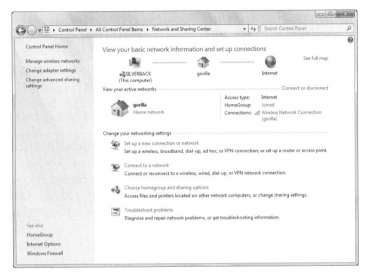

If it's a wired network:
▶ Is the cable plugged in and free of kinks?

If it's a wireless network:
▶ **Is the network card turned on?** Often computers, especially laptops, have a switch to disable and enable wireless.
▶ **Is the network password correct?** Select **Manage wireless networks** on the left, then double click on the network to connect to (if it's not listed see the next suggestion), select the **Security** tab and check **Show characters** to show the password in plain text. If it's wrong, change it.
▶ **Is the network being seen?** Go to the bar graph (network) icon in the notification area, click it and see if the network is listed; if it is, select it and click the **Connect** button. If it's not listed, restart the wireless router. If the network is hidden, add it using **Connect to a network** in the Network and Sharing Center.

Network problems

Tip: The wizard is by far the best way to fix network problems in Windows 7, but if you feel you really want to do it yourself and you'd like a little help there are some good tutorials at ehow.com.

If there's a red **X** between the network and the Internet then try the following:

▶ Restart the wireless router and (if there is one) modem. This is an age-old solution: making the router and modem re-register with the ISP.

▶ Check with the ISP that their service is available.

Using the troubleshooting wizard

The easiest way to fix network problems with Windows 7 is to use the network troubleshooting wizard. This can be started by going to **Start > Control Panel > All Control Panel Items > Network and Sharing Center** and selecting **Fix a network problem**. It includes fixes for:

▶ Internet connections.
▶ Shared folders.
▶ HomeGroup.
▶ Network adapters.
▶ Incoming connections.
▶ Printing.

The wizard runs automated checks over each component in the process of making a connection to ensure it's working. Eventually it'll suggest a possible solution to your problem. If this doesn't do the trick the wizard will continue working through the process until it finds the actual issue. The Internet connections wizard should be the one that yields the best results when looking for a connection problem.

Hardware problems

32

Resolving problems with hardware can be a tricky business since as well as potential problems with the hardware itself, the problem could just as easily be software related. Each piece of hardware, like hard drives, graphics cards, webcams and the like often also has an associated driver or application that makes it work. Windows has built-in troubleshooting wizards to make this process easier, but there are some things it's worthwhile knowing that'll make trying to fix the problem yourself or with the wizards easier.

Hardware issues are usually easy to spot because they normally lead to an all-out failure rather than a slow down. Of course when some pieces of hardware fail, for example the motherboard or the hard disk drive where Windows is installed, there's little Windows can do to help you find the fault because it'll be out of action itself.

Some rules of thumb

These simplified rules will give you an idea of what might be wrong, but they're all things that the troubleshooting wizards won't be able to help with if Windows itself isn't available:

- ▶ If it doesn't turn on – Check the power is connected, switched on and there is power reaching the PC. If it still doesn't turn on

Hardware problems

then there is likely to be something wrong with the motherboard, a failed power supply, or a loose connection somewhere between the power supply, case and motherboard. Consult an expert or the manufacturer of the PC.

▶ **If the PC turns on and starts beeping** – It's possibly a motherboard, memory or graphics card failure. If you feel comfortable doing it (and know how to do it safely) then make sure everything inside the PC is plugged in correctly. If that doesn't work, then consult an expert or the manufacturer of the PC.

▶ **If the PC turns on, and something appears on screen** – Go to Chapter 28 for more help.

▶ **If there is smoke** – Turn it off, immediately! Obviously this indicates a dangerous electrical fault. Seek expert advice.

Troubleshooting wizards are available for almost any problem you face in Windows 7. A quick way to launch them is to type "troubleshooting" into the Start menu search box.

Don't attempt any unnecessary maintenance yourself if your PC is still under warranty; call the manufacturer and get their help.

Hardware wizards

The hardware wizards in Windows 7 are available from **Start > Control Panel > All Control Panel Items > Trouble-shooting > Hardware and Sound** and cover every conceivable aspect of fixing a hardware problem. The most general is **Hardware and Devices**, which is able to identify and resolve problems for the widest range of hardware.

The **Printer** wizard is detailed in the types of problems that it can tackle, for example it can determine simple things – if there isn't enough ink or if the paper has run out – through to more complicated issues such as the Print Spooler service having problems (when printing has completely crashed).

If the hardware wizard, or any more device-specific wizard, can't resolve the problem it'll make suggestions as to where else to get help, such as the Microsoft support site or asking a friend for help using remote assistance. Select **Explore additional options** when the wizard finishes.

Fixing manually

Wizards aren't the only way to locate the source of a hardware problem. Device Manager is more useful in finding broken hardware than almost any other application; launch it from **Start > Control Panel > All Control Panel Items > Device Manager**. Every single bit of hardware that's connected to the PC that Windows can see is listed, providing a detailed view of your system. Any item with a yellow exclamation mark next to it has a problem.

Many issues can be fixed by removing the piece of hardware and then plugging it back in again. For anything connected via USB this is fine to do whilst the PC is turned on, but for anything else it's safest to power down first. Another common fix is to update the driver software for the problem device to the latest version. Right click on the faulty device and select **Update Driver Software**. A wizard walks you through the process of updating the drivers and will also check the Internet for the latest versions. If newer drivers aren't found, visit the hardware manufacturer's website and find the drivers manually; download them and then point the wizard at them using the **Browse my computer for driver software** option.

Tip: After substantially changing hardware, for example replacing a motherboard or something equally as drastic, you may be asked to activate Windows again. This happens because the hardware signature of the PC is used by Windows Activation to match the licence to the PC. As long as it's a genuine installation of Windows there's nothing to worry about; to check your copy is legitimate go to Start > Control Panel > All Control Panel Items > System and look for the "genuine" logo.

Improving performance

The performance of Windows can start to degrade over time for a number of reasons. Installing lots of applications can lead to many programs running in the background at once and more programs running automatically at startup, each consuming a little bit more memory or taking a little bit more processor time. Performance can also decrease when Windows finds it hard to locate files on hard disks or when hard disk space gets consumed by temporary files. We tend to buy PCs to fit our needs at a specific moment in time and yet when we get them home we find that they're capable of more, so we do more and more with the same PC until it starts to struggle.

This chapter will help to manage the PC you already have and identify which areas need to be upgraded for it to continue to perform.

Tip: You might see some applications claiming to defragment the memory on your PC. Don't bother with these, as there really is no need. Every time the PC reboots the memory is wiped clean so fragmentation never really gets that bad. If it ever did, it would only be because the PC had been booted up for too long and a reboot would probably help in other ways.

Hard disk performance

Hard disk performance is often the easiest issue to spot as files and folders load slowly and processes such as Windows loading from hibernation (a method of standby) will also be slow. The main issues affecting hard disk performance are files becoming fragmented and running out of space, or the computer building up too many temporary files. There are a couple of good tools built into Windows to help with these.

Defrag

Defrag is a term that gets thrown around a lot when fixing PC problems, but the only problem this helps fix is where the PC is under-performing in terms of reading or writing files to the hard disk. Defragging won't help if there's a physical problem with a hard disk or if the PC is rebooting constantly. However, if the PC is slow at opening files or saving them then it may have an effect; it can also speed up gaming.

A defrag is actually "Disk defragmentation". When a file is written to the hard disk, Windows has to make do with whatever space it can find and often that space isn't in one solid block. Defragging pulls fragments of files back together to be stored in one location so that the hard drive doesn't have to skip around retrieving them from all over the place.

To launch defrag go to **Start > All Programs > Accessories > System Tools > Disk Defragmenter**. By default a defrag should already be set to run at a scheduled time. Obviously, though, the PC needs to be turned on for this to work; so if it's not usually on at the time scheduled, click the **Configure schedule** button to choose a time when the PC is likely to be on but not being used.

The middle section shows the current status of all the hard disks in the PC, when the last defrag ran and how far it got. From here it's possible to run defrag at any time; just select the drive to work on and click **Analyse disk** or **Defragment disk**. The Analyse disk button makes the tool look at the disk to work out if a defrag is neces-

Hard drives get fragmented over time as files are written and deleted and this can affect performance, especially when opening large files. Select a disk to defragment and click Analyse disk. If the report returns with more than twenty percent fragmentation, click Defragment disk.

sary; a high percentage of fragmentation (above twenty percent) means it's worth clicking the **Defragment disk** button. Defragmentation can take hours on large hard disks, whereas running an analysis can take just a few minutes so it's always worth doing first.

It can be worth running defrag after installing games as they often contain large files like maps or levels that Windows finds hard to locate a single space for. The more a file is split the longer it takes Windows to put all the pieces back together and so the slower the game. The same is true of any file, including documents or photos.

Disk Cleanup is very straightforward and quite safe, but it's worth taking a minute just to check what's in the recycle bin before you empty it to make sure nothing's been deleted by accident.

Disk Cleanup

Found in **Start** > **All Programs** > **Accessories** > **System Tools** > **Disk Cleanup**, this tool can automatically delete temporary files from the most common places that are created whilst using the PC, empty the recycle bin or delete information files about old problems that the PC has experienced. It's possible to clear up any of these left-over files yourself, but Disk Cleanup is a one-stop shop that can safely delete any of these common files for you. Simply tick the types of files to remove and click **Clean up system files** to create some space; the tool lets you know how much space will be gained.

Other ways to increase disk speed

There are other ways to increase disk performance, but most will require some form of hardware change, like replacing the hard disk with one that spins faster or with a solid state drive, or even replacing the motherboard and the hard disk. It's best to seek specialist advice before doing this, however. If you are looking at these options, the chances are a gaming PC will suit your needs.

Startup performance

Startup speed is a bugbear for many; Windows 7 was designed to start up faster than previous versions, but that's difficult to ensure with all the extra stuff we load onto our PCs. The most common slow down at boot is when too many things start at the same time. The applications that load alongside Windows take a few extra fractions of a second, which soon start to add up. Reducing startup applications is a great way to speed things up, but be careful as there can be adverse effects, such as programs not being there immediately when you want them, or your PC not being protected by antivirus software.

Configuring startup programs

A program called MSCONFIG can help you work out what's going on at startup. Type **MSCONFIG** into the **Start** search box to start it. It's an advanced tool for working with Windows settings and is great for troubleshooting; but for the purposes of speeding up boot time the **Startup** tab is all that's needed. This lists the items that are set to start at the same time as Windows; to stop an item from starting, remove the tick to its left. But how do you work out which to disable? Often there will be entries for things you don't need immediately; for example, do you need your webcam software to start automatically or when you need to use your webcam? A good rule of thumb is not to disable anything if you don't know what it is. Changes can easily be undone, though, so if you disable a program and then find problems after the next reboot, just enable it again. Click **Apply** to make the changes, and reboot to see the difference.

Tip: Having every program on your PC run at startup might make it easy to get to some applications, but it can make Windows take forever to become usable. Startup Delayer is a great solution and it does exactly what it says on the tin; it delays some programs at startup, the net result being that you're able to start using the PC faster and then after a period of time you set, these other programs load automatically. Get it at r2.com.au.

MSCONFIG allows any program that runs at startup to be easily turned on or off. Just click Start and type "MSCONFIG".

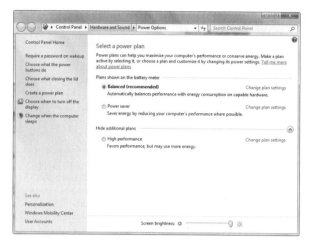

Selecting the Power saver plan affects how much battery your laptop uses and how much processing power it can use. For desktops the default "Balanced" plan is the best, but for gaming select High Performance.

Tip: Dimming the screen brightness on a laptop is one of the best ways to improve battery life and Windows 7 will do it automatically for you. If in doubt press ⊞ + X to launch Mobility Center and reduce the brightness with the slider. The power profile can be swapped here quickly too.

Battery life

Special attention is required for laptops because the more electricity they need, the less time the battery will last. Windows 7 is good at extending battery life, but it's worth knowing what can be tweaked. Control Panel > All Control Panel Items > Power Options **is the control centre for everything power related.**

Power plans

Power plans define exactly what can be turned off or have power reduced to it and when. Modern CPUs can function at a lower level of performance and use less power when not in use, which is great if you have a laptop running low on battery. The same is true of network adapters, hard disks and other components that can be turned off when they aren't needed.

Windows has three in-built power plans to cater for all eventualities:

▶ Balanced – the default, cuts performance to decrease power usage and places equal emphasis on both.
▶ Power saver – places emphasis on decreasing power usage, which is great for laptops, but will impact performance on desktops.
▶ High performance – best used on a desktop PC, it prevents components from being turned off for longer periods of time.

If you use your PC for high-performance tasks such as gaming, it's best to use the High Performance plan, but remember that suspend or sleep modes will be disabled.

Index

Index

Index

Index

Index